Sports
31385003975701

IT HAPPENED TO ME

Series Editor: Arlene Hirschfelder

Books in the It Happened to Me series are designed for inquisitive teens digging for answers about certain illnesses, social issues, or lifestyle interests. Whether you are deep into your teen years or just entering them, these books are gold mines of up-to-date information, riveting teen views, and great visuals to help you figure out stuff. Besides special boxes highlighting singular facts, each book is enhanced with the latest reading lists, websites, and an index. Perfect for browsing, there are loads of expert information by acclaimed writers to help parents, guardians, and librarians understand teen illness, tough situations, and lifestyle choices.

SPORTS

THE ULTIMATE TEEN GUIDE

GAIL FAY

IT HAPPENED TO ME, NO. 33

THE SCARECROW PRESS, INC.
Lanham • Toronto • Plymouth, UK
2013

Published by Scarecrow Press, Inc.
A wholly owned subsidiary of The Rowman & Littlefield Publishing Group, Inc.
4501 Forbes Boulevard, Suite 200, Lanham, Maryland 20706
www.rowman.com

10 Thornbury Road, Plymouth PL6 7PP, United Kingdom

British Library Cataloguing in Publication Information Available

Library of Congress Cataloging-in-Publication Data

Fay, Gail.
    Sports : the ultimate teen guide / Gail Fay.
        p. cm. — (It happened to me ; no. 33)
    Includes bibliographical references and index.
    ISBN 978-0-8108-8217-1 (cloth : alk. paper) — ISBN 978-0-8108-8218-8 (electronic)
    1. Teenage athletes—Training of. 2. High school athletes—Training of. I. Title.
    GV711.5.F39 2013
    796—dc23

                                                                            2012028320

∞™ The paper used in this publication meets the minimum requirements of American
National Standard for Information Sciences—Permanence of Paper for Printed Library
Materials, ANSI/NISO Z39.48-1992. Printed in the United States of America.

To my sister, Lori,
for encouraging me to give writing a shot

Contents

Acknowledgments

First and foremost, I want to thank all the current and former high school and college student-athletes who contributed to this book: Alyssa, Amberlee, Andy, Anna, Annalise, Anthony, Austin, Caitlin, Cameron, Corey, Dane, David, Davon, Derek, Emily, Evan, Jacque, Jamie, Janira, Jessica D., Jessica H., Jessica U., Joseph, Josh, Kirsten, Lauren, McKenzie, Megan, Mikalla, Nathan, Noah, Rachel, Requan, Roger, Samantha, Taylor, and Yamil. I truly appreciate the time you invested in answering my survey questions and e-mails; this book would not be the same without your real-life sports experiences. Special thanks to the athlete bio subjects—Anthony, Derek, Jacque, Jessica D., Jessica U., Kirsten, McKenzie, Nathan, Noah, and Roger—for taking time to talk with me at length, whether in person, through e-mail, or via Skype.

I also want to thank Aaron Cantrell, Mike Doyle, John Gottschalk, Saralyn Hannon, Jose Moreno, and Paul Rave—all current and former coaches who shared insights from their coaching experience; Laura Atkinson, for sharing her experiences as a massage therapist working with injured athletes; Robyn Kaczynski, fitness instructor, for answering my questions about personal training; and Alison Bell, director of college counseling at Holy Trinity Episcopal Academy, and Lenny Paoletti, athletic director at Holy Trinity Episcopal Academy, for providing excellent information on getting recruited to play in college.

Thanks to the photographers who contributed their work: Alycia Collins, Robert Fay, Brad Hagen, Pogos Kuregyan, Nick Lyon, Alice Phangkhayan, Ryan Seeloff, and Elise Stearns-Niesen. Special thanks to Elise for helping me track down model release forms.

Thanks to the Wolitarsky family, for providing interviews, connecting me with photographers, and helping me track down permission forms. Nathan, I wish you a speedy recovery so you can continue your shot putting career.

Thanks to my editor, Arlene Hirschfelder, for patiently answering all my questions and for providing valuable feedback.

Finally, I want to thank my husband and best friend, Bob, for listening to all my fascinating sports facts and for understanding that normal life would resume "after the book."

INTRODUCTION

···

"I love softball with all my heart. It's what I was born to do!"
—*Megan, 16, softball*

If you're reading this book, then you already know that sports play a huge part of the high school experience. According to the National Federation of State High School Associations (NFHS), 55.5 percent of all high school students join at least one athletic team. During the 2010–2011 school year alone, over 7.6 million U.S. teenagers played sports for their school—nearly forty thousand more than played the year before. In fact, the number of U.S. high school student-athletes has increased every year since the 1989–1990 school year.[1]

If you've played your sport for a while, then you know the thrill of winning a big race or pulling together as a team to win when it counts; you probably also know the disappointment of losing, possibly because you choked when the pressure was on. You probably know the struggle of studying for a test when you're

Ten Most Popular Sports for High School Boys in 2010–2011[2]

1. Football (eleven players)
2. Track and field (outdoor)
3. Basketball
4. Baseball
5. Soccer
6. Wrestling
7. Cross-country
8. Tennis
9. Golf
10. Swimming and diving

> "What I like most about football is the adrenaline rush you get when you step onto the field and the crowd in the stands are hooting and hollering. I just get so pumped up."—Requan, 16, football

Ten Most Popular Sports for High School Girls in 2010–2011[3]

1. Track and field (outdoor)
2. Basketball
3. Volleyball
4. Softball (fast-pitch)
5. Soccer
6. Cross-country
7. Tennis
8. Swimming and diving
9. Competitive spirit squads
10. Lacrosse

falling asleep because you just played a ninety-minute soccer game or ran a three-mile cross-country race. You might also know the temptation of trying new and possibly illegal supplements to get bigger, stronger, faster.

This book is written for anyone who loves to compete. It's for those who feel like playing _____ (you fill in the sport) is just part of who they are. It's written for athletes of all levels—from the high school freshman who's still deciding what to play, to the junior or senior being recruited by Division I universities. My goal is to provide you with answers to a variety of questions; for example, does it matter what I eat the night before my game? How do other high school athletes cope

> "I like [basketball] so much because you can never be the best; there's always new things to do—new defense, new offense, new way to dribble—and there's always new opponents. You never really get used to the people you play against."—Jessica D., 16, basketball

with the pressure to perform? Are all performance enhancers illegal? How can I improve my speed during the off-season? What's the best way to approach college coaches about playing for their team? You'll find practical tips as well as suggestions on where to go to learn more.

Each chapter is self-contained; in other words, you don't have to read chapter 5 to understand chapter 6. If chapter 4 ("Eat to Win") sounds the most interesting, start there. If you really want to play in college but don't know where to start, skip to chapter 8. Here's a summary of what you'll find in each chapter to help you decide where to start:

> "I like that I can just let my mind be quiet and ski and go somewhere while also strengthening my body and lungs. It's nice to have direction from coaches, but also be able to do it alone."—Annalise, 18, Nordic skiing

- Chapter 1 celebrates the sheer joy of competing—why you do what you do on the field, on the ice or snow, on the court, on the track, or in the pool. It contains tips for new athletes who are still deciding what sport to play, as well as quotes from fellow teens who share what they love about their sport. You'll also get a brief history lesson on Title IX and how it affects you today.
- Chapter 2 covers the life of the student-athlete. Studies, practice, competition, family commitments, spending time with friends—how do you balance it all? What have others tried that works? This chapter also discusses the advantages and responsibilities that come with being a student-athlete.
- Chapter 3 addresses mental toughness: What is it? How do you get it? How can you consistently get yourself mentally prepared before every game or race? Mental toughness is an attribute that can help you thoroughly enjoy your sport and successfully participate at higher levels of competition. Student-athletes share what they do to prepare themselves mentally.
- Chapter 4 provides sport-by-sport advice on eating and drinking so that you perform at your best. Most people know it's important to eat certain things before a race or game, but what about after? This chapter also covers the eating disorders that high school athletes sometimes suffer from.
- Chapter 5 covers steroids and other performance enhancers. Are they all illegal? Why do athletes use steroids and risk getting caught? What are the potential negative side effects of using steroids? This chapter will help you make an informed decision on whether or not to try performance enhancers.

- Chapter 6 presents information on common sports injuries—how they happen, how they can be avoided, and what to do if you do get injured. This chapter also provides detailed information on more serious injuries such as concussions and the importance of not playing when you're injured.
- Chapter 7 provides training suggestions for those who want to get to the next level athletically. You'll find tips on increasing various physical fitness factors such as speed, strength, power, and endurance. Whether you're trying to jump from JV to varsity, get recruited to play at the college level, or just increase your overall fitness, this chapter can help.
- Chapter 8 outlines specific suggestions for those of you hoping to play in college. Did you know that there are three separate intercollegiate athletic associations with opportunities to earn scholarship money to play in college? Did you know there are pre-recruiting steps you can (and should) start taking in your freshman or sophomore year of high school? Current and former college athletes share their experiences playing at the college level.

> "[I love] the rush/exhilaration you feel while running the bases (after a great hit of course!)."—Taylor H., 15, softball

Less Common High School Sports That Gained the Most Participants in 2010–2011[4]

Boys:

1. Fencing (38 percent increase over the 2009–2010 school year)
2. Weight lifting (12 percent increase)
3. Badminton (9.4 percent increase)

Girls:

1. Wrestling (19.8 percent increase over the 2009–2010 school year)
2. Badminton (14 percent increase)
3. Weight lifting (11 percent increase)

"I liked being part of a team and knowing your teammates have your back. The best part of it was it kept me in shape."—Anthony, 20, basketball

- Chapter 9 discusses ways to stay involved in sports for life. You'll find ideas for playing in recreation leagues, challenging yourself in endurance sports, volunteering in youth sports, and securing a sports-related part-time job or full-time career.

Within each chapter you'll find similar features:

Sport-specific historical facts
Interesting statistics
Helpful hints
Summaries of sports-themed young adult novels, including life applications
Athlete biographies featuring former and current high school and college athletes
Quotes from current and former high school athletes from across the country
List of resources (books, online articles, websites, organizations, etc.) for more information (Note: I found most of the books listed at the public library, so there's no need to go out and buy them all.)

So, where are *you* going to begin? Pick a chapter and start reading!

"I love hitting. . . . It's exciting when you are at the plate and everybody starts screaming for you to hit a home run."—Yamil, 14, baseball

Notes

1. National Federation of State High School Associations (NFHS), "2010–11 High School Athletics Participation Survey," p. 52, www.nfhs.org/content.aspx?id=3282 (accessed October 13, 2011); NFHS, "High School Sports Participation Continues Upward Climb" (press release, August 23, 2011), www.nfhs.org/content.aspx?id=5752 (accessed October 13, 2011).
2. Based on the number of participants; NFHS, "2010–11 High School Athletics," 52.
3. Based on the number of participants; NFHS, "2010–11 High School Athletics," 52.
4. NFHS, "High School Sports Participation Continues Upward Climb."

PLAY BALL!

"I love the fast pace of the sport. You never stop doing something in the water; either you're swimming to the other side, egg beating, guarding someone, or you could be taking a shot."—Samantha, 17, water polo

"I am a center defender, so I love to feel control of the whole back field and being the leader of the defense."—Evan, 15, soccer

For me, there's nothing like walking onto a freshly lined softball field on a warm summer evening. I love hearing the soft crunch of dirt under my cleats as I jog toward the outfield. I love listening to the lights crackle and hum as they sputter to life. And, of course, there's nothing like chasing down a fly ball and hearing it *thunk* into my glove.

What do you love about your sport? Is it the roar of the crowd as your team kicks off and races downfield or the sweet sound of *swish* as your shot hits all net? Is it the freedom of running alone on the course or the thrill of racing others side by side down the track? Is it being part of a team or facing the individual challenges that come with each game?

> "The thing I like most about playing softball is that it is never easy. You will always come across a difficult task and always need to improve on something!"—Megan, 16, softball

This chapter is dedicated to the celebration of sports and competition. Many athletes share what they love about their sport. You may find yourself nodding and saying, "Me too! I love that about _____." If you haven't found *your* sport yet or if you're looking for a new sport to try, this chapter can help.

"I like tennis because it's the best of both worlds. Although we have a 'tennis team,' it is still an individual sport. . . . I get to focus and work on my own and I don't have to rely on another person's performance, but then if the whole team does well we can win a tournament."—Caitlin, 16, tennis

Where Did Sports Begin?

People have been challenging each other to athletic competitions for around four thousand years. Egypt seems to be the place where it all began, both for primitive track and field meets and for wrestling. It was the ancient Greeks, however, who took competition to a whole new level when they introduced the Olympics. The first games took place in 776 BC in the city of Olympia, Greece, and involved track and field events, including the marathon. The word *athlete* comes from the Greek word *athlos*, which means competition.

These ancient Greek competitions were for men only; ladies weren't even allowed to watch, probably because the athletes raced in the nude. Some historians believe the running naked tradition started because someone tripped over his loincloth. Others believe the Greeks just wanted to show off their bods. Another theory is that running naked made everyone equal; without clothes, one couldn't

History of the Marathon

The modern marathon is named after a city in Greece. Legend has it that in 490 BC, a Greek soldier named Pheidippides ran 24.85 miles (40,000 kilometers) from a battlefield in Marathon to Athens. When he arrived, he shouted, "Niki!" (victory) and then collapsed and died. The route of the present-day Athens marathon follows Pheidippides' run.

At the 1908 London Olympics, the marathon distance was changed to 26.2 miles so the runners would finish in front of the royal family's viewing box in White City Stadium, and that's been the distance of the race ever since. Marathon runners in the 2004 Athens Olympics ran from Marathon to Athens just like Pheidippides.[1]

History of Wrestling

Wrestling has been around since around 1850 BC, making it the world's oldest sport. Egyptian tombs from this time period show pictures of competitors using wrestling moves that are still used today. In ancient Greece, wrestling was considered a combat sport that was part of a soldier's military training. As a result, the wrestling that was part of the first Olympics in 776 BC was much more violent than today's version. Men's wrestling has been part of the modern Olympics since 1896; women's wrestling became an Olympic sport in 2004.

Today, girls' high school wrestling is becoming more popular. Between the 2002–2003 and 2010–2011 school years, girls' participation in high school wrestling nearly doubled; some of those girls are competing with the guys if their schools don't have teams.[2]

tell who was rich or poor. Whatever the reason, it's true that ancient Greeks ran naked, much to the surprise of their non-Greek competitors.[3]

Why Play Sports?

"When I step out onto that field I lose myself in the game. I don't think about anything outside of softball. I think that's why people play sports . . . it's the time they can be themselves and lose themselves in the game they love."
—*Taylor H., 15, softball*

So, why have people been participating in sports for almost as long as they've been on the planet? What is it about sports that appeals to people of all ages, and particularly young adults? Here are a few suggestions.

Sports Are Fun

This is the reason for playing that's given most often by athletes of all ages. By definition, a sport is a form of recreation, a "physical activity engaged in

"I like having fun while learning [new skills] and playing with my friends."—Janira, 15, softball

What Do You Think?

In August 2009, fifteen-year-old Peter Barston of Darien, Connecticut, started surveying young athletes in his hometown.[4] He wanted to find out the answer to one simple question: Why do you play sports?

Peter had seen the results of the 1989 survey done by researchers at Michigan State University, and he wondered if the answers would be the same today. (In that 1989 survey, "to have fun" was the number-one reason given and "to win" didn't even make the top ten.) So, Peter went out and talked to football, basketball, baseball, and softball players in Darien youth leagues. He gave them a one-page survey with the following potential reasons for playing sports:

> To stay in shape and get exercise
>
> To improve my skills
>
> To have fun
>
> To be a part of a team and learn teamwork
>
> To go to a higher level of competition
>
> To earn a college scholarship
>
> To increase my self-confidence
>
> To win
>
> To make friends
>
> For the excitement and challenge of competition
>
> Because my parents asked me to play

Peter surveyed around one thousand athletes in grades 4–8, and as with the Michigan State survey, one answer stood out above all the others: to have fun.

Do you think this reason becomes less important as athletes move into high school? If so, why is that? If you were to give high school athletes the same survey, which reason do you think would be number one?

For a copy of Peter's survey or for information on doing a similar survey in your hometown, go to www.sportsreasons.com and check out the links on the left-hand side.

for pleasure."[5] Sports can give you a break from school, homework, and the other un-fun activities in life. Even grueling two-a-day practices and intense interval training are somewhat enjoyable because you're sharing the experience with others. Whether you're all celebrating a big win or laughing about the goofy way you held your glove to make the catch, sports provide a great outlet to relax and enjoy yourself with others.

If your sport isn't fun anymore, maybe you need to stop and ask yourself why. Are you feeling too much pressure to win? If so, can you identify the source of the pressure; is it your coach, your parents, or maybe even yourself? Chapter 3 has suggestions for developing mental toughness, which might help you handle this pressure in a constructive way.

Are sports no longer fun because they're taking up all of your free time? Maybe you need to go from three sports to two or take a season off travel ball. Are you just burned out on that particular sport? Maybe it's time to try something new. There's no rule against trying out for a different sport partway through your high school career.

Sports Help You Stay in Shape

Some of you may truly enjoy working out, whether it's running, swimming, cycling, or weight lifting. For some of you, however, exercising may not be on

History of Field Hockey

Field hockey is one of the world's oldest sports. Drawings on a four-thousand-year-old tomb suggest that some form of the game was played by ancient Egyptians. There's also evidence that games involving a ball and stick were played thousands of years ago by the Persians, Greeks, and Romans. Over time these games evolved in different directions, with field hockey as we know it developing in England in the mid-nineteenth century.

In 1901, a woman named Constance Applebee brought the game to the United States, when she came from England to take a summer course at Harvard. Though field hockey was played by men and women in England, in the United States it developed primarily as a women's sport at the high school and college levels. During the 2010–2011 school year, only 12 U.S. high schools had boys' field hockey teams, while 1,808 high schools fielded girls' teams.[6]

> "[Sports] helped me meet new people and make friends as well as keeping me in shape by giving me a motivation to exercise."—Jamie, 18, swimming

your top-ten list of ways to spend an hour or two. This is where sports come in. Exercise is built into the very nature of the activity, so you're getting cardio and strength training while you're having fun. In field hockey, for example, players often run three to five miles per match; soccer players often run five or six miles. But somehow getting those miles in while sprinting toward the goal or jogging back to midfield is not as overwhelming (or boring) as just setting out on a five-mile run.

Depending on your sport, you're probably jogging, sprinting, jumping, swimming, skiing, or treading water just by going to practice and playing the games, and all of these are great cardio workouts. In addition, you probably do some degree of throwing, hitting, passing, and serving, all of which require muscle power and burn calories, especially if performed repeatedly. In order to perfect the skills in your sport, you undoubtedly endure hours of drills, which most likely involve more cardio and strength or resistance training.

You just can't get around the fact that you're going to get a great workout if you play sports. Table 1.1 contains a summary of calories burned per hour in various sports. Compare these numbers to those given in table 1.2, which shows how many calories someone burns per hour while performing everyday activities

Table 1.1 Calories Burned per Hour of Playing Time*

Sport	130-Pound Athlete	180-Pound Athlete
Baseball	295	409
Basketball	472	654
Cross-country	531	735
Cross-country (Nordic) skiing	826	1144
Downhill (alpine) skiing	472	654
Field hockey	472	654

Sport	130-Pound Athlete	180-Pound Athlete
Football	531	735
Golf	266	368
Gymnastics	236	327
Ice hockey	472	654
Lacrosse	472	654
Soccer	590	817
Softball	295	409
Swimming (backstroke)	413	572
Swimming (butterfly)	649	899
Tennis (singles)	472	654
Track and field (high jump, pole vault)	354	490
Track and field (hurdles)	590	817
Track and field (shot put, discus)	236	327
Volleyball	472	654
Water polo	590	817
Wrestling	354	490

Source: Adapted from NutriStrategy, "Calories Burned during Exercise, Activities, Sports and Work," www.nutristrategy.com/caloriesburned.htm.

*The calories counts refer to the number burned during an hour of competitive activity (a game or race); these numbers are higher than those for calories burned during practices, pickup games, vacation activities, and so on.

Table 1.2 Calories Burned per Hour of Everyday Activity

Activity	130-Pound Person	180-Pound Person
General housework (moderate)	207	286
Mowing the lawn (walking with power mower)	325	449
Raking the lawn	254	351
Shoveling snow by hand	354	490
Taking out the trash	177	245
Walking the dog	236	327

Source: Adapted from NutriStrategy, "Calories Burned during Work, Occupations and Hobbies," www
.nutristrategy.com/caloriesburnedwork.htm.

such as raking the lawn or taking out the trash. While some everyday activities involve burning a fair number of calories, in general, you burn a lot more playing a sport. Plus, it's much more fun to get in shape playing basketball rather than mowing lawns.

Sports Have Other Health Benefits

Have you ever heard of the "runner's high"? The term refers to the happy, isn't-life-wonderful feeling athletes get after a hard workout. This feel-good state is caused by a rush of endorphins (chemicals produced in the pituitary gland) released into the bloodstream after twenty to thirty minutes of strenuous exercise. Because of this endorphin rush, exercise is an excellent natural way to deal with depression, anger, anxiety, and a whole list of other emotional issues.

Other health benefits include the following:[7]

> "[I like that] it's legal for me to take my anger out without getting in trouble."
> —Roger, 16, football

- Athletes are less likely to take up smoking.
- Female athletes are less likely to develop breast cancer and osteoporosis (brittle bones) later in life.
- Exercise improves sleep.
- Sports provide a healthy way to vent and "reboot."

Sports Novels

Throughout this book you'll find Good Read sidebars highlighting young adult novels that involve sports and characters dealing with real-life issues. These suggestions are based on my own reading; I focused on books in which sports play a big role in the plot. However, there are literally hundreds more out there on a variety of sports—everything from baseball and wrestling to skateboarding and surfing. Here are a few websites you can search to find interesting titles. I suggest using the websites for research and then check to see if your local library has the books.

Barnes and Noble (browse.barnesandnoble.com/browse/nav.asp?visgrp=fiction&bncatid=716220). In the category Teen Fiction—Sports, Barnes and Noble lists over six hundred titles in which sports are part of the plot to varying degrees. You can get a brief summary by clicking on the title. You can also sort books by "bestselling" and "newest to oldest."

GoodReads (www.goodreads.com/list/show/2151.YA_Sport_Novels#50055). This website has a list of over one hundred sport-themed novels along with brief summaries and reviews by other readers, many of whom are teenagers.

InfoSoup (info.infosoup.org/lists/TeenSportsAll.asp?BooklistID=56). InfoSoup divides its Teen Sports Fiction booklist into categories so it is easy to find a novel involving a specific sport. Categories include Baseball, Basketball, Football, Soccer, Swimming, and Other Sports.

TeenReads (www.teenreads.com/reviews/index). Once you find a book that sounds interesting, you can find more reviews on this website. Type the title into the search bar at the top of the "Find a Book" page.

Athletes Get Better Grades Than Nonathletes

Your parents will appreciate this little factoid: in general, athletes do better in school and have fewer absences than nonathletes. According to a 2007 study of three hundred Minnesota high schools, student-athletes had an average GPA of 2.84, while students who didn't participate in sports averaged 2.68. According to a 2001 study of North Carolina high schools, the mean GPA for student-athletes was even higher—2.91—versus 2.71 for nonathletes.[8]

What is the connection between sports and improved performance in the classroom? For one thing, regular exercise improves the quality of your sleep, which has a direct influence on your ability to concentrate in class. Better concentration means you are better able to learn and remember. Also, most if not all high schools have attendance and GPA requirements for student-athletes. If you don't show up for class and maintain the required GPA, you don't play; it's that simple. That fact alone is motivation for many athletes to study, and grades improve as a result.

Sports Provide a Way to Make Friends

If you're a high school freshman or if you've just moved to a new school, joining a team can ease the transition. You're immediately connected with a group of peers who have at leave one interest in common: your sport. You'll probably find yourself hanging out after practice and even after the season is over. That's not to say you're going to hit it off with everyone on your team, but there's something about suffering through workouts together and winning a big game together that creates a bond. As Josh, a football player from California, puts it, "Battling together on the field with my teammates really bonds you together as brothers in a similar way that going into battle bonds soldiers together."[9]

> "I enjoy having something to be committed to that represents my high school and I really enjoy the team aspect of it."
> —Mikalla, 15, soccer

Being part of a team involves trust—trust that your teammate will back you up if you dive for a fly ball, trust that your teammate will be there for the kill if you set the ball to her, trust that your teammate remembers the play and will be there when the pass arrives—and trust is a huge part of friendship as well. Sports can give you the opportunity to make friends that last a lifetime.

Sports Can Give You a Sense of Purpose

Some of you may be looking for something to give your life meaning—something you can throw yourself into or someplace where you feel like you belong. You may not think of it in those exact words. Maybe you would say that you're looking for

a place where you fit in,
a reason to get up in the morning,
a way to escape _____ (you fill in the blank), or
a way to fight loneliness or depression.

> "The competition was the main thing that I played for. I feel the need to compete in almost anything, just to prove what I'm able to accomplish/achieve."
> —Austin, 15, football

Whatever you call that need to find meaning or purpose, sports can help. Physically, sports can give you a positive outlet for your anger, hurt, anxiety, or frustration. Emotionally, sports can give you a sense of being needed; when you're part of a team, it matters that you show up to practices and games. Mentally, sports can give you something to focus on instead of your breakup, your parents' divorce, the foreclosure of your home, or whatever. The Good Read sidebar on page 12 features a novel about a young man with a rough childhood who finds purpose and meaning in basketball; his sport keeps him from throwing his life away.

> "When I get on the field, all my worries and problems just fade away."—Requan, 16, football

Sports Can Teach You Important Life Lessons

The most important lesson is probably teamwork. No matter where you live or what you do after high school, you will need to know how to work with others to achieve a goal. In high school that goal might be a league championship. As a college student, you might need to work with roommates to pay bills and keep the apartment clean. As an employee, you might need to resolve personal problems with a coworker in order to finish the project your boss gave you to work on together. As a parent (think long term!), you might need to rally your children to make a cool birthday gift for your spouse. You'll never run out of opportunities to practice the teamwork skills you learn in sports.

Good Read: Ball Don't Lie by Matt de la Peña

Sport: Basketball

Life apps: Sports as a way of coping with life, obsessive-compulsive disorder, living in foster homes, playing in college

Summary: Seventeen-year-old Sticky has not had an easy childhood. He's been neglected by his mom, abused by his mom's boyfriend, and shuffled between foster homes. He's even lived on the streets of Los Angeles. But the skinny white kid can play basketball, and he's found a new "family" among the mainly black men he plays ball with at Lincoln Rec. Sticky sees basketball as his way out of his sorry life; as he puts it, "I think God put me here to play ball."

Ball Don't Lie is narrated in a unique style, alternating between the present and the sad past events that brought Sticky to this point. Author Matt de la Peña played basketball at University of the Pacific, and his book contains realistic dialogue and play-by-play basketball descriptions. *Ball Don't Lie* was named an ALA-YALSA Best Book for Young Adults and ALA-YALSA Quick Pick for Reluctant Readers.

Delacorte Press, 2005
280 pages

Sports can also teach you how to set realistic yet challenging goals. This is a skill you'll probably learn from your coach, so listen up. At the beginning of each season, the coach may share what he or she wants you to achieve both as a team and as individuals. Almost guaranteed, reaching those goals will not be easy, which is where perseverance comes in—another life skill learned on the court, on the field, on the ice, or in the pool. Sports can teach you the valuable lesson of not giving up when something gets hard—and life gets tough sometimes, whether it's a college class, a relationship, or a job.

> "I love the team atmosphere. I love the fact that in order to be successful you have to have seven or eight girls who are playing with the same goal in mind. You can't win without your teammates."—Jacque, 22, volleyball

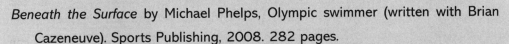

Sports Biographies, Memoirs, and Autobiographies

Here's a short list of inspiring nonfiction books written by or about athletes and coaches, all of which include important life lessons gained from playing or coaching:

Beneath the Surface by Michael Phelps, Olympic swimmer (written with Brian Cazeneuve). Sports Publishing, 2008. 282 pages.

Figure It Out: How I Learned to Live in a Digital World without Digits by Mark Speckman, Willamette University head football coach who has no hands. Willamette University Press, 2009. 126 pages.

Go for the Goal: A Champion's Guide to Winning in Soccer and Life by Mia Hamm, U.S. soccer star (written with Aaron Heifetz). It Books, 2000. 256 pages.

The Other Side of the Mountain by E. G. Valens. The story of Jill Kinmont, a talented downhill skier who became paralyzed from the neck down after a skiing accident. HarperCollins, 1989. 352 pages.

Quiet Strength by Tony Dungy, former head coach of the Indianapolis Colts (written with Nathan Whitaker). Tyndale House, 2008. 352 pages.

Sayers: My Life and Times by Gale Sayers, former Chicago Bears running back (written with Fred Mitchell). Triumph Books, 2007. 240 pages.

Something for Joey by Richard E. Peck. The story of the relationship between former NFL running back John Cappelletti and his younger brother, Joey, who was suffering from leukemia. Laurel Leaf, 1983. 192 pages.

Soul Surfer: The True Story of Faith, Family, and Fighting to Get Back on the Board by Bethany Hamilton, surfer who lost an arm to a shark attack. MTV Books, 2006. 240 pages.

They Call Me Coach by John Wooden, former head basketball coach at UCLA (written with Jack Tobin). McGraw-Hill, 2003. 272 pages.

Through My Eyes by Tim Tebow, NFL quarterback (written with Nathan Whitaker). Harper, 2011. 272 pages.

Wins, Losses, and Lessons by Lou Holtz, former head football coach at Notre Dame. Harper Entertainment, 2007. 318 pages.

What Do You Think?

I love sports, and I know the positive impact they had on my life in high school. However, I also know that there are inherent risks involved in athletics. Some people believe certain risks outweigh the positive aspects. Here are two arguments against sports—or at least, some aspects of sports. Compare the pros I just presented with the cons that follow and decide if sports are right for you, and if so, what precautions you should take as you get involved.

Sports Can Be Dangerous

Football is still considered the most dangerous sport. According to one report, between 1997 and 2007 at least fifty high school or junior high school football players sustained serious head injuries, some of which resulted in death. While I was writing this book in October 2011, a sixteen-year-old player from New York died after a hard hit to the head.[10]

Football is not the only sport with action-related deaths. In November 2011, for example, a sixteen-year-old hockey player named Kyle Fundytus was hit in the neck with a puck and then died of cardiac arrest (his heart stopped beating). Kyle had regularly performed that same sliding block; according to Kyle's coach, it was a "'once in a 10 million' accident that cost Fundytus his life."[11]

Even if it's not immediately life threatening, a head injury can negatively affect you for the rest of your life. Repeated concussions can cause persistent headaches, an inability to concentrate, and a tendency to pass out at the slightest hit to the head. They can also result in something far more serious: a degenerative brain disease (a condition that gets progressively worse) called chronic traumatic encephalopathy (CTE). People with CTE suffer from deteriorating memory, confusion, slowed muscle movements, dementia (progressive loss of brain function), and other symptoms that are usually seen in older people with Alzheimer's disease. In 2009, professional football player Chris Henry died in a car accident. When scientists studied Henry's brain afterward, they found signs of CTE—a surprising finding since Henry was only twenty-six when he died. Henry's case provides more evidence that repeated hits to the head can cause permanent brain damage.[12] Though most common among football players, concussions are also on the rise among basketball players who hit their head on the gym floor. (For more information on concussion safety and symptoms, see chapter 6.)

Girls, there's one sports-related risk that applies specifically to you; it's called the female athlete triad. The "triad" refers to three connected conditions: disordered eating, amenorrhea (not having your period), and osteoporosis (brittle bones). In some sports, having a thin figure is considered beneficial—running, gymnastics, and diving, for example. Female athletes in these sports can develop eating disorders such as anorexia and bulimia in their attempt to keep their weight down. In combination with intense training, weight loss can lead to amenorrhea, which may seem very convenient; however, a lack of periods also means your hormones are out of whack, which can negatively affect the strength of your bones. Athletes with amenorrhea are more likely to develop stress fractures and other injuries.[13] (For more information on eating disorders, see chapter 4.)

Sports Lower Self-Confidence and Increase Stress

According to this argument, sports do exactly the opposite of what they're supposed to do. They're supposed to be a fun way to relax with friends. They're supposed to increase your self-esteem as you learn new skills, achieve new goals, and set new personal records. However, sports can actually cause extreme anxiety and emotional distress.

Some parents contribute to the problem. They spend a lot of money on club teams, personal trainers, and equipment, all with the goal of having an all-star. But the pressure can be too much for the player. Consider this situation, for example: A varsity softball player struck out three times during one game. When the player got home, her parents made her take batting practice for three hours. Instead of helping, the extra practice just put more pressure on the player and she ended up striking out in the next game too. She hung her head as she headed for the dugout, her expression clearly showing she was not having fun.[14]

Along with losing the joy of playing, athletes such as this softball player can develop sleeping or anxiety disorders as a result of the pressure to win, to attract the attention of the college scout, or to earn a full-ride scholarship. They can feel worthless in general just because they can't perform as expected in one area of life. Unfortunately, many athletes quit when sports become so stressful.

Finally, sports can teach you good sportsmanship, a quality people admire on and off the field. In the sports context, sportsmanship involves playing by the rules, treating your opponent with respect, and being gracious whether you win or lose. In everyday life, sportsmanship translates to being honest and fair.

Ashley, a volleyball player from Rhode Island, wrote an essay about life lessons she learned from her sport. In particular, Ashley and her teammates have learned trust and communication on the court: "In volleyball, there is no time to second-guess. Players have to develop a trusting bond and be sure their teammates will lead them in the right direction." Ashley also says that "volleyball, like life, is full of mistakes, but when we make them, we can't complain and fall apart." Ashley concludes her essay by saying, "Everything I needed to know in life I learned in volleyball."[15]

> "[I like wrestling because] I'm the only one that has control over whether or not I win. I can't blame anyone else besides myself."—Derek, 18, wrestling

Picking a Sport

Many of you are probably set on your one to three sports. Some of you, however, might be looking for a new sport,

Samantha says, "My dad told me that I had to pick a different sport other than volleyball so I wouldn't roll my ankle and miss another big softball tourney. So I remembered that a couple of my friends were trying out for water polo and I decided to try out with them." Samantha made the team and became a leading scorer. *Photo courtesy of Elise Stearns-Niesen.*

Sports across the Country

Did you know that 787 U.S. high schools had a boys' weight lifting team in 2010–2011? Or that 188 high schools had a girls' riflery team? According to a survey conducted by the National Federation of State High School Associations (NFHS), high school students across the United States participated in at least forty different sports during the 2010–2011 school year. Table 1.3 presents some results of that survey. You might be surprised at the wide variety of sports played by your fellow high schoolers.

Table 1.3 Results of the NFHS 2010-2011 Athletics Participation Survey

| Sport (number of states reporting for boys/girls) | Boys | | Girls | | Combined |
	Number of Schools	Number of Participants	Number of Schools	Number of Participants	Number of Participants
Air Riflery	46	561	46	433	994
Archery	43	486	44	428	914
Badminton	224	4,693	417	12,083	16,776
Baseball	15,863	471,025	63	698	471,723
Basketball	18,150	545,844	17,767	438,933	984,777
Bowling	2,454	28,265	2,436	25,753	54,018
Competitive Spirit Squads	433	2,846	4,266	96,718	99,564
Canoeing	56	1,291	59	1,516	2,807

Sport (number of states reporting for boys/girls)	Boys		Girls		Combined
	Number of Schools	Number of Participants	Number of Schools	Number of Participants	Number of Participants
Crew	74	2193	78	2,144	4,337
Cross-Country	14,097	246,948	13,839	204,653	451,601
Dance/Drill	59	2,177	1,216	21,487	23,664
Drill Team	37	384	251	4,379	4,763
Equestrian	65	200	206	1,585	1,785
Fencing	98	2,027	95	1,801	3,828
Field Hockey	12	192	1,808	61,996	62,188
Flag Football	11	335	179	5,654	5,989
Football—11 player	14,279	1,108,441	241	1,395	1,109,836
6-player	214	4,158	0	0	4,158
8-player	770	16,595	43	161	16,756
9-player	250	5,183	6	5	5,188
Golf	13,681	156,866	9,609	71,764	228,630
Gymnastics	121	2,472	1,506	19,719	22,191
Ice Hockey	1,612	36,912	578	9,022	45,934

Sport (number of states reporting for boys/girls)	Boys		Girls		Combined
	Number of Schools	Number of Participants	Number of Schools	Number of Participants	Number of Participants
Judo	51	745	47	412	1,157
Lacrosse	2,192	95,683	1,999	74,927	170,610
Riflery	226	2,375	188	1,237	3,612
Rodeo	40	115	45	128	243
Skiing—Alpine	553	5,772	542	4,713	10,485
Skiing—Cross-Country	353	4,374	328	4,797	9,171
Snowboarding	53	827	48	469	1,296
Soccer	11,503	398,351	11,047	361,556	759,907
Softball—Fast-Pitch	77	1,522	15,338	373,535	385,028
Softball—Slow-Pitch	1	26	656	15,920	15,946
Swimming & Diving	6,899	133,900	7,164	160,881	294,781
Synchronized Swimming	0	0	30	557	557
Team Tennis	1,414	28,415	1,457	30,310	58,725

Sport (number of states reporting for boys/girls)	Boys		Girls		Combined
	Number of Schools	Number of Participants	Number of Schools	Number of Participants	Number of Participants
Tennis	9,839	161,367	10,181	182,074	343,441
Track and Field—Indoor	2,638	70,289	2,598	60,397	130,686
Track and Field—Outdoor	15,954	579,302	16,030	475,265	1,054,567
Volleyball	2,078	50,016	15,479	409,332	459,348
Water Polo	768	20,757	762	18,603	39,360
Weight Lifting	787	22,161	445	8,237	30,398
Wrestling	10,407	273,732	1,215	7,351	281,083
Other	155	2,549	161	1,356	3,905

Source: Reprinted from "2010–11 High School Athletics Participation Survey," conducted by the National Federation of State High School Associations, www.nfhs.org/content.aspx?id=3282; used with permission.

either because you want to add another sport during the off-season, or because you're injured and need to find a sport that emphasizes a different muscle group, or because you're new to team sports and you're trying to figure out what to play. This section can help you make a decision.

Know Yourself

Here are four questions to consider when choosing a new sport. Remember: These are just guidelines. You should also talk to your parents, your coaches, and other athletes, and then go for it. You can always change directions if you discover the sport isn't what you thought it would be.

1. What skills and abilities do I have?

Skills and abilities can be divided into three categories: technical, physical, and mental. *Technical skill* refers to the ability to perform a specific sport-related task, for example, dribbling a soccer ball, doing the splits, hitting a baseball, or lifting your body up over a high jump bar. Some technical skills just come naturally. Have you been doing backflips into the pool since you were five? Maybe you should consider gymnastics or diving. Are you an ace at miniature golf? Maybe you're a natural putter and should consider golf as your new sport. Maybe you have great hand-eye coordination and should consider taking up tennis. You can also look for sports that don't involve skills you lack. In the athlete bio, you'll read about McKenzie Cooper, who chose crew precisely because it *didn't* involve hand-eye coordination.

Athlete Bio: McKenzie Cooper, Crew

Before joining the crew team as a freshman in 2008, McKenzie Cooper was not much of an athlete. In fact, she says, "the strongest muscle in my body was my thumb from changing the channel on our remote." By the time she was a senior, however, McKenzie was competing in both crew seasons (fall and spring), and she rowed in four- and eight-person sprints as well as individual long-distance races.

McKenzie decided to try crew after using a rowing machine during freshman registration. "It seemed to come pretty naturally," McKenzie says, adding, "I have no hand-eye coordination whatsoever. [In crew] I don't have to catch anything, I don't have to throw anything. I just have to hold on tight and pull."

At McKenzie's Florida high school, crew is a club sport, which means it's not funded by the school even though they get to wear the school logo. Unlike football or baseball players, rowers (and their parents) raise money to pay for all equipment, uniforms, and transportation—and crew is not cheap. Each boat costs up to thirty thousand dollars! Also, crew regattas always take place off campus; the closest racing spot for McKenzie's team is over twenty-five miles away. As a result, McKenzie says, "we completely go unseen. We don't really get a lot of recognition around the school because we are considered a club sport. . . . The thing with crew is it's not a sport that's widely known if you're not involved in it. It's not like you can turn on the TV and be like, 'Oh, hey, there's rowing on today.' No, you turn it on and you're like, 'Oh, there's a football game, there's a basketball game, there's a baseball game.' It's not a sport that you can grow up knowing that you can try out for."

McKenzie graduated from high school in May 2012 and was accepted into the Sports and Wellness Scholars Program at Ohio State University. She received a full

McKenzie says the two crew seasons are like cross-country and track: "In the fall season we're like cross-country—we row the long distances with endurance and pace—and then in the spring season it's all out." *Photo courtesy of the author.*

academic scholarship as well as an invitation to row on Ohio State's novice crew team. In just four years, McKenzie went from self-proclaimed couch potato to college athlete; that's quite an accomplishment![16]

Physical fitness refers to your overall physical condition, but it also includes several specific factors:[17]

- Speed: the ability to move very quickly in one direction
- Strength: the force a certain muscle group can produce

Did You Know?

In 1852, Harvard defeated Yale in an eight-man rowing competition held on New Hampshire's Lake Winnipesaukee. The race marked the first American intercollegiate athletic competition in any sport.

- Power: a combination of speed and strength, especially needed for jumping, throwing, and hitting
- Endurance: also known as stamina, or the ability to continue physical activity for a long period of time
- Agility: the ability to change direction quickly without slowing down
- Flexibility: the range of motion around a joint

Are you the fastest wide receiver on your team? Maybe you should consider going out for track as a sprinter. Do you have the highest number of blocks on your volleyball team? Maybe you should consider trying the high jump or long jump. Strong soccer kick and nerves of steel? Try out for placekicker on the football team. (For information on which sports involve which technical, physical, and mental skills, check out the book by Francois Fortin listed in the Find Out More section at the end of this chapter.)

The last skill category involves *mental toughness*, which includes "concentration, commitment, control, and confidence."[18] Mental toughness involves the ability to stay focused and tune out the crowd. In basketball, for example, you might have opposing fans screaming and waving their arms as you're trying to make a free throw. Individual sports require a lot of mental toughness because it's just you out there on the wrestling mat or tennis court. You must be confident and controlled under pressure. The mental aspect also involves your personal phobias. If you're afraid of falling, you probably don't want to try pole vault or diving. If you don't like being pushed underwater, you probably don't want to try water polo. (For more on mental toughness, see chapter 3.)

> "I love the competitive aspect of golf and its challenges. It is a game of pure skill and mental strength. You are learning to control your emotions constantly while playing."
> —Rachel, 18, golf

2. What skills and abilities do I want to improve?

Let's say you're a young football player, and you want to increase your overall strength and power. The most obvious

> "I am a pitcher, and I honestly loved having control over the game. I loved having people focus their attention to me, and the added pressure is what helped me focus and ultimately be successful."—Kirsten, 20, softball

It's Never Too Late to Start

Some of you may feel like you're too late to become a successful athlete. Maybe you haven't found a sport you love or maybe you haven't been playing since you were five like some of your teammates. Well, you're in good company. The following professional athletes were late starters just like you, and they have accomplished great things. Don't let your lack of experience keep you from trying a new sport; you might not become the next Michael Jordan, but then again, you might. You'll never know until you try.

Allyson Felix—Felix had never run track competitively when she joined the high school team as a freshman. She showed up for tryouts wearing baggy shorts and clunky basketball shoes, and she still flew down the track. Felix had a gift she never knew she had. Four years later, she broke the U.S. junior (age nineteen and under) record at 200 meters. One year after that, Felix broke the *world* junior record and won a silver medal at the 2004 Olympics. In 2012, Felix participated in her third Olympics and won three gold medals.[19]

Michael Jordan—When he was a high school sophomore, Jordan had to settle for playing on the JV basketball team. Instead of pouting about it, however, he just worked harder; he would think of that team list without his name on it and then give a little extra in the weight room or at practice. Jordan played varsity his junior and senior years of high school, earned a scholarship to the University of North Carolina, and then turned pro after his junior year. The rest, as they say, is history.[20]

Hakeem Olajuwon—Olajuwon played professional basketball for eighteen years, seventeen of those with the Houston Rockets. He was picked ahead of Michael Jordan in the 1984 draft and went on to become a one-time league MVP (1993–1994), twelve-time NBA all-star, and two-time MVP of the NBA finals (1994, 1995). But get this—Olajuwon had never even touched a basketball before he turned fifteen.[21]

You may be thinking, "OK, those are *really* talented athletes. With that kind of talent, they could have started even later and turned pro." True; some athletes have a tremendous amount of natural ability to work with. So, here are a few "regular" athletes who started playing their sport in high school and still succeeded because they put in a lot of hard work.

David—David started playing football as a sophomore in high school, and he didn't see much playing time until his senior year. He was voted Most Improved his senior year and then went on to be the starting mike linebacker during his redshirt freshman year at Moorpark College (redshirt players can work out with the team but they can't play in actual competitions). After that season, Occidental College took an interest in David and began recruiting him. Had David not been deployed to Afghanistan, he probably would have ended up playing at Occidental. As of 2012, David was the defensive coordinator at a California high school.[22]

McKenzie—McKenzie went out for crew as a freshman with no previous experience in *any* sport. That same year, McKenzie and her freshman-four team placed third overall and second scholastically (meaning that among the crew teams connected to a high school, they placed second in the state). As a sophomore, McKenzie and her JV-four team placed third at state and first among school teams, so they earned a trip to Saratoga, New York, for the nationals. At the beginning of her senior year, McKenzie won the 5,000-meter varsity single race at a big regatta in Jacksonville, Florida. At the end of her senior year, McKenzie and her varsity-eight team placed sixth at the state championship regatta—the best performance of a women's varsity-eight team from her high school in eighteen years.[23]

Samantha—As a high school freshman, Samantha decided to join a couple friends who were trying out for water polo; she knew absolutely nothing about the sport. By the end of her freshman year, however, Samantha was awarded MVP of her frosh/soph team. During her sophomore year, Samantha was bumped up to varsity as a starter, and she earned the team's Best Offensive Award as well as all-league honorable mention. As a junior, Samantha won varsity MVP, was named second team all-league, and joined a club water polo team. As a senior, Samantha was named one of the top players in her division of the California Interscholastic Federation, Southern Section—the first time someone from her school had won that honor in eleven years.[24]

option is to hit the weights, but some of you might get sick of the weight room after a while. Another option is to add a sport that emphasizes strength building—wrestling, for example. As an added bonus, wrestling can improve your self-confidence, speed, and agility, all of which will make you a better football player. The same principle applies to other sports. If you have a physical fitness area that needs work, find a sport that can help you improve it. Obviously, you need to check your school's athletic calendar to make sure the new sport doesn't overlap with your current one.

3. What is the best sport for my body type?

In other words, consider looking for a sport that favors the physique you've been given. For example, if you are tall and have long arms, you can use those features to your advantage on a rowing or volleyball team. On the other hand, being short might give you an edge in gymnastics and diving.

That's not to say short people can't row and tall people can't dive; physical attributes such as height do not automatically make or break your future in sports. Even though basketball players are usually tall, there have been some incredible "short" players. Take Nate Robinson, for example. He's five foot nine (by some accounts, he's only five foot seven) in a league where the average height is around six foot seven. But Robinson won the 2009 NBA Slam-Dunk Contest by jumping *over* six-foot-eleven Dwight Howard for the slam. Robinson had a successful college career at the University of Washington, and he's played professionally since 2005.[25]

> "[I like] the fact that it takes more than one person to encounter any sort of achievement, whether it's an effective pass or a goal."
>
> —Amberlee, 16, soccer

4. What are my personal preferences?

In other words, what do you want to play? Do you prefer team sports or individual sports? Outdoor sports or

"What I like about playing golf is that it is all individual and if something goes wrong you can't blame anyone but yourself for not practicing harder."—Jessica H., 20, golf

Ten Personal Essays

In each of the following essays, teens discuss their personal experiences with their sport—what they have learned, why they compete, or what their sport means to them. By reading their stories, you might be reminded of why you love your sport or you might be motivated to try something new.

B., Ashley. "A Practice Session for Life." *Teen Ink*. teenink.com/nonfiction/sports/article/15141/A-Practice-Session-for-Life/. Ashley describes various aspects of her favorite sport and then makes connections to everyday life. She concludes by saying, "Everything I needed to know in life I learned in volleyball."

C., Kim. "The Game of Golf." *Teen Ink*. teenink.com/nonfiction/sports/article/15161/The-Game-of-Golf/. At her mom's suggestion, Kim took up golf and now is so glad she did.

J., Kristyn. "Who's Watching." *Teen Ink*. teenink.com/nonfiction/sports/article/15149/Whorsquos-Watching/. Kristyn's basketball coach asked the team, "What are you doing when no one is watching?" In her essay, Kristyn shares how this question has changed her perspective during off-season conditioning workouts as well as in everyday situations.

K., Caitlin. "Finding Myself on the Mat." *Teen Ink*. teenink.com/nonfiction/sports/article/15171/Finding-Myself-on-the-Mat/. Caitlin shares how joining the boys' high school wrestling team changed her life in positive ways.

L., Brandon. "Life on My Feet." *Teen Ink*. teenink.com/nonfiction/sports/article/15170/Life-on-My-Feet/. Brandon has been running since he was four years old, and he still loves every minute of it.

M., James. "One Hundred Meters." *Teen Ink.* teenink.com/nonfiction/sports/article/15151/One-Hundred-Meters/. James describes the joy and pain involved in swimming the hundred-meter breaststroke.

P., Al. "What Makes a Gymnast." *Teen Ink.* teenink.com/nonfiction/sports/article/15135/What-Makes-a-Gymnast/. According to Al, "gymnastics is one of the most dangerous sports in the world," and that's why he loves it.

R., Renee. "Cheerleading Is a Sport." *Teen Ink.* teenink.com/nonfiction/sports/article/15172/Cheerleading-is-a-Sport/. Renee argues convincingly that competitive cheerleading is a sport with rules and intense physical activity just like gymnastics or volleyball or basketball.

W., Ben. "Gold Buckle Dreams." *Teen Ink.* teenink.com/nonfiction/sports/article/15136/Gold-Buckle-Dreams/. Ben's sport is rodeo, and he describes the adrenaline rush of successfully staying on a buckin' horse—the "1,300 pounds of raw power [that's] trying to pitch you into the dirt."

W., Eric. "Brothers." *Teen Ink.* teenink.com/nonfiction/sports/article/15147/Brothers/. Eric is a football player who views his teammates as brothers. In this essay, he describes the bond that forms through training, playing, and sacrificing to achieve a common goal.

indoor sports? Winter sports or spring sports (this might depend on the season that's already taken by your current sport)? Is it important to be with friends, or do you want to meet new people? Do you want to run a lot or not so much? Another option is to try something that's exactly the opposite of what you would normally choose. You might find you actually like it.

The Last Lap
The clock is ticking
Time increases
Close to the wall
The last lap
I catch a glimpse of light
through the clear water
Butterfly kick
the fastest way to get through the water
Stroke, Stroke, Breathe
Stroke, Stroke, Breathe

I'm close to the end
I dare not distract myself
with other swimmers
at this point in the race
I need to finish first!
So close, So close
and . . .
Done!
I'm out of breath
The clock says I win
The crowd says I'm the best.
—Jamie, 18, swimming[26]

Good Read: Dairy Queen *by* Catherine Gilbert Murdock

Sport: Football

Life apps: Family dynamics, friendship, communication, importance of hard work

Summary: D.J. lives on a farm in the small town of Red Bend, Wisconsin. She grew up playing football with her two older brothers, both of whom are playing football in college. They trained hard during the off-season, and D.J. used to join in their workouts—running sprints, catching passes, making tackles. She knows the sport as well as anyone, which is why a family friend (who happens to be the football coach at the rival high school) asks her to train Brian, the rival's quarterback, to get him into shape.

After the summer of training, D.J. decides to try out for her own high school team, though she doesn't tell Brian or her parents. She makes the team and ends up facing Brian on the field, which puts a little strain on their friendship.

Narrated by D.J. in a sarcastic, conversational voice, *Dairy Queen* is thoughtful and honest, as well as laugh-out-loud funny. The author has written two sequels: *The Off Season* (2007) and *Front and Center* (2009).

Houghton Mifflin, 2006

275 pages

Title IX and You

There haven't always been so many sports to choose from—at least not for girls. Up until the early 1970s, most high schools only had three girls' teams—swimming, tennis, and track—and colleges had even fewer options. To make matters worse, girls who wanted to play on boys' teams usually weren't allowed to do so. Hundreds of thousands of would-be high school athletes were forced to sit on the sidelines and watch the boys run around the bases and dribble down the court.

Then came Title IX. This little law really changed everything in high school and college athletics, and the effects are still being felt today. Here's how.

What the Law Says

Title IX is part of a larger education bill passed in 1972. It specifically addresses discrimination based on sex in school programs and activities: "No person in the United States shall, on the basis of sex, be excluded from participation in, be denied the benefits of, or be subjected to discrimination under any education program or activity receiving Federal financial assistance."[27]

In other words, schools receiving money from the government have to provide the same opportunities for boys and girls—both in the classroom and on the playing field. Before 1972, many high schools discouraged girls from taking advanced math and science courses, and many universities didn't even accept female students. Both high schools and colleges limited girls' athletic options. Schools that

Did You Know?

During the 2010–2011 school year, 241 U.S. high schools had girls' eleven-player football teams. Texas had the most girls playing football, yet according to the NFHS survey, the state did not have one girls' team. That means all 316 girls played on the boys' teams.[28]

A few girls playing on guys' teams made headlines in 2011. For example, Jackie Kasburg from Ohio kicked three extra points in her first game and was later crowned homecoming queen; Brianna Amat from Michigan kicked the game-winning field goal shortly after being crowned homecoming queen; and Jaline DeJesus from Florida became the first girl to play football in Florida's top high school division (she went in at cornerback).[29]

What Do You Think?

Girls are allowed to wrestle on boys' teams. In 2011, two girls made it to the Iowa state championships wrestling against boys.[30] Girls are also allowed to kick field goals and extra points; they're even allowed to play cornerback on boys' football teams.[31] But what about guys playing on girls' teams?

In 2011, Brandon Urbas made his Michigan high school cheerleading team. He cheered at football games all fall. But when the team entered its first competitive event of the season, Brandon's team was disqualified because Brandon is a boy.

According to the Michigan High School Athletic Association (MHSAA) rules, "girls can compete on boys' teams in sports where a girls' team is not offered, but boys are not allowed to compete on any girls' squads in competitive sports where a male option is not offered." After Brandon's team was disqualified, the MHSAA issued this statement: "Boys may not participate on a girls' team in MHSAA sponsored postseason meets and tournaments. . . . Schools have adopted this position to preserve participation opportunities for the historically underrepresented gender."[32]

But are girls really underrepresented in cheerleading? Do you think this is an example of gender discrimination, the very thing Title IX was trying to stop? Or does this rule make sense? Many high schools have a volleyball team for girls but not for guys, but it probably makes sense to prohibit guys from joining the girls' team. If this is the case, should the rule be applied consistently to every sport, including competitive cheer?

had girls' teams treated them like second-class citizens. Whereas boys' coaches were paid, girls' coaches were volunteers. Girls got hand-me-down equipment from the boys, and they didn't have buses provided for transportation to away games; instead, they had to carpool and pay for gas themselves. According to Title IX, if schools didn't start making things more even, they would lose federal funding.

How the Law Has Been Applied

Basically, Title IX requires schools to provide equal opportunities for guys and girls. Practically, that means

- girls and guys must enjoy the same quality of locker rooms, equipment, and coaching;
- girls and guys must have the same access to playing fields and school-funded transportation; and
- girls must have the same opportunities to play even if schools spend more money on boys' athletics (some sports, such as football, cost more to run).[33]

High schools started adding girls' sports during the 1972–1973 school year, and hundreds of thousands of girls across the country jumped at the chance to play. In 1971–1972 just 294,015 girls participated in high school athletics (compared to 3,666,917 boys); in 1972–1973, girls' participation soared to 817,073. That's an increase of over 520,000; comparatively, the increase in boys' participation was just 103,720.[34]

Good Law, Bad Rap

College sports changed more slowly. It wasn't until the early 1990s—nearly twenty years after Title IX passed—that the NCAA (National Collegiate Athletic Association) finally made real progress in adding more women's teams and athletic scholarships. These changes partly resulted from changes in how Title IX was enforced. Instead of looking for clear signs that a school was discriminating against women, the U.S. Department of Education's Office of Civil Rights (OCR) began using proportionality as the standard; that is, if a college campus has a student body that's 50 percent female and 50 percent male, there should be an equal number of men's and women's athletic teams. If the campus is 60 percent female, women should have more athletic teams than men. The same proportionality rule

? Did You Know?

In Oklahoma during the 2010–2011 school year, the number of girls playing high school sports exceeded the number of boys who participated. That's the first time girl participants have exceeded boy participants in any state in the thirty-eight years that participation statistics have been kept.[35]

The Battle of the Sexes

Perhaps the most significant victory for women's sports happened on a tennis court in Houston, Texas. Bobby Riggs was a fifty-five-year-old former professional tennis player who had won Wimbledon in 1939. He was also a self-proclaimed male chauvinist pig—someone who believed women were inferior to men in every way, athletic talent included. To prove his point, Riggs challenged several professional women's tennis players to a match. On Mother's Day 1973, Riggs slaughtered his first female opponent, Margaret Court. He had also challenged Billie Jean King, a twenty-nine-year-old tennis player who had already won two Wimbledon titles. King had turned him down a couple times because, as she said, "I thought it would set us back 50 years if I didn't win that match. . . . It would ruin the women's tour and affect all women's self-esteem." After Riggs beat Margaret Court, King accepted finally his challenge.

On September 20, 1973, King not only beat Riggs, she destroyed him in straight sets (6–4, 6–3, 6–3) in front of 50 million television viewers. The so-called Battle of the Sexes was a huge victory for women's sports. King proved that women could be talented, hard-hitting athletes just like men. Girls across the country started playing tennis and other sports because King had shown them that it was OK to be a "jock."

Over the course of her tennis career, King won thirty-nine Grand Slam titles. She also became a crusader for women's athletics, starting a women's sports magazine and a women's sports foundation. In 1990, she was named one of the *Life* magazine's "100 Most Important Americans of the 20th Century."[36]

applies to the money available for athletic scholarships, though today the proportions are mostly determined by the NCAA and not individual schools.

With a limited amount of money available and a quota to meet, many colleges and universities have dropped men's athletic programs in order to add programs for women. Since the 1990s, more than two hundred successful men's athletic programs have been cut at universities across the country, mainly in sports like gymnastics, swimming, and wrestling.[37] In the men's sports that remain, there's a cap on the number of athletic scholarships that can be handed

Women in the Summer Olympics[38]

The first modern Summer Olympics were held in 1896, but women could not compete until four years later. Even then, only three events were available. The following chart shows when selected women' events were added to the Olympics, followed by the year the corresponding men's event was added. Notice that only volleyball debuted as a medal event for men and women in the same year.

Olympic Event	Women's First Year	Men's First Year
Tennis, golf, yachting	1900	1896
Swimming, diving	1912	1896
Gymnastics, track and field	1928	1896
Volleyball	1964	1964
Basketball	1976	1936
Field hockey	1980	1908
Marathon	1984	1896
Soccer	1996	1908
Water polo	2000	1900
Wrestling	2004	1896
Boxing	2012	1904

out so that money can be used for women's scholarships. Almost without exception, women end up having more available scholarships than men in any NCAA Division I sports where there's both a men's and women's team. For example, as of 2012, women's basketball had 15 (versus 13 for men), women's gymnastics had 12 (versus 6.3), women's volleyball had 12 (versus 4.5), and women's crew had 20 (versus zero).

"For women in this sport [crew] there are a lot more college scholarships available because of Title IX. . . . But there are not nearly as many women in the sport as there are men. . . . Girls really don't want to have rougher hands or bigger muscles than their boyfriends."—McKenzie, 17, crew

Some people blame Title IX for limiting men's options at the college level. Before you jump on that bandwagon, consider this: First, the original intent of Title IX was to end discrimination against women, not to make athletic opportunities proportional to the male-female ratio of a student body. In many cases, the proportionality rule doesn't make sense. For example, consider the situation at California State University, Bakersfield. In the mid-1990s, female students outnumbered male students by about a 60–40 percent ratio, so according to the proportionality rule, women should have had more athletic options than men. However, at least half of those female students were over forty years old; they were most likely not interested in playing intercollegiate soccer or basketball. Yet there was still talk of cutting Cal State Bakersfield's successful men's wrestling team to give female students that opportunity. Why cut men's programs to achieve proportionality for women who aren't going to play anyway?[39] (As of the 2010–2011 school year, the male-female ratio was about the same at Cal State Bakersfield—38 percent male, 62 percent female[40]—and the wrestling team was still competing.)

Athlete Bio: Noah Davisson, Volleyball

Noah is one of thousands of male athletes affected by the current implementation of Title IX. He played volleyball throughout high school, both at his school and on a club team. As a senior, Noah and his club team won the 2009 Boys' Junior National Championships.

Yet when it came to playing in college, Noah's choices were slim—not because colleges weren't interested in him, but because very few NCAA schools even have a men's volleyball program due to Title IX. There are around 350 NCAA Division I schools; as of 2012, only 23 of those colleges have men's volleyball programs (while 329 have volleyball for women). Each of those 23 programs has only 4.5 scholarships to offer incoming freshmen each year, and teams generally recruit more than 4.5 players. As a result, Noah wasn't offered anything close to a full-ride scholarship by any of the ten or so colleges that recruited him. The highest offer was 40 percent, but because this was from an out-of-state school, it would have barely covered the out-of-state fees and Noah would have been stuck with a big college tuition bill.

Ultimately, Noah ended up at UCLA: "Once I knew UCLA was interested, I just kind of stopped talking to everybody else. I was going to take an official [visit] to Hawaii. I was going to take an official to Long Beach [State]. But once I took my official to UCLA I just kind of made a decision." Noah actually turned down the partial athletic scholarship because he got more money through nonathletic financial aid, and you can't accept both.

At UCLA, Noah found the competition for playing time was fierce. Because there are so few volleyball programs, each team is stacked with some incredible talent. As a result, Noah says, coaches usually want the freshmen to redshirt. Even after his freshman year, however, Noah still didn't see any playing time. He says this was one of the hardest parts about his college experience: "The toughest part is definitely coming in and realizing how much you need to develop. Most guys don't play for their first three years. Most guys will red-

Noah (number 33) says the fact that he had a 4.3 GPA made college coaches very happy. They knew they didn't have to worry about his academic eligibility. *Photo courtesy of Brad Hagen.*

shirt, not play, not play, suit up and maybe play, and then senior year they'll slowly play. Those first three years are rough because you're used to constantly playing."

As it turned out, Noah injured his back halfway through his second year and ended up leaving the team. After taking a whole summer off volleyball, Noah started training for the U.S. beach volleyball team. As of 2012, he was also coaching a girls' high school club team and was set to graduate in 2013. Noah says, "I didn't know the nature of the men's volleyball program until I got here obviously [i.e., fact that it would be so competitive to get playing time], but I'm content that I'm attending such a decorated institution."[41]

Second, schools are not required to cut men's programs to make room for women's; they just need to find ways to spend less money on men's sports so they have enough for women's. So, are there other ways to save money on men's sports? Writer Andrew Zimbalist thinks so; here are a few of his suggestions:[42]

1. Reduce salaries for men's coaches, especially in sports such as basketball and football, where a head coach often makes more than the president of the university. Zimbalist suggests that doing so would save many schools around $1 million a year—enough to finance two Division I swimming and diving teams.
2. Reduce the number of coaches in sports where there's an excessive number—football, for example, where the average team has 10.3 assistant coaches each making more than sixty thousand dollars plus benefits. Zimbalist suggests that cutting three coaches would pay for a men's Division I tennis team.
3. Reduce the number of football scholarships offered each year. Right now, that number is eighty-five. Because this number is so high and because women must be given proportional numbers of scholarships, other men's sports have very few scholarships to offer. If you total the number of football players on offense, defense, and special teams, you come up with about thirty-five. Add twenty players in case of injuries, and you still only come up with fifty-five. Why do coaches need to recruit eighty-five players each year? Even NFL teams only carry forty-five. Zimbalist suggests that by reducing the number of recruited football players to sixty, each school would save around $350,000—enough to field a Division I wrestling team.

With these factors in mind, it seems like it's actually the OCR's enforcement of Title IX and colleges' funding choices that have limited men's options—not Title IX itself.

It's a Fact

Like it or not, the fact is that, overall, men are more interested in sports than women. Even with more scholarships and sports available to them, fewer women are involved in college athletics than men. As of the 2010–2011 school year, NCAA schools fielded 9,746 women's teams and 8,568 men's squads (a difference of 1,178 teams), yet male athletes still outnumbered female athletes—252,946 men verses 191,131 women.[43]

Find Out More

Books

Berman, Len. *The Greatest Moments in Sports*. Naperville, IL: Sourcebooks, 2009.

Blumenthal, Karen. *Let Me Play: The Story of Title IX*. New York: Antheneum Books, 2005.

Fortin, Francois, ed. *Sports: The Complete Visual Reference*. Willowdale, ON: Firefly Books, 2000.

Human Kinetics, with Thomas Hanlon. *The Sports Rules Book: Essential Rules, Terms, and Procedures for 54 Sports*. 3rd ed. Champaign, IL: Human Kinetics, 2009.

Platt, Richard. *They Played What?! The Weird History of Sports and Recreation*. Minnetonka, MN: Two-Can, 2007.

Smith, Roger. *Teens and Rural Sports: Rodeos, Horses, Hunting, and Fishing*. Broomhall, PA: Mason Crest Publishers, 2008.

Summers, David, ed. *The Sports Book: The Games, the Rules, the Tactics, the Techniques*. London: DK Publishing, 2007.

Chapters

Olson, Walter. "Title IX Is Unfair to Men's Sports." In *Sports and Athletes*, ed. Christine Watkins, 139–46. Detroit: Greenhaven Press, 2009.

Zimbalist, Andrew. "Title IX Is Not Unfair to Men's Sports." In *Sports and Athletes*, ed. Christine Watkins, 147–53. Detroit: Greenhaven Press, 2009.

Online Article

The Nemours Foundation/KidsHealth. "Choosing the Right Sport for You." TeensHealth, reviewed January 2011. kidshealth.org/teen/food_fitness/exercise/find_sports.html?tracking=T_RelatedArticle#.

Notes

1. Apostolos Greek Tours, Inc., "History: The Athens Marathon," www.athensmarathon.com/marathon/history.html (accessed October 7, 2011).
2. Francois Fortin, ed., *Sports: The Complete Visual Reference* (Willowdale, ON: Firefly Books, 2000), 328; History World, "History of Sports and Games," www.historyworld.net/wrldhis/PlainTextHistories.asp?historyid=ac02 (accessed April 2, 2012); National Federation of State High School Associations (NFHS), "Participation Statistics," www.nfhs.org/Participation/SportSearch.aspx (accessed April 1, 2012).

3. Sean Stewart Price, *Sports: Truth and Rumors* (Mankato, MN: Capstone Press, 2011), 6–7.
4. Mark Hyman, "A Survey of Youth Sports Finds Winning Isn't the Only Thing," *New York Times*, January 31, 2010.
5. *Merriam-Webster Online*, s.v. "Sport," www.merriam-webster.com/dictionary/sport?show=1&t=1320959571 (accessed November 10, 2011).
6. Theresa Castellone and Christina Dimauro, "History of Field Hockey," The Game of Field Hockey, www.uri.edu/personal/tcas8605/ (accessed March 31, 2012); Fortin, *Sports*, 234; NFHS, "2010–11 High School Athletics Participation Survey," p. 51, www.nfhs.org/content .aspx?id=3282 (accessed March 31, 2012).
7. The Nemours Foundation /KidsHealth, "Five Reasons for Girls to Play Sports," Teens Health, last reviewed May 2011, kidshealth.org/teen/food_fitness/sports/girls_sports.html (accessed November 22, 2011).
8. Both studies cited in NFHS, "The Case for High School Activities," pp. 4, 8, www.nfhs.org/content.aspx?id=3262 (accessed November 22, 2011).
9. Josh Cohen, e-mail to author, March 10, 2012.
10. Jonathan Zimmerman, "The Place of Sports in American Culture Is Too Extreme," in *Sports and Athletes*, ed. Noël Merino (Farmington Hills, MI: Greenhaven Press, 2011), 21; Jonathan Wall, "Football Player Dies from Head Injury Sustained during Game," *Pep Rally: A Y! Sports Blog*, October 16, 2011, rivals.yahoo.com/highschool/blog/prep_rally/post/Football-player -dies-from-head-injury-sustained-?urn=highschool-wp7202 (accessed November 25, 2011).
11. Greg Wyshynski, "After 16-Year-Old Hockey Player Dies, Safety Debate Begins," *Puck Daddy: A Y! Sports Blog*, November 15, 2011, sports.yahoo.com/nhl/blog/puck_daddy/post/After -16-year-old-hockey-player-dies-safety-deb?urn=nhl-wp17481 (accessed November 25, 2011).
12. Terry Ziegler, "Chronic Traumatic Encephalopathy (CTE)," SportsMD, February 1, 2012, www.sportsmd.com/Articles/id/44.aspx (accessed May 26, 2012).
13. The Nemours Foundation/KidsHealth, "Female Athlete Triad," TeensHealth, last reviewed February 2010, kidshealth.org/teen/food_fitness/sports/triad.html (accessed November 25, 2011).
14. Christine Watkins, "Introduction," in *Sports and Athletes*, ed. Christine Watkins (Farmington Hills, MI: Greenhaven Press, 2009), 15–16.
15. Ashley B., "A Practice Session for Life," *Teen Ink*, teenink.com/nonfiction/sports/article/15141/A-Practice-Session-for-Life/ (accessed November 23, 2011).
16. McKenzie Cooper, interview with author, December 3, 2011; Kelly Humphreys, e-mail to author, May 28, 2012.
17. Clive Gifford, *Sports* (Mankato, MN: Evans Brothers, 2010), 10–11.
18. Youth Sport Trust (Great Britain), *The Young Athlete's Handbook* (Champaign, IL: Human Kinetics, 2001), 4.
19. Bonnie D. Ford, "Learning Curve," ESPN.com, sports.espn.go.com/espn/eticket/story?page=allysonfelix (accessed December 1, 2011).
20. Larry Schwartz, "Michael Jordan Transcends Hoops," ESPN.com, espn.go.com/sports century/features/00016048.html (accessed November 14, 2011).
21. ESPN.com, "Hakeem Olajuwon Biography," espn.go.com/nba/player/bio/_/id/619/hakeem -olajuwon#5 (accessed November 14, 2011).
22. David Schuster, e-mail to author, November 14, 2011.
23. Cooper, interview; Humphreys, e-mail.
24. Samantha Buliavac, e-mails to author, November 19 and 22, 2011; Jeff Tully, "Two Indians Named All-CIF," *Burbank Leader*, March 14, 2012, www.burbankleader.com/sports/tn-blr -sp-allcif-20120314,0,3073300.story (accessed March 15, 2012).

25. "Sprite 2009 Dunk Contest Winner," *Yo! Magazine.net*, February 21, 2009, www.yo
magazine.net/sports/2009/feburary/21_02_09/Sprite%202009%20Dunk%20Contest%20
Winner.htm (accessed December 1, 2011).

26. Jamie wrote "The Last Lap" when she was a freshman. Reprinted with permission.

27. "Title IX, Education Amendments of 1972," United States Department of Labor, www.dol
.gov/oasam/regs/statutes/titleix.htm (accessed December 6, 2011).

28. NFHS, "2010–11 High School Athletics," 51, 61.

29. Cameron Smith, "Ohio Girl Is Homecoming Queen and Star Kicker on Same Night," *Pep
Rally: A Y! Sports Blog*, October 9, 2011, rivals.yahoo.com/highschool/blog/prep_rally/
post/Ohio-girl-is-homecoming-queen-and-star-kicker-on?urn=highschool-275126 (accessed April 2, 2012); "Homecoming Queen Kicks Winning FG," *FOXSports.com*, October 3, 2011, msn.foxsports.com/other/story/Homecoming-queen-kicks-game-winning
-field-goal-100311?GT1=39002 (accessed March 1, 2012); Cameron Smith, "Female Cornerback Breaks Florida 6A Football Glass Ceiling," *Pep Rally: A Y! Sports Blog*, rivals
.yahoo.com/highschool/blog/prep_rally/post/Female-cornerback-breaks-Florida-6A-football
-gla?urn=highschool-272241 (accessed March 1, 2012).

30. Associated Press, "Teen Wrestler Refuses to Compete against Girl in State Tourney Match,"
New York Post, February 17, 2011, www.nypost.com/p/news/national/teen_wrestler_forfeits
_state_tourney_9D4ha5zDBXowUkd3rd5nwI (accessed March 1, 2012).

31. "Homecoming Queen Kicks Winning FG"; Smith, "Female Cornerback Breaks Florida 6A
Football Glass Ceiling."

32. Cameron Smith, "Male Cheerleader Gets Team Disqualified . . . Because He's a Boy," *Pep Rally:
A Y! Sports Blog*, December 16, 2011, rivals.yahoo.com/highschool/blog/prep_rally/post/Male
-cheerleader-gets-team-disqualified-8230-?urn=highschool-wp10098 (accessed March 1, 2012).

33. Karen Blumenthal, *Let Me Play: The Story of Title IX* (New York: Antheneum Books, 2005),
69–71.

34. NFHS, "2010–11 High School Athletics," 52.

35. NFHS, "High School Sports Participation Continues Upward Climb" (press release), August
23, 2011, www.nfhs.org/content.aspx?id=5752 (accessed October 13, 2011).

36. Larry Schwartz, "Billie Jean Won for All Women," ESPN.com, espn.go.com/sportscentury/
features/00016060.html (accessed March 3, 2012).

37. Elizabeth Arens, "Title IX Is Unfair to Men's Sports," in *Sports and Athletes: Opposing Viewpoints*, ed. Laura K. Egendorf (San Diego, CA: Greenhaven Press, 1999), 128.

38. FunTrivia.com, "Fun Trivia: O: Olympics History," www.funtrivia.com/en/subtopics/
Olympic-Sport-Debut-Years-115147.html (accessed October 17, 2011); Blumenthal, *Let Me
Play*, 54.

39. Arens, "Title IX," 129–30.

40. "California State University—Bakersfield," *U.S. News and World Report*, colleges.usnews
.rankingsandreviews.com/best-colleges/csub-7993 (accessed May 19, 2012)

41. Noah Davisson, interview with author, February 3, 2012.

42. Andrew Zimbalist, "Title IX Is Not Unfair to Men's Sports," in *Sports and Athletes*, ed.
Christine Watkins (Farmington Hills, MI: Greenhaven Press, 2009), 151–52.

43. National Collegiate Athletic Association, "NCAA Participation Rates Going Up," NCAA
.com, November 2, 2011, www.ncaa.com/news/ncaa/article/2011-11-02/ncaa-participation
-rates-going (accessed May 19, 2012).

THE LIFE OF A STUDENT-ATHLETE

"The hardest thing is trying to balance school, swim, work, and church as well as getting enough sleep. You have to figure out what things you want to/have to sacrifice to participate in everything at the same time."—Jamie, 18, swimming

Balancing Act

Chapter 1 emphasized the positive aspects of sports—the thrill of running the bases after a great hit, the rewards of working together as a team to win a game, the mental and emotional boost gained from intense physical activity. But as you all know, sports also involve a lot of hard work and not just on the field or in the weight room. Being part of a team involves a big-time commitment, making it difficult to keep up with homework, tests, and papers, let alone hang out with friends and sleep. Such is the life of the student-athlete. It's a balancing act that requires effective time management, discipline, and sacrifice.

As a student-athlete there are the things you *have to do* (go to school, study, write papers, practice, attend team dinners, participate in games, attend "required" family functions, sleep, etc.) and the things you *want to do* (hang out with your friends, go to the movies, sleep in on weekends, spend time with your

---

! It's a Fact

Of the student-athletes I surveyed, over half said they spend (or spent) ten to twenty hours per week involved in practice, training, competitions, and travel to and from competitions. Those on club or travel teams spend/spent up to fifty hours a week since more practice and travel is involved. How do these numbers compare with your experience?

> "There is no way you can have family, sports, school, friends, and, most importantly, sleep. It's literally impossible. So I've had to cut out the friends and replace them with teammates and even at times removed the family and replaced them with coaches. . . . But I've found that if my daily routine is just school, sports, food, homework, sleep, I am fairly successful."
> —Caitlin, 16, tennis

> "I find that if I were to skip practice in order to study, I would just procrastinate more and probably get just as much done and not have fresh air or exercise all day."—Annalise, 18, Nordic skiing

boyfriend/girlfriend, etc.). The key is learning to prioritize and do the most important things first. However, the reality is that you often have several have-to-do things happening at the same time—a championship game to prepare for, a biology test to study for, an English paper to write, and sleep to squeeze in.

So how are you supposed do it all? I surveyed more than thirty current and former high school student-athletes and asked how they did it. Here are some tips that have worked for them:

1. *Keep your goals in mind*—both academically and athletically. Remember that you are a *student*-athlete; the student part comes first. Those of you hoping to play in college on scholarship, consider this: If you don't keep your grades up, you don't play. If you don't play, you don't get noticed by college scouts. Also, college coaches don't want athletes they have to babysit. They want student-athletes who can manage their own time and keep up on their school assignments. Keeping these goals in mind makes it easier to do the hard thing—like staying home to finish a paper instead of going to the movies—when you need to.

> "At our school we have to have a 2.0 GPA to stay on the team. A lot of the time I have to stay up late to get my homework and studies finished."
> —Andy, 15, swimming

"In high school I focused a lot of my time and attention to softball, so I often would give up hours of study time. I maintained a 3.5 in high school, but I know if I dedicated more time to my studies, I would have had a higher GPA and also had more options for different colleges."—Kirsten, 20, softball

2. *Be willing to make some sacrifices.* This point goes along with the first one, and as most of you know, giving up free time during season is one of your biggest sacrifices.
3. *Take advantage of every free moment you have.* For example, use bus rides to and from competitions to finish an assignment, study for a test, or catch up on sleep. While waiting for your ride, pull out your book for English and read a little. When you don't have big blocks of time, every little bit helps.
4. *Get as much done in class as possible.* That means schoolwork, not sleep!
5. *Create a calendar* with due dates (papers, projects, book reports, etc.), test dates, competitions, practices, family commitments, work hours, and anything else you have to do. Keep the calendar with you at all times and look at it often. You might even make two versions—a wall calendar for your bedroom and a pocket size for your backpack.
6. *Set a study place and time.* The place might be your bedroom, the dining room table, a spare room, or the public library. The time might be after practice, before dinner, or after dinner. You need to pick the place and time that works best for you; the quieter, the better so you can work without distraction and finish more quickly. If you're old enough to drive and your parents will loan you the car, you might try the public library to get away from the distractions of home—TV, Xbox, and so on.
7. *Ask for help.* If you find yourself overwhelmed or if you keep missing important due dates, it might be time to ask someone to keep you accountable—a coach, parent, tutor, teammate, friend, or older sibling. Show him

"The hardest part for me is just being exhausted all the time. During school it's difficult to balance homework and practicing because when you get home all you'd like to do is get some food and sleep. But during summer the hardest part is having to cancel plans with friends because you have no time to hang out or do something during your only school break in the year."
—Samantha, 17, water polo

What Do You Think?

Should homeschooled athletes be allowed to join varsity teams at public schools? Since the rise of NFL quarterback Tim Tebow, the legislatures in many states have been debating this issue. Tim was homeschooled by his mom and played football for a public school in Florida—one of twenty-five states that allow homeschooled student-athletes to play with public high school teams. Tim Tebow is probably the most famous homeschooled athlete ever.

As of 2012, Virginia, Mississippi, and Alabama were all considering legislation that would allow homeschoolers to play on public school teams. Many people are against this idea; here are some of their arguments:[1]

- When students choose to be homeschooled, they give up their privilege of participating on public school teams.
- Homeschoolers might take the place of public school students on the roster.
- It's very difficult to hold homeschooled students to the same academic, attendance, and discipline requirements that public school students must meet in order to compete.
- It could create a recruiting war between schools who want a certain homeschooled student-athlete to play for them.

On the other hand, even homeschooling families pay taxes, and those taxes help pay for public school athletic teams. Should this give homeschooled students the right to play varsity sports?

or her your schedule. Ask for suggestions on how to make it work better. Just knowing that someone else is going to ask if you studied or finished the paper might be motivation to get it done on your own.

During the course of your high school career, you're undoubtedly going to give up some things to maintain your student-athlete balancing act. I asked my survey takers what they've given up due to their busy school and sports schedule; the most common answers were sleep, free time, spending time with a girlfriend or boyfriend, hanging out with friends, and sleeping in on weekends. Some mentioned missing a specific event. For example, Megan, a sixteen-year-old softball player, had to miss her sister's wedding reception because her team made it to the championship game of the little league state tournament. Mikalla, a fifteen-year-old soccer player, had to give up a spot in her school's show choir, which was something she had to try out for. Others mentioned missing out on football games, school dances, and church youth groups because they were playing in a game or traveling to a tournament.

After a couple years of this balancing act, some of you might decide that it's too much and that your sport is the thing that has to go. Your high school years are a time for figuring out what you really like to do; for you, it might be theater or music and not soccer or wrestling. During her first two years of high school, nineteen-year-old Anna tried to balance track and field with the rest of her activities and then decided it just wasn't working for her: "I would have a full school day, track practice,

> "In high school I think I gave up a little bit of a 'life' in order to balance the pressure of sports and studies, but at the same time I do not regret or feel like I missed out on a lot."
> —Jacque, 22, volleyball

tutor students, and then go home to do my own homework and music practice. Then on the weekends we had all-day track meets, and then an all-day orchestra rehearsal on Sunday. I ended up having to drop track my junior and senior year of high school to have more free time."[2] Remember: Sports are supposed to be fun. If you're always tired or stressed or just not enjoying your sport, maybe it's time to take a break and reevaluate.

It's a 24/7 Thing

> *"We are not trying to interfere with what happens outside of schools, . . . [but] if you're going to represent the school we expect you to uphold that image 24/7."*
> —*Superintendent Joseph F. Casey, Massachusetts*[3]

Maybe you've never thought of it this way, but being a student-athlete carries a lot of responsibility. Everywhere you go—another school's campus, a tournament, the movies, a party—you represent your team and your school. Being a student-athlete is part of who you are no matter where you are.

Athlete Bio: Jessica Doyle, Basketball

Basketball is a tradition in the Doyle family. Jessica's two older brothers played, her dad played, and Jessica joined them playing in the driveway when she was seven or eight. Jessica joined her first rec league team when she was around nine and was coached by her dad until she reached high school.

In 2011, in between her sophomore and junior years, Jessica decided to transfer—not for athletic reasons, but for academic ones. She had been in honors English at her first high school, but she wanted more of a challenge—something to better prepare her for college. The new school offered two such programs: the Cambridge Program and the Sports Medicine Academy. The Cambridge Program is part of AICE (Advanced International Certificate of Education) and is overseen by the University of Cambridge in the United Kingdom. The courses are specifically designed to prepare students for advanced degree programs in college. The Sports Medicine Academy is basically a school within the high school. Jessica takes courses in first aid, CPR, health science, sports psychology, and anatomy, and when she's done, she'll graduate with a certificate in sports medicine.

The new programs didn't add more work, but Jessica says the work is definitely harder. Plus she has to keep a higher GPA than her teammates who aren't in the Cambridge Program. To keep on top of all her assignments, Jessica uses every spare minute, including bus time and waiting during JV games: "Our whole team does some homework [on the bus], and we usually have some of the same classes so we try to help each other out." Jessica also says, "My

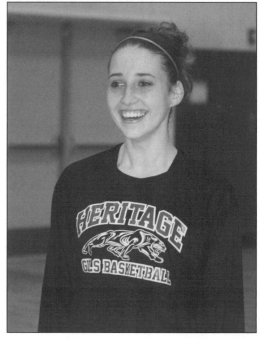

Jessica says a key lesson she learned in basketball is to work hard no matter who's watching you. *Photo courtesy of the author.*

mom's usually the one who's like 'don't forget, don't forget.' She reminds me a lot 'cause I forget."

Though she's only a junior, Jessica is thinking about college. Her dream school is the University of Tennessee, both for its academics and for its basketball program. She says, "I went to their camp two years in a row when I was younger and I got to meet Pat Summit." At those basketball camps, Jessica found out about being a practice player for college teams. Even if she doesn't get recruited, being a practice player would be a way to keep playing while getting a college education. For Jessica, "school is most important, really. You can't slack off in that."[4]

What Is the Hardest Part of Playing Your Sport?

"Having a job while being in school and playing a year-round sport."—Jessica H., 20, golf

"Trying to be the best I can be."—Cameron, 17, baseball

"Learning to control my anger/competitiveness."—Alyssa, 16, softball

"Staying focused during school on game days."—Davon, 19, football

"The hardest part is probably keeping everyone happy and in shape to do the best of their abilities for the team to do its best as a whole. Which includes having everyone at practices!"—Jessica U., 16, competitive cheer

"Maintaining the constant weight."—Derek, 18, wrestling

"Learning to work as a team and keeping the drama off the field."—Taylor H., 15, softball

"Balancing school and football. I always gave football first priority and that always caused more problems for me than anything. It's very, very hard doing both school and football, especially in college. It gets worse as the season goes because you get so tired after practice too and doing homework sucks."—David, 23, football

Role Model

Who are the most popular or well-known students at your high school? My guess is that many of them are athletes, particularly athletes in the most popular sports. Some of you may be part of that crowd, and there's nothing wrong with that. If classmates know who you are because you give 100 percent on every play,

Linsanity!

If you listened to the news in February of 2012, you no doubt heard about Jeremy Lin, the twenty-three-year-old benchwarmer who skyrocketed to stardom on the basketball court. The press had a field day with his last name, coming up with a long list of words: Linsanity, Linderella, and, unfortunately, Linsurgery (Lin had knee surgery in April 2012, ending his Lincredible season). Lin went from being number fifteen on the New York Knicks' roster to being on the cover of *Sports Illustrated* in less than three weeks. How did he do it? Hard work, lots of hard work.

If you're looking for a positive role model, consider Lin. He went undrafted out of Harvard, signed with the Golden State Warriors, got waived by the Warriors and picked up by the Houston Rockets, who then let him go before the 2011–2012 season even started. Then the New York Knicks picked him up, but they soon sent him down to the D-League, where he stayed until shortly before he got his chance to play on February 4, 2012. Lin says, "The journey was very different. Getting waived twice, going to the D-League four times, just fighting for a spot in any rotation, and being basically a 15th guy on a roster, that's tough at times." But he didn't give up, and it finally paid off.

How has Lin reacted to his sudden stardom? Has he rubbed it in people's faces, saying, "See?! I told you I was all that!"? Not even close. He's about as humble as you can get, and he's just happy to be playing the game he loves. According to his teammate Jared Jeffries, Lin "has inspired us to play harder because he gives it his all every day." Former coach Mike D'Antoni says, "He's a good guy, it's all about the team. . . . His defense is good, his energy is good, his personality rubs off on everybody." That's the kind of role model you want to be.[5]

you score goals, you make diving catches, you lead the team in assists, you hustle up and down the court, and you give your school and community something to cheer about—good for you! That's exactly the kind of role model your classmates need—someone who's a hardworking, self-sacrificing team player.

However, some high school athletes let that popularity go to their heads. They become arrogant and boastful. They think of themselves as being untouchable; like they can get away with things just because they play _____ (you fill in the blank). They act like the school rules don't apply to them, and they bully younger, smaller, weaker students just because they can. Characters in the sports novel *Leverage* (2011) by Joshua C. Cohen illustrate this type of negative role model. Cohen paints an intense picture of what can happen when high school athletes see themselves as invincible.

As a high school athlete, you have a chance to positively influence a lot of people simply because they know who you are. You can use your popularity for

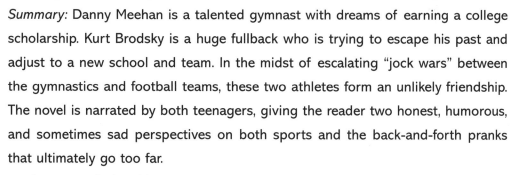

Good Read: *Leverage by Joshua C. Cohen*

Sports: Football, gymnastics

Life apps: Bullying, steroid use, pranks between sports, friendship

Summary: Danny Meehan is a talented gymnast with dreams of earning a college scholarship. Kurt Brodsky is a huge fullback who is trying to escape his past and adjust to a new school and team. In the midst of escalating "jock wars" between the gymnastics and football teams, these two athletes form an unlikely friendship. The novel is narrated by both teenagers, giving the reader two honest, humorous, and sometimes sad perspectives on both sports and the back-and-forth pranks that ultimately go too far.

Leverage deals with some serious, hard-hitting issues in blunt and sometimes crude language. As a former gymnast and current football fan, author Joshua Cohen describes both sports in true-to-life terms. Girls: Though the main characters are mainly guys, don't be put off. I found the book hard to put down.

Dutton Books, 2011

425 pages

Who's Your Favorite Professional Athlete and Why?

"Bethany Hamilton [surfer] . . . she always has a positive attitude and no matter what she goes through she still gets back on her board."—Taylor H., 15, softball

"My favorite sports figure is Ray Lewis because when he's playing, he dominates and plays like no one's better than him."—Requan, 16, football

"Suzann Pettersen—she is clearly very hardworking and plays because she loves the sport and wants to be the best she can be."—Rachel, 18, golf

"Tim Tebow is my favorite professional sports figure because his drive to win is spectacular and he has great team leadership."—Corey, 20, wrestling

"Evan Longoria. I like the way he handles himself on the field. He is very serious and wants to win, but the minute he steps into the dugout you will see him smiling and laughing and being there for his teammates."—Kirsten, 20, softball

"My favorite is definitely Reggie White from the Green Bay Packers. He was so unstoppable and feared and could literally take over the game from the defensive end position. But how he lived his life was always what I admired most. He . . . preached the gospel, opened shelter homes, witnessed, and had an incredible impact on the Green Bay Packers while he was there."—David, 23, football

"Paula Creamer because as far as she has come and all that she has accomplished, it is still not just another thing to have her picture in a magazine. She is still impressed by it."—Jessica H., 20, golf

"Chad Ochocinco because he goofs around but gets the job done. He has style."—Davon, 19, football

"Sam Bradford . . . he is a Heisman winner and NFL quarterback, but he stands out in my opinion because he graduated with a 3.95 GPA and is unashamed about his relationship with Jesus Christ."—Anna, 19, track and field

"Probably Tom Brady, because he was faced with many obstacles but was able to keep his head up and make it to the NFL to be one of the best quarterbacks ever."—Austin, 15, football

good. Think about athletes you look up to and why. For the most part, the reasons are positive. When I asked my survey takers,"Who's your favorite professional athlete and why?" no one said, "Because she talks trash about her teammates" or "Because he's a selfish ball hog." People want positive role models, and you have the chance to be just that, whether it's for a younger brother following in your wrestling footsteps or a middle school girl who wants to run the 100 meters just like you. They can learn hard work from you. They can learn what a true leader looks like. They can learn how to perform under pressure. Or they can learn how to take advantage of people who are half their size, a skill that really doesn't take much practice.

You might be thinking, "Hey. I didn't ask to be a role model. That's too much pressure." True. It might not be fair to expect athletes at any level—high school, college, or professional—to be role models. But if you just work hard, play your game, and treat others with respect, you'll be a positive role model without even realizing it.

Good Sport

Being a student-athlete also means being a good sport, whether you win or lose. The TeensHealth website defines sportsmanship as playing fair, following the rules

Don't Be a Show-Off

On its website, the National Federation of State High School Associations (NFHS) posts a weekly Student-Athlete Tip of the Week. Here's the tip for the week of December 5, 2011:[6]

A confident student-athlete does not need to chest pound and showboat following an outstanding play during a game. Does a good student brag and jump up and down when getting 100% on an exam?

Tom Brady, three-time Super Bowl winner and quarterback of the New England Patriots, said that his coach, Bill Belichick, had the following advice for him. "When you win, say very little. When you lose, say even less."

This is just another way of saying, don't be surprised or get overly excited following a good play or good game. This should be something you expect as a result of your constant preparation.

of the game, respecting the judgment of referees and officials, and treating opponents with respect.[7] It's a general attitude of common courtesy that will carry
you far in life.

A good sport is someone who

- congratulates other team after a win or a loss.
- cheers for teammates, both in response to a good play and to encourage
  after a mistake.
- acknowledges when an opponent makes a good play.
- cheers when an injured teammate or opponent is able to walk off the field.
- lets it go when the refs make a bad call—and they will.
- doesn't need to rely on cheating or cheap shots to get a win.

What Would You Have Done?

Here's a display of sportsmanship you don't see very often: In 2011, a
girls' cross-country team from the Bolles School in Jacksonville, Florida,
gave up its second-place medals and trophies because the girls felt another team
deserved them more. And this wasn't just any meet—it was the state championship.

The American Heritage team from Plantation, Florida, had actually finished
second, but it was knocked down to fifth place because of a mix-up with the
timing chips on the girls' shoes. As a result, the Bolles team from Jacksonville
was bumped up to second.

The Bolles team stepped down from the podium, huddled up, and then
walked over to the disappointed American Heritage team; the girls didn't even
talk to their coach about what they were about to do. One Bolles runner said
that "there was no debate among the Bolles team about what to do because
they all knew that the American Heritage runners deserved the honor more than
they did." So the Bolles runners took off their medals and put them around the
necks of the American Heritage girls.

After seeing the overjoyed reaction of the American Heritage team, one
Bolles runner said, "This was worth so much more than a state championship."[8]

A good sport does not

- trash-talk the other team or refs, even if everyone else is doing it.
- pout after a loss; losing is part of life, so learn to deal with it.
- deface the campus of the opposing team.
- vent anger by trashing the bus, restaurant, or locker room. Not only does this reflect poorly on your team and your school, but it could go on your

What Not to Do

In 2012, the New Orleans Saints were being penalized for a so-called bounty program in which players were paid for injuring their opponents. Do I need to say that trying to injure, maim, or otherwise take out an opponent doesn't qualify as good sportsmanship? Football involves hard hits. But it's one thing to flatten your opponent and then help him up; it's another to flatten him so he doesn't get up.

Unfortunately, the bounty mentality is showing up in high school sports as well. Players might not be getting paid for taking out an opponent, but coaches have been overheard encouraging such behavior and players have been caught on video committing flagrant fouls. And it's not just the guys. In 2011, Samantha and her water polo team were winning 13–1, in large part because of Samantha's performance. With around thirty seconds left in the match, Samantha called for a pass from the other side of the pool; she was nowhere near the ball. An opposing player came over to guard her, but instead turned around and punched Samantha square in the face, effectively taking her out of the play.[9]

Not only is such violent behavior unsportsmanlike, it could have legal ramifications. In a 2012 high school soccer match in South Carolina, a girl from Chester High School tripped a girl from Lewisville High School. (If you look at the video, it actually looks like the two players' feet just got tangled.) The girl on the ground got up and attacked the girl who tripped her. She pulled the Chester girl's hair and repeatedly punched her, even switching hands to get a better grip on the girl so she could keep punching. The attacker didn't just get ejected from the match; she was charged with simple assault, which is a criminal offense.[10]

record—not something you want a college recruiter or future employer to see.

- blame a loss on teammates, referees/umpires, coaches, and so on. Take responsibility for your part in losses as well as wins.
- engage in excessive celebrations after a score or good play.
- rub it in when his or her team wins.

As mentioned in the first chapter, sportsmanship is valued in real life as well as in sports. You will never run out of opportunities to treat others fairly and with respect.

Teammate

Whether you play football, field hockey, or water polo, you're part of a team and you have teammates who depend on you, just as you depend on them. For the team to perform at its best, each player needs to be well rested, focused, and ready to give 100 percent. Even in sports that are more individual—tennis, golf, and swimming, for example—you're still part of a team; the individual scores add up to determine which team wins. Bottom line: As a member of a team, your actions during a game or race affect your teammates.

> "[The hardest part is] striving to be your best, especially in the middle of the game when everyone's watching and you feel like your lungs are going to burst but you have to keep going, because that's your team and basically your high school family."—Mikalla, 15, soccer

But what about off the field? As a member of a team, do your actions away from school affect your teammates? Consider the following situations:

A crew team is a good representation of what a team should be: one unit working together toward a goal. *Photo courtesy of the author.*

> "The thing about golf is that it is very individual but you need to rely on many other people such as teachers, coaches, and even golf buddies to watch your swing and point out what is wrong or different about it. Golf is a game you can't teach yourself."—Jessica H., 20, golf

In May of 2011, administrators at Melrose High School (Massachusetts) found out that eleven varsity athletes were involved in underage drinking and smoking. The athletes were identified from photos that someone had downloaded from Facebook onto a thumb drive and turned in to school officials. The penalty: Each athlete missed up to 60 percent of the next athletic season. Some of the athletes were captains on their teams; they lost those leadership positions.[11]

Some of you might be tempted to blame the person who turned in the photos. Or the person who posted them on Facebook in the first place. But is that really the issue? My guess is that all eleven drinking/smoking students knew the legal

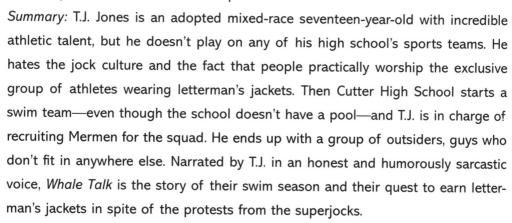

Good Read: *Whale Talk by Chris Crutcher*

Sport: Swimming

Life apps: Team bonding, social outcasts, racism, adoption, father-son relationship

Summary: T.J. Jones is an adopted mixed-race seventeen-year-old with incredible athletic talent, but he doesn't play on any of his high school's sports teams. He hates the jock culture and the fact that people practically worship the exclusive group of athletes wearing letterman's jackets. Then Cutter High School starts a swim team—even though the school doesn't have a pool—and T.J. is in charge of recruiting Mermen for the squad. He ends up with a group of outsiders, guys who don't fit in anywhere else. Narrated by T.J. in an honest and humorously sarcastic voice, *Whale Talk* is the story of their swim season and their quest to earn letterman's jackets in spite of the protests from the superjocks.

Greenwillow Books, 2001

220 pages

drinking age and knew there was a penalty for underage drinking. By choosing to party anyway, they lost sight of the fact that they're part of a team; their actions affected their teammates, who were forced to play a good part of their next season without their shortstop or goalkeeper or whatever position each of the eleven played.

Here's another example: In the summer of 2011, several basketball players from a different Massachusetts high school were involved in a disgusting hazing incident (hazing is illegal in Massachusetts). They forced two freshmen to eat Oreo cookies covered in bodily fluid. When the basketball coach found out in November 2011, he immediately reported it to the school administrators, who took action against the players. Two were expelled from school and several others were suspended; none of them played basketball for their school in the 2011–2012 season. Given that the disciplined players were all upperclassmen, they were probably among the varsity starters. That means the rest of the team had to pick up the slack because of their teammates' horribly inconsiderate actions.[12]

A year earlier, in 2010, several female soccer players from another Massachusetts school were suspended for hazing freshmen players. The hazing incident

What Is Hazing?

Here's how the Massachusetts state law defines hazing:

Any conduct or method of initiation into any student organization, whether on public or private property, which willfully or recklessly endangers the physical or mental health of any student or other person. Such conduct shall include whipping, beating, branding, forced calisthenics, exposure to the weather, forced consumption of any food, liquor, beverage, drug or other substance, or any other brutal treatment or forced physical activity which is likely to adversely affect the physical health or safety of any such student or other person, or which subjects such student or other person to extreme mental stress, including extended deprivation of sleep or rest or extended isolation.

Each state has its own rules about hazing. In Massachusetts, anyone found guilty of participating in hazing can spend up to one year in jail and be fined up to three thousand dollars. Anyone found guilty of watching a hazing without reporting it can be fined up to one thousand dollars.[13]

itself was very mild compared to the basketball players' "ookie cookie game," but it was considered hazing nonetheless. With some of their top players suspended, the girls lost 7–1 in their first state playoff match.[14]

The moral of the story is *stop and think*: Is what I'm about to do legal? If someone finds out that I _____ (you fill in the blank), will it affect my ability to play? Will it affect my teammates' ability to play? As a student-athlete, your actions really do affect others, no matter where you are.

Aside from doing illegal things that could get you suspended, there are other ways you can take yourself out of the game and leave your teammates hanging:

- If you don't keep your grades up, you could be declared academically ineligible to play. Your teammates depend on you to study for your exams and turn in your papers.
- If you lose your cool during a game, you could get ejected for unsportsmanlike conduct. Your teammates depend on you to keep your anger in check.
- If you disobey team rules (don't show up for practice, don't show up for class, etc.), you might be forced to sit out a game. Again, this hurts your teammates; they depend on you to be part of the team and follow the rules like everyone else.

Being a student-athlete is an awesome experience. You will take away friendships, study habits, organizational skills, and positive qualities such as good sportsmanship. Just try to keep in mind that it's a privilege you get to enjoy 24/7 and not just when you're on the field.

No Shaving Allowed!

Sports involve rules. Even if you don't understand or agree with the rules, you have to follow them so that you and your teammates don't get penalized. In 2012, one Maryland swim team found this out the hard way. According to the NFHS, swimmers, divers, and water polo players may not shave at the competition site before, during, or after a meet. One Broadneck High School swimmer either forgot or ignored this rule, and someone found out. After winning the county championship meet, the Broadneck girls' team retroactively lost its title because this swimmer had shaved on-site. Just another example of how your actions affect your teammates.[15]

Good Read: Black and White *by Paul Volponi*

Sport: Basketball

Life apps: Friendship, learning from mistakes, racial tension, learning that your actions affect others

Summary: Marcus and Eddie are the stars of the Long Island High School basketball team. They're also best friends, and they're always together—so much so that people started calling them Black (Marcus) and White (Eddie). They bring out the best in each other on the court, and they're hoping to play at the same college next year. Then they start robbing people to get a little extra cash and things go terribly wrong. They discover that one event could change their lives and their friendship forever.

Marcus and Eddie both narrate this story, giving the reader two perspectives on the same events. The author describes the racial tension, basketball action, and verbal exchanges between characters in realistic terms.

Viking, 2005

185 pages

Good Coach, Bad Coach

A big part of your experience as a student-athlete involves your coaches. As you probably already know, a good coach can make high school sports a fantastic experience; a not-so-good coach can make it a challenging four years. How you deal with the second kind of coach is up to you. One option is to go out for a differ-

> "The hardest part of wrestling was balancing school, sports, and work. The coach of the wrestling team was also hard to deal with because he only believed in technique and not going to the weight room."
> —Corey, 20, wrestling

"I ended up going to play in college, and due to my coach I wanted to quit after my freshman year, but my parents—more specifically, my dad—pressured me into staying and to continue playing because of my education. . . . But during my sophomore year, she [the coach] really took a toll on me and my motivation to keep playing softball so I finally told my parents regardless of the school I go to, that my happiness is the most important."—Kirsten, 20, softball

ent sport; even at the college level, some players find they just can't play under certain coaches and choose to go elsewhere (see Lauren's story in chapter 8). The other option is to stay and play in spite of the coach's negativity, lack of expertise, different philosophy regarding weight training, or whatever it might be. (Note: If your coach is doing something illegal or unsafe, that's another matter. At that point, you really need to talk to the principal or athletic director so someone doesn't get hurt.)

Here are some suggestions to make the most of a team with less-than-ideal coaching. These suggestions may or may not work; it partly depends on your coach's personality and the particulars of your conflict with him or her. Keep in mind you always have the option to walk away if it's just not working out.

1. Always be a good sport. Remember, good sportsmanship involves showing respect to your teammates, the other team, the officials, and the coaches. If you want any chance of having your opinion heard, you need to maintain a respectful attitude toward the coach because of his or her position.
2. If you want to talk to the coach about changing something (about practice, about using the weight room more, whatever), do it in private. No one wants to be called out or challenged in public; the coach might reject your idea just because he or she feels like you challenged his or her authority.
3. If you bring an idea to the coach, word it in such a way that you emphasize the positive about your idea, not the negative about the coach's current way of doing things. You might point out how going to the weight room could help decrease the number of injuries or how a team chant could boost morale and create more team chemistry.
4. Be a positive leader on the team. Don't be the one who's leading the trash talk against the coach; be the one who's trying to make the best of the situation.

Even if you're respectful and positive, there's no guarantee the coach is going to change. Josh found this out when he played college football:

> The hardest and worst part of my college career was playing on a team that did not play together as a team. There was no team chemistry, there was a lack of that overall brotherhood. Practices were filled with fights, shouting matches, and discipline. As the team captain, I did all I could to help promote team unity, including taking the team out to eat several times on

History of Softball

On a cold, windy day in November 1887, alumni from Yale and Harvard gathered in Chicago's Farragut Boat Club waiting to hear the outcome of the annual Harvard–Yale football game. After hearing that Yale won, as the story goes, one excited young man picked up an old boxing glove and tossed it to one of the Harvard guys. The Harvard alum picked up a broom and hit the glove away, giving a young man named George Hancock a brilliant idea. Hancock grabbed some chalk, drew foul lines and a home plate on the gym floor, and tied the boxing glove laces together to create a big, soft ball. He divided the group into two teams, and they played what was probably the first game of softball, though they called it indoor baseball. Final score: 41–40.

Indoor baseball was a hit (pun intended); it was something people could play during Chicago's harsh winters. Eventually the game moved outside during the warmer months, where it was played on fields that were too small for playing baseball. The game soon spread to Minneapolis, Minnesota, where it became a popular way for firemen to pass the time in between calls. One fireman, Lewis Roper, is credited with developing some of the rules softball follows today. For example, Roper shortened games to seven innings so that they lasted about an hour.

By the early 1900s, the game had spread to many states in the Midwest and Canada, and it was known by several different names, including cabbage ball, mush ball, diamond ball, and pumpkin ball. In 1926, a YMCA official from Denver, Colorado, suggested the name softball and it stuck.[16]

my own dime and organizing times when we could all hang together. The most frustrating part was the coaching staff, which did NOTHING to help promote this unity. As a matter of fact, the head coach called me into his office one day and actually told me to stop doing a pre-game chant that we had all come up with that the team actually liked and fired us up. The coach said he hadn't approved it and that he was the coach and not me and that I should just concentrate on playing. . . . I have played under many coaching staffs and I have NEVER heard or seen of a team being run the way he ran our team. The thought of quitting crossed my mind several times because of that.[17]

Josh did finish out his career at this college, and he is thankful for the relationships that he developed with his teammates in spite of the poor coaching.

Whatever you do, try not to let a bad coach steal your love of the game. This might seem hard and even impossible at times. Kirsten, age twenty, ultimately decided to quit her college softball team rather than let her coach take away her motivation to play. Now Kirsten plays recreational softball and is an assistant coach for a high school softball team.[18]

Find Out More

Chapters

Malone, Christian. "Professional Athletes Should Be Role Models." In *Sports and Athletes*, ed. Christine Watkins, 46–51. Farmington Hills, MI: Greenhaven Press, 2009.

Standen, Jeffrey. "Athletes Should Be Role Models Only for Athletics." In *Sports and Athletes*, ed. Christine Watkins, 52–57. Farmington Hills, MI: Greenhaven Press, 2009.

Notes

1. Jeré Longman, "Home Schoolers Are Hoping to Don Varsity Jackets in Virginia," *New York Times*, February 8, 2012, www.nytimes.com/2012/02/09/sports/virginia-home-schoolers-make-a-play-to-join-high-school-teams.html?_r=2&pagewanted=all (accessed March 6, 2012).
2. Anna Schuster, author's sports survey, September 9, 2011.
3. Quoted in Sean Teehan, "Facebook Photos Bring Suspensions," *Boston.com*, May 8, 2011, www.boston.com/sports/schools/articles/2011/05/08/substance_abuse_photos_cost_11_melrose_high_athletes/?rss_id=Boston+High+School+Sports (accessed March 6, 2012).
4. Jessica Doyle, interview with author, January 4, 2012.

5. Sam Gardner, "Lin Outshines Kobe, Continues to Wow," *FOXSports.com*, updated March 12, 2012, msn.foxsports.com/nba/story/Jeremy-Lin-New-York-Knicks-outshine-Kobe-Bryant-Los-Angeles-Lakers-021012 (accessed April 3, 2012).

6. Billy Shepherd Sports Inc., "Student-Athlete Tip of the Week (12-5-11)," National Federation of State High School Associations, www.nfhs.org (accessed December 8, 2011).

7. The Nemours Foundation/KidsHealth, "Sportsmanship," TeensHealth, reviewed October 2011, p. 1, kidshealth.org/teen/food_fitness/sports/sportsmanship.html# (accessed December 16, 2011).

8. Cameron Smith, "Florida Runners Donate Medals, Trophy to Disqualified Foes," *Pep Rally: A Y! Sports Blog*, November 23, 2011, rivals.yahoo.com/highschool/blog/prep_rally/post/Florida-runners-donate-medals-trophy-to-disqual?urn=highschool-wp9079 (accessed December 15, 2011).

9. taylornottyler, *Water Polo Punch* (video), YouTube, December 22, 2011, www.youtube.com/watch?v=5Lq1beGq42g (accessed March 6, 2012).

10. Cameron Smith, "South Carolina Teen's Brutal Attack Earns Assault Charge," *Pep Rally: A Y! Sports Blog*, March 29, 2012, sports.yahoo.com/blogs/highschool-prep-rally/south-carolina-teen-brutal-soccer-attack-earns-assault-103322121.html (accessed March 29, 2012).

11. Teehan, "Facebook Photos."

12. Cameron Smith, "Hoops Hazing Back in the Crosshairs after Disgusting Mass. Incident," *Pep Rally: A Y! Sports Blog*, December 1, 2011, rivals.yahoo.com/highschool/blog/prep_rally/post/hoops-hazing-back-in-crosshairs-after-disgusting-mass-incident?urn=highschool,wp9312 (accessed December 16, 2011).

13. David Abel and Erica Noonan, "Hazing Penalty Defended," *Boston.com*, November 11, 2010, www.boston.com/sports/schools/soccer/articles/2010/11/11/school_athletic_officials_defend_hazing_suspensions/ (accessed December 16, 2011).

14. Abel and Noonan, "Hazing Penalty."

15. Cameron Smith, "Maryland Swim Team Retroactively Loses County Title because of Bizarre Shaving Violation," *Pep Rally: A Y! Sports Blog*, February 22, 2012, sports.yahoo.com/blogs/highschool-prep-rally/maryland-swim-team-retroactively-loses-county-title-because-153508295.html (accessed March 5, 2012).

16. "History of Softball and the ASA," Amateur Softball Association of America, www.softball.org/about/asa_history.asp (accessed November 12, 2011); "History of Softball," Softball Performance.com, www.softballperformance.com/softball-history/ (accessed November 12, 2011).

17. Josh Cohen, e-mail to author, March 10, 2012.

18. Kirsten Frame, author's sports survey, November 30, 2011.

3

IT'S ALL IN YOUR HEAD

"If you can't deal with failure then you don't deserve a victory."
—*Mikalla, 15, soccer*

You've gone hitless for a few games in a row, once when a single would have won the game. You overhear the coaches talking about your slump. You spend hours working on your swing in batting practice. The next game, you come up to the plate with a huge knot in your stomach. You don't want to mess up, but you're so tense that you lunge at a bad pitch and pop up . . . again. You hang your head and jog back to the dugout, beginning to wonder if you're ever going to get a base hit again.

Sound familiar? Maybe your sport isn't softball or baseball, but you probably know the cycle of failure, self-doubt, anxiety, and more failure. It's so hard to break out of a slump. It's not something you can fix with more sprints, squats, or dribbling drills. The problem is all in your head.

Sports involve your brain as much as your body: you have to understand plays, see the field and know your next move, block out the crowd, and concentrate on executing skills. You also need to control anxiety and negative thoughts. It takes conditioning and practice to develop these mental skills, no different from the development of physical skills. Dr. Alan Goldberg, a sports psychologist, says that

> "Sometimes the pressure does get to my head and it affects my performance. I have some anxiety issues so it really just takes me calming down and getting in the zone to perform and win."—Caitlin, 16, tennis

most performance problems that athletes and other performers struggle with are not a result of poor conditioning, inadequate coaching or a lack of physical skills or technical ability. . . . When the heat of competition is turned up high, the individual performer or team that falls apart most often does so because of mental factors like runaway nervousness, intimidation, poor concentration, negativity, lack of confidence or an inability to let go of mistakes or bad breaks.[1]

This chapter is all about learning how to train your mind so all your physical training doesn't go to waste.

History of Golf

Way back in the 1400s, Scottish shepherds played a game in which they used wooden sticks to hit small rocks toward specific targets. Over time, the targets became holes that were dug into the ground where it was relatively flat. The rough, uneven playing surfaces were nothing like the neat, manicured courses we have today.

Late in the fifteenth century, Scotland was preparing for an invasion from England. However, the people were so busy playing this new game that they weren't training for battle, so the king banned the sport. The ban wasn't officially lifted until 1502, when King James VI took up golf himself. After the king started playing, the game's popularity grew very quickly and so did its social status. Over the next two hundred years, golf was introduced to France and England. By this time, rocks had been replaced with wood balls and then balls made out of animal hides stuffed with goose feathers; balls with a rubber core came later. Also, players had stopped using sticks and started using clubs with heads made out of wood and iron. Because this equipment was handcrafted and expensive, golf was mainly played by the wealthy. It wasn't until the mid-1800s that clubs and balls became mass produced and average people could afford to play.

Golf is one of the few sports that women started playing soon after the men. In fact, Mary Queen of Scots probably introduced golf to France when she studied there in the 1500s. Golf became an Olympic sport for men in 1896 and for women in 1900.[2]

Under Pressure

Part of the thrill involved in sports is being challenged mentally and physically—of scoring a goal or touching the wall first when your team really needs you to do so. The right amount of stress can get you psyched up, energize you, and cause you to perform to the best of your ability. However, too much pressure can turn you into a basket case. It can make you nauseous, give you anxiety attacks, make you choke at key moments, and cause you to lose the joy of playing.

Pressure comes from a variety of sources. If you're involved in individual sports such as tennis or skiing, you might feel pressure to win every time you play or race. In a team sport, you might feel pressure to perform up to various expectations—a certain number of rebounds or strikeouts, for example. If you're hoping to play in college, you might feel pressure to impress college scouts. If you're a freshman or sophomore, you might feel pressure to impress the coach in order to earn a starting spot or move up to varsity. If you have super-involved parents who have poured a lot of time and money into your sport, you might feel pressure to please them. Above all these sources, however, is the pressure you put on yourself. Some of you expect perfection from yourselves every time you're out there—a super goal, but one that's guaranteed to stress you out since no one is perfect.

> "Sometimes winning the meet rests upon only a couple of points and if you lose your event, it can make the difference of losing and winning."
> —Andy, 15, swimming

> "Learning how to deal with the pressure to perform or win was tough and it took a long time. Mostly I just try to have fun regardless of how I am playing. Also I try to keep things into perspective. I know that a lot of athletes, including myself, hate when people tell you it is just a game because to most of us it is our lifestyle and defines a huge percentage of who you are but at the same time you have to be able to not take it too seriously. Very rarely will you have a perfect performance or perform at the level you think you should, but I think that constantly reminding yourself not to take the game or yourself too seriously is important."
> —Jacque, 22, volleyball

No One Is Perfect

Next time you make a mistake or lose a race, remember that everyone blows it now and then—even the professionals:

- Usain Bolt—the fastest man in the world as of 2012—false started at the 2011 World Track and Field Championships and was disqualified.[3]
- During the championship match of the 2011 FIFA World Cup, several players on the U.S. women's soccer team failed to put the ball in the net when it came down to penalty kicks.[4]
- During his career, Michael Jordan missed more than nine thousand shots—twenty-six of them would have won the game.[5]
- During the 2006 Winter Olympics, snowboarder Lindsey Jacobellis made a mistake that cost her a gold medal. As she neared the finish line all by herself, Jacobellis decided to show off a little on her last jump. She fell, and someone else got the gold.[6]
- Two years in a row (2010 and 2011), Alex Rodriguez ended the Yankees' season in the playoffs by striking out.[7]

Developing mental toughness can help you deal with these pressures. If you learn to keep the stress at an energizing but not overwhelming level, you can control nervousness and negativity, play relaxed and confident, perform better, and have more fun. Mental toughness can also help you deal with everyday situations—for example, taking a big test, writing college admission essays, or interviewing for a new job. It's definitely a skill you'll use long after you stop playing high school sports.

What Is Mental Toughness?

Dr. David Yukelson, coordinator for sports psychology services at Penn State University, asked several collegiate student-athletes to define mental toughness; here are some of their responses:

Mental toughness is not being affected by anything but what's going on in the game or competition no matter what the coaches, other players, or refs are doing. It's being able to block out what's not important.

? Did You Ever Want to Quit?

"There were definite times when I wanted to quit, but only because I couldn't balance everything in my life, not because I didn't love to run. I felt pressure from my coach to keep running. He was never one to accept any excuse, even a family emergency or serious injury."—Anna, 19, track and field

"I thought about quitting once. But I could never let down my teammates because I made a commitment to them and my coaches had worked so hard with me. It wasn't anyone who gave me pressure to keep playing, it was more the fear I had inside me of letting them down. So I never quit."—David, 23, football

"I was going through a phase where I was playing badly. I took a break for a week and realized how much I missed playing, so I continued to practice hard."—Rachel, 18, golf

"My reasons for wanting to quit many, many times are all for different things. Whether it be the way my coach disrespectfully treated or talked to me, the stress it put on my body, wanting more free time with friends or trying to focus more on school, as much as I love to cheer . . . sometimes that wasn't enough to keep me doing what I love most."—Jessica U., 16, competitive cheer

Mental toughness is not letting anyone break you.

Mental toughness is doing whatever is necessary to get the job done including handling the demands of a tough workout, withstanding pain, or touching an opponent out at the end of a race.[8]

Citing a 2002 article by Graham Jones and colleagues, Dr. Yukelson defines mental toughness as "having the natural or developed psychological edge that enables you to

- cope better than your opponents with the many demands (e.g., competition, training, lifestyle) that are placed on you. . . .
- be more consistent and better than your opponents in remaining determined, focused, resilient, and in control under pressure."[9]

Making a technical foul shot, as Jameeshia is here, requires mental toughness. Even though it's a "free" shot, it's easy to let nerves and negative thoughts prevent you from putting the ball in the net. *Photo courtesy of the author.*

Mental toughness is something internal that drives your outward actions. It's a frame of mind, an outlook, an attitude. It's also an ability to control your thoughts, keep yourself focused, and stay motivated. Some people describe this quality as playing with heart, desire, or drive. Mental toughness is the somewhat intangible quality that makes the difference between two equally trained and talented athletes. The one with mental toughness—who is able to stay calm and relaxed under pressure, recover quickly from mistakes, maintain self-confidence, and stay focused in spite of distractions—is the one who will be the better overall player and enjoy his or her sport to the fullest.

How Do You Become Mentally Tough?

Some people are just born that way; they thrive on pressure and put in their best performance when the game or meet is on the line. You might be like this; the rest of us have to work at it. The good news is that anyone can develop mental toughness—that is, anyone who really wants to. Just like anything else in sports and in life, learning something new takes work. Here are some tips for developing mental toughness.

Always Give 100 Percent

"Confidence is about who puts it on the line, who has the courage to compete like a warrior without fear of failure."—Dr. Jerry Lynch, sports psychologist[10]

Are You Mentally Tough?

Dr. Goldberg poses the following questions on his website, Competitive Advantage. Answering yes to one or more means you—like thousands of other high school and college athletes—could benefit from a little brain training. Sports psychologists like Dr. Goldberg agree that mental toughness is just as important as physical strength and skill.

- Do you suffer from slumps, choking, psych-outs, runaway emotions, negativity, or a lack of confidence?
- Do you perform better in practice than at "crunch time" when it counts the most?
- Do you consistently underachieve in your performance arena?[11]

Mentally tough athletes are confident—not in an arrogant kind of way but in a I've-worked-my-butt-off-and-I-know-I-can-do-this kind of way. This step toward mental toughness is pretty simple: leave it all on the field (or in the pool or on the ice) every time. If you give 100 percent in every drill, every time trial, every scrimmage, every preseason race, and every match, you'll be confident in your ability to perform when it really counts. You'll know that you can block that

"I handled myself in pressure situations very well; those were times when I would perform my best. I love pressure and the feeling of people looking for you to make a positive move for the team."—Kirsten, 20, softball

"It took me a long time to learn how to handle pressure because I would tighten up and be very ineffective. Once I learned to relax and play like I did in practice and I put my mind in a relaxed state, I played a lot better and got significant more playing time and a lot more of the coaches' trust."
—David, 23, football

"For me it's [i.e., dealing with pressure] about being confident, positive thinking, praying, and knowing that my team is there to back me up. . . . I also believe that I was blessed with these gifts and am so grateful for the opportunities I am given to go out and glorify Him through my playing. My team also played a big part in taking off the pressure because I was able to build such a strong bond with them and we knew we were in it together no matter what the outcome was."—Emily, 23, volleyball

hit, make that diving catch, or sink that free throw simply because you've done it over and over at practice and in other competitions.

Part of giving 100 percent all the time is learning everything you can from your coaches. If the coach wants the team to work on strength training, do it. If the coach wants you personally to work on exploding out of the starting blocks, do it. Self-confidence comes from thorough preparation, from knowing you are ready to succeed because you have done everything you possibly can to get there. Listening to and learning from your coaches is part of that preparation.

I can almost guarantee that some of your teammates won't understand your day-to-day work ethic. They'll wonder why you're putting so much effort into preseason conditioning or doing whatever the coach tells you. Mentally tough athletes give 100 percent even if no one else is.

Note: If you're injured or sick, you might have to give less than 100 percent physically until you recover—not because you want to but because it's what's best for your body and overall health. It's the mental state of wanting to give your best effort every time that's important, even if you're not physically able to do so. Giving less than 100 percent because you're sick is much different than slacking off because you're lazy or unmotivated.

Set SMART Goals

"I was never the fastest, I wasn't the biggest, the strongest. I just did everything I could to outwork everybody. I stayed a little longer or whatever it was to get myself ready so I could be the best I wanted to be on the field."
—Maurice Jones-Drew, Jacksonville Jaguars running back[12]

Mentally tough athletes are self-motivated. That means they don't need someone else reminding them to practice, train, or work on a certain skill. They have a goal—maybe it's to break a certain record, make varsity as a sophomore, or play at a Division I school—and they are motivated to do whatever it takes to get there. This kind of desire or heart will keep you going on those days when you're just not feeling up to the work, and everyone has those days. U.S. track and field star Allyson Felix has won six Olympic medals (four gold, two silver) and ten World Championship medals (eight gold, one silver, one bronze), yet she admits, "I definitely have those moments where I wake up and I'm just not feeling it. . . . But you don't want to have any regrets; you don't want to slack off at all. So I try to just push through anything that comes up."[13]

If you're struggling with lack of motivation more than just once in a while, maybe you need to set some goals. Goals give you something to focus on in practice and training, a reason for your hard work and sacrifice. Coaches and parents can help you think of goals, but in the end, the goals really need to be your own.

❓ Did You Ever Want to Quit?

"I don't like to quit. I think what makes a good player is being able to finish on a good day and a bad day."—Jessica H., 20, golf

"Yes. One day I told my coach I quit after practice because I kept missing my assignment."—Davon, 19, football

"I've wanted to quit several times. Especially when I'm running laps in the over 100 degree heat . . . bleck . . . but I'm definitely not a quitter and it would be embarrassing to me to give up on something."—Caitlin, 16, tennis

"There were moments where things got very stressful, especially in college, but every time I think about not having volleyball in my life I can't imagine it. . . . There is always a lot of pressure from coaches and parents but I think for myself at least I put a lot of pressure on myself to be great."—Jacque, 22, volleyball

"Yes. Although I had a very successful career in high school I felt that because I played year-round for so many years that I wanted to focus on my schooling and not play softball anymore. I wanted to just be done and play recreationally and just enjoy the sport that I love."—Kirsten, 20, softball

There are basically two kinds of goals. *Outcome-based goals* are focused on a particular outcome, for example, winning your race. When you set outcome goals, you are motivated by something outside of yourself—a first-place medal, the praise of your coach, the title of state champion—rather than your performance. It's good to have outcome goals, but focusing solely on things outside yourself often leads to disappointment, which in turn makes it harder to stay motivated. Factors you have no control over can sometimes prevent you for meeting a goal—a better prepared opponent, for example. If you focus only on winning, you could beat your best time and still feel like a failure because you came in second place. In addition, a winning-is-the-only-thing attitude can lead to cheating (e.g., using illegal supplements) in a desperate attempt to meet your goal.

To avoid these pitfalls, you should have *performance-based goals* in addition to your outcome goals, that is, goals for your personal performance. A volleyball player might aim to hit a certain number of kills per match; a gymnast might shoot for a floor exercise score that's higher than her last one. Having performance goals will help decrease anxiety and stress since the goal isn't just to win. There's nothing wrong with aiming to be the best, but you can be also be happy with a new personal best even if you come in third.

You can set goals for all aspects of your athletic performance: physical conditioning, technical skills and abilities, and even mental toughness. The key is to make your goals SMART:[14]

*S*pecific
*M*easurable
*A*chievable
*R*ecorded
*T*ime-framed

Make your goals *specific*, not vague. For example, shoot for a specific time in the 200 meters or a specific percentage of completed passes, not "I want to have a good game" or "I want to play better than last week." If your goals are specific, they will be *measurable*. You will know right away if you got the time or the

"I try to calm myself down by saying that you either win or lose as a team. It's one or the other and you have to be happy with what you did. As long as you tried your hardest, that's all that matters. Even though winning is a great feeling, you have to lose to know what it's like to be a team and a proper athlete."—Jessica U., 16, competitive cheer

percentage. It's also important to make goals *achievable*. For example, you might want to swim a 49.82-second 100-meter butterfly (the men's world record time), but if you're a high school girl, that's probably not going to happen. Why not pick something that's physically possible for you to achieve—maybe shaving .50 seconds off your best 100-meter butterfly time. You want it to be something that will push you, not kill you.

When you make your goal, *record* it somewhere. Write down both the date you made the goal and the date you achieved it. Seeing in writing how you've accomplished goals will do wonders for your motivation and your self-confidence. Finally, give yourself a set amount of time to meet your goal, again making it realistic. If you're not sure what's realistic, talk to your coach. Adjust your *time frame* as necessary if you get sick or injured.

Visualize Success

Mentally tough athletes know how to use mental imagery. The terms *visualization*, *mental imagery*, *guided imagery*, and *mental rehearsal* are used interchangeably to

Good Read: **Athletic Shorts: Six Short Stories** *by* **Chris Crutcher**

Sports: Football, wrestling, swimming, basketball

Life apps: Father-son relationships, death, racism, homophobia, competition

Summary: Five of the six short stories feature characters from some of Chris Crutcher's novels, including Louie Banks (from *Running Loose*) and Lionel Serbousek (from *Stotan!* and *Ironman*). The stories feature a wide variety of high school athletes: an overweight football player who becomes prom king; a wrestler whose next opponent is a girl; a swimmer whose whole family was killed in a boating accident; a unique young man with decent basketball skills; a wrestler with a demanding father; and a football player who befriends a young man with AIDS. The stories are set in states across the country, from Montana to New Jersey.

Greenwillow Books, 2002

208 pages

"Usually the night before the game before I go to sleep I just visualize what I'm going to do during the game to help the team out."—Samantha, 17, water polo

describe this skill. Basically, visualization is the process of creating a mental picture of what you want to happen. People use this skill in all areas of life—school, work, relationships, and so on. In relation to sports, mentally tough athletes use visualization to picture themselves successfully performing in competition, whether that's hitting the perfect dismount from the balance beam, deflecting a shot on goal, or clearing the high jump bar. The picture of success is different for each athlete—even athletes competing in the same sport.

Here are some guidelines for creating a mental image:

1. Pick a specific task related to your sport. You might start with something that you accomplish successfully in practice and then choke on in real competition.
2. Close your eyes and see yourself successfully performing the task step by step, just like you've done in practice.
3. Create a picture using the senses of sight, sound, and touch. See yourself extend your arms as you swing the bat; hear the roar of the crowd (*only if* that positively motivates you; if the crowd freaks you out, then imagine silence); feel the cool air as your body lifts out of the water for a shot.
4. Rehearse your mental picture often—at night before you go to bed, as you're lacing your shoes before practice, while you're waiting to step onto the ice before a match. Always see yourself as focused and confident as you successfully perform the task.
5. Add positive self-talk to your mental image. That doesn't mean you have to talk to yourself out loud. It just means you tell yourself what you are going to do. Use positive statements that start with "I can . . ." and "I will . . ." Dr. Yukelson says that visualizing success involves focusing "on those things you want to occur, rather than things you're afraid might go wrong."[15]

Here are two examples of mental images. Remember, these are only examples; you need to make your picture very personal.

- If you have a problem choking at the free throw line, try visualizing yourself making the shot step by step. See yourself step up to the line, relaxed and confident. You receive the ball from the referee, bounce it a few times,

"The way I deal with the pressure to perform is blocking everyone around me out and focusing on the game and what exactly is going on. For instance, if I am up to bat, I think of the ball hitting my bat and me running around the bases. If I am in the field, I repeat the play that needs to be done to get the out, over and over again."—Megan, 16, softball

hold it, look up, lift your arms, let the ball roll off your fingertips, and watch the ball drop into the net. Imagine the feel of the ball in your hand and the *swish* sound of ball hitting net. See yourself blocking out every distraction—the crowd, the other team, the coach, the ref. It's just you and the basket, and you've done this a hundred times at practice. Tell yourself, "I can make this shot."

• If you're in a hitting slump, picture yourself coming to the plate calm and confident. See yourself clear the dirt with your right foot or dig your back foot in or tap the plate with your bat—whatever your batting ritual entails. Feel the bat in your hands as you raise your arms. Tell yourself to stand up and drive it, keep your eyes on the ball, wait for your pitch, or whatever it is you're struggling with. See the pitcher wind up and deliver a strike. You swing, stepping with your front foot, turning your hips, fully extending your arms, eyes focusing on the ball. Hear the ball connect solidly with the bat, and see yourself sprinting to first.

Focus on What's Important

"Imagine you are in a pure white room, it is silent, and there is nothing in the room except for you, four snow white walls and an apple on the one wall. Now focus all your energy on that apple, your entire consciousness is thinking of that apple, and as you do that you will get a taste of what we do before a race."
—Brendon Dedekind, former Olympic swimmer[16]

Mentally tough athletes can control their point of focus or concentration. They can focus on one thing and block out everything else, or they can concentrate on several things at once—the ball, the position of a teammate, their next move. They can also switch back and forth as needed. The key is knowing what's important at any given moment in the competition.

Switching Your Focus

Here's an exercise to illustrate what it means to switch your focus between external objects and events and internal thoughts and feelings:[17]

1. Pick up a ball and focus all your attention on the logo or lettering.
2. Stand on one leg and focus on the feeling of your body balancing on one foot.
3. Remain standing on one leg, but switch your focus back to the logo; block out the feeling of your leg.
4. Think of a positive statement you say to yourself during a match or race.
5. Picture yourself in a game situation when you would say that positive statement to yourself.
6. Switch your focus back to the leg.
7. Change legs and focus on the other leg.
8. Think of a strategy or plan you used in your last competition (e.g., keep your head up while skating with the puck, explode out of the blocks, make a smooth turn at the wall).
9. Picture yourself in a competition, successfully completing the strategy or plan.
10. Focus back on the ball.

No matter what sport you play, you need to be able to focus on external elements (e.g., the goal, the lane, the player you're guarding) as well as your own internals thoughts (e.g., the play, what the coach wants you to do in this situation, when you're going to start your final kick). Sometimes you need to have a narrow focus; that is, you need to focus all your attention on one or maybe two external items. For example, a pitcher needs to focus first on the catcher's hand giving him the sign and then on the catcher's glove—and that's it. He's

> "I really try to focus on what I'm doing and forget about everyone else."
>
> —Evan, 15, soccer

In order to make this play, Taylor B. uses narrow focus. She watches the ball go into her glove and blocks out everything else. *Photo courtesy of Elise Stearns-Niesen.*

not paying attention to the crowd, the umpire, the other team cheering for the batter. Mentally tough athletes know how to block all of that out when they need to focus on one thing. Similarly, if a player is taking a penalty shot, the goalie needs to focus all her attention on the girl taking the shot—not the crowd, her teammates, or the referee.

At other times, you need to have a more broad focus in order to take in additional information; for example, the position of teammates and/or opponents or the strength and direction of the wind. A pitcher, for example, needs to broaden his focus if there is a runner on first base. He needs to focus on the catcher's glove, while also making sure he checks the player at first. If a girl is

"I try to keep composed at all times while playing. I don't think about winning; just try and play my best shot each time."—Rachel, 18, golf

taking a corner kick, the goalie needs to focus on the kicker as well as opposing players coming behind her for a header. There's a danger of making your focus too broad, especially if the crowd makes you nervous. Some people thrive on playing in front of cheering and/or booing fans; they're energized by broadening their focus to include the crowd. Other players find they tense up when they take

> "I make sure that anything that could possibly bother me is taken care of before I play. This consists of cleaning out my golf bag, laying out my clothes, shaving, cutting my nails, and cleaning my room. I don't want anything that could possibly bother me to be on my mind."
> —Jessica H., 20, golf

in the crowd. If this describes you, don't make your focus so broad that you get distracted by the crowd.

When a particular play is over, you need to switch gears and broaden your focus: How many outs are there? What's my next move? How much time is left? You don't have time to think of these things while the next play is actually happening. For example, if the ball is hit back to the pitcher, he needs to know the number of outs and the position of players so he knows where to throw the ball; once the ball is hit, he's back to a narrow focus: watching the ball go into his glove.

For many players, the biggest obstacle to absolute focus is not the crowd or other external factors; it's internal things like nervousness, anxiety, and negative thoughts. Everyone gets nervous; everyone makes mistakes and then worries about them. But mentally tough players know how to turn off these distracting, off-task thoughts and stay focused. Here are a few suggestions for keeping your

What Were You Thinking?!

It was the 2012 Sugar Bowl. University of Michigan versus Virginia Tech. The game was tied 20–20 when it went into overtime. Virginia Tech got the ball first but missed a thirty-seven-yard field goal. All Michigan's kicker had to do was make his thirty-seven-yard attempt. So how did Brendan Gibbons calm his nerves and get himself focused? What was going through his head as he lined up his kick? Brunette girls.

"Every time we were struggling in kicking," Brendan said in an interview, "coach always tells me to think about girls on a beach or brunette girls. So that's what we did."[18]

If nothing else is working for you when you step up to the starting line or set up for a penalty shot, maybe you should try thinking about something completely different. It worked for Brendan.

thoughts in check so they don't break your concentration:

> "I would listen to a song before a game and just memorize the beat and play it over and over in my head so it would take the pressure off my shoulders."— Requan, 16, football

- Recognize that you are anxious or thinking negatively. It sounds cliché, but admitting there's a problem really is the first step to fixing it.
- Stop dwelling on past mistakes, whether they happened last match or last inning. You can't do anything to fix that loss or error now, so just let it go. Frustration will only cloud your focus, making it more likely that you'll make another mistake.
- Talk to yourself using positive statements such as "I can do this."
- If you're really nervous or anxious, take a few slow, deep breaths to calm down and regain focus. (More on relaxation breathing in the next section.)
- Learn to turn negative thoughts into positive suggestions for what to do in the future. For example, instead of thinking, "I can't hit that shot if my life depended on it," a basketball player could say to himself, "OK. Get a good look at the basket. See it. Feel it. Trust it." Instead of thinking, "This girl is so quick. I can't shake her," a field hockey player could say to herself, "I'm just going to win the tackle, be aggressive to the ball, do the simple."[19]

Sometimes the whole team can get caught in negative thinking and play way below its potential as a result. Basketball coach Mike Doyle says teams can go into a game with a defeated attitude if the opponent has always won. When that happens, Coach Doyle says,

> you're going to go in there with your shoulders sulking and thinking, "Oh, they're going to win anyway." You're not going to give it 110 percent. You have to play to win, not play not to lose. A lot of teams are up by a couple points and they really can't believe that they're beating whoever and then the reality sinks in—"There's eight minutes left and oh my gosh we're winning"—and then you play a little scared rather than to win.[20]

Whether as a team or as an individual, you need to clear your head of negativity and nervousness so you can focus on what's important and play to the best of your ability.

Cup for a Day

Each year, the Stanley Cup is awarded to the National Hockey League champion. According to tradition, each member of the winning team gets to have the cup for a day, and as a result, the cup has been all over the world, accompanying players to their home countries. Interesting things have happened during the 118 years of this tradition. Here are a few highlights:

- 1907: The Stanley Cup was stolen from a photographer's home by a young man who tried to turn around and sell it. He had no takers, so he gave the cup to a lady who used it as a flower pot for a few months before it was finally retrieved by the Montreal Wanderers.
- 1924: Montreal players were driving to a victory party when they got a flat tire. They took the cup out of the trunk so they could get to the spare tire. However, they forgot to put the cup back into the trunk when they were finished and left it by the side of the road. Hours later they realized their mistake and returned to find the cup sitting in the snow where they had left it.
- 1996: When it was his turn with the cup, Sylvain Lefebvre of the Colorado Avalanche used it to baptize his first child.[21]

Develop a Game-Day Routine

Mentally tough athletes are able to put themselves in a confident, focused frame of mind. You've probably heard of putting on your game face; well, this is putting on your game mind. By doing the same things in the same order before every game, you can consistently get your mind as well as your body into a state of readiness.

Some parts of your game-day routine are going to be the ordinary steps of preparing for "battle": putting on

"Before the games I listen to my music and pick my favorite song that gets me ready to play."—Davon, 19, football

your uniform, protective gear, socks, shoes, and so on. Putting everything on in the same order every time can signal to your mind that it's time for action. Jacque, age twenty-two, put her gear on the same way before every volleyball practice or match throughout high school and college: "Left ankle brace, right ankle brace, left knee pad, right knee pad, then my shoes."[22] Some athletes go so far as to eat the same things and wear their hair the same way. Kirsten, age twenty, says, "If we had a home game I would always get Slurpees and sour gummy worms. It was not the most nutritious but I didn't feel right if I didn't. If we had away games, I would always bring a Dr Pepper for a little caffeine boost. Also, when we would have home games I would always keep my hair straightened and when we would have away games I would always wear it curly."[23]

According to many of my survey takers, listening to music is a big part of their game-day routines. Some athletes listen to certain songs to get them ready. Derek, a wrestler, says, "Before every match I listen to my music and stretch. The song I always play when I step on the mat is 'All I Do Is Win.'"[24] David, a football player, always listened to a game-day mix while getting his ankles taped. A few minutes before taking the field, he says, "I changed the song to 'Move Along' by All-American Rejects. I always went out on the field with that song in my head. I always seemed to play best after I did that."[25] Jacque says that her whole team listened to music as part of their pre-game routine: "We always did the same thing. . . . We started off with a pre-game talk from our coach, then we would all get in a circle and say a prayer for the game. The last thing we did was to get ourselves fired up. We would put on some music, dance and yell and bang on the walls on the way out of our locker room."[26]

> "Before a game I usually eat a hearty breakfast, think positive, and listen to upbeat music."
> —Amberlee, 16, soccer

Other parts of your routine will involve conscious mental preparation. Sports psychologists have different terms and techniques for this part of your game-day routine; you can find some suggestions in the Find Out More section at the end of

> "During game day, I didn't talk unless I had to. I listened to my game-day mix, put my pants on, got my ankles taped, and then put tape on my wrists and fingers. Then I put on any wristbands I had decided upon for that game and then put my pads on and listened to music and envisioned me making plays."—David, 23, football

this chapter. I'm going to suggest three basic techniques, which you can perform in whatever order works best for you.[27]

1. Breathing—Focus all your attention on taking slow, deep breaths. It might help to close your eyes and block everything else out. Or you can practice your breathing while lacing your shoes or having your ankles taped—whatever helps you focus on your breathing and calm your nerves. If you feel you need to get more pumped up, change to quick, shallow breaths. In action-packed sports like football, volleyball, and basketball, players often feel the need to get psyched up. Just make sure your nervous energy doesn't become overwhelming. You don't want to be overly anxious and tense when the whistle blows.

2. Visualizing—Bring to mind the mental pictures of success you have created. Rehearse them over and over in your mind. Again, you can combine this technique with putting on certain parts of your gear, or you can just sit quietly with your eyes closed, or you can be stretching and shaking out your muscles. As you visualize success, you can also talk to yourself in positive terms. Remind yourself that you can do this, you have done it. Get yourself into a confident frame of mind.

3. Relaxing—Tense and relax the different muscle groups: shoulders, arms, legs, and so on. Tense the muscles and hold for a few seconds, then let the tension out. Focus on feeling your muscles relax completely. You can combine this step with your breathing.

"As a team, before the game day we usually played fun, silly games at practice to relieve the pressure of the upcoming day."—Caitlin, 16, tennis

Developing a personal game-day routine is an important part of mental toughness. It may take some trial and error in finding what works best for you. The key is to be consistent so you can consciously put your game mind on before every competition. Your team may have group routines, but these should not take the place of your own personal routines.

Learn from Your Mistakes

"It's actually more helpful for me to lose a race than anything else. . . . After having a bad race or if I lose, I work even harder to get back so that doesn't happen again."
—Michael Phelps, U.S. Olympic swimmer[28]

"I've failed over and over and over again in my life. And that is why I succeed."
—Michael Jordan, former NBA star[29]

Mentally tough athletes know how to rebound from failure and move on. In fact, how you deal with failure plays a big part in determining how far you go as a competitive athlete.

If you participate in a solo sport, an individual loss is all on your shoulders. But instead of beating yourself up over it, sit down with your coach and discuss what happened and what you can do differently next time. Did you stand up too soon coming out of the blocks? Should you have started your final kick

> "I always repeat to myself, 'This is what I'm here to do. Let's get it done!'"—Jessica H., 20, golf

earlier? Was your backhand off all day? Did you drag your leg going over the bar? Knowing what you need to correct gives you a specific goal (remember the *S* in SMART goals) for your next training session.

If you play a team sport, a loss is suffered as a group. However, you might know in your heart that your error(s) contributed to that defeat. Again, it doesn't do any good to keep thinking, "If I would have just . . ."—what's done is done. After the game, assess what happened and what you can do to avoid making that mistake next time. Did you tense up as the grounder came toward you? Did you

> "Usually right before we start we give what I like to call 'criticism of wisdom'—just letting each other know what can be improved to help us all."—Mikalla, 15, soccer

> "I was very competitive when it came to the actual race, but I never let it get to me that bad. Track and field was something I did for fun; it was not my life. And I was never the one superstar, but I did score points every meet for winning a heat. . . . If I got 2nd, 3rd, or 4th, I would be bummed for a bit, but I would move on and enjoy the meet after that. The nice thing about track and field is that you have so many events, you can usually redeem yourself pretty quick."—Anna, 19, track and field

Put It behind You

Here's another Student-Athlete Tip of the Week (for November 28, 2011) presented by the National Federation of State High School Associations:[30]

Can you put a bad game or performance behind you? How would you react if you missed a last second shot or made a foolish play costing your team a chance to win a game? How about just playing a poor game?

It happens all the time. Most sporting [events] aren't decided until the last few minutes of play. Don't be afraid to take the shot, make the last out, or be that defensive stopper that decides the game.

However, don't make excuses if you fall short. Accept the responsibility in knowing that you did your best and try to learn from the experience.

Never dwell on the negatives! Remember, the first play of the game is just as important as the last play of the game. That's why you should play hard and smart all game long!

Don't take yourself out of the game mentally by dwelling on a mistake. Put it behind you, and get your head back in the game. *Photo courtesy of Ryan McVay/Thinkstock.*

lean back too far and send your shot over the goal? Did you let the crowd get to you and miss the game-winning field goal? Get with your coach and develop a plan to work on the issue at the next practice.

It's even more important to stop dwelling on a mistake if the game is still going. Even if you just fumbled the ball or missed a game-tying penalty shot, you need to shake it off. Mentally tough athletes don't get stuck in negative thinking; they know how to turn off the instant replay of disaster that's playing in their heads and refocus. This is where you can use visualization to remind yourself of what you know you can do.

One thing mentally tough athletes don't do is make excuses for a mistake or blame other people for a loss. Did you fault on your serve? Don't blame it on the sweat spot on the gym floor. Did the ref miss the holding call? Probably; refs make mistakes too. Did your goalie blow an easy save? Possibly, but what good does it do to chew her out? She probably feels bad enough as it is. Mentally tough athletes take responsibility for their own mistakes and leave it at that.

> "I am very competitive and try my hardest. But I don't cry when we lose. I move on to the next game and try to win."
> —Joseph, 20, basketball

So, are you mentally tough? If not, do you want to be? You can get that psychological edge if you're willing to work at it.

Have You Ever Heard of Jianzi?

- In China, the sport is also called *tijianzi*, or "kicking the shuttle."
- The goal is to kick a badminton-like shuttle between players without letting it hit the ground. Points are scored for each successful pass; points are lost when the shuttle hits the ground.
- Jianzi started in ancient China. Today it is played mainly in China and Vietnam, although it is becoming more popular in Europe.
- Jianzi is also known as Chinese hacky sack. As in hacky sack, players may use any part of their body except hands and arms to pass the shuttle.[31]

Find Out More

Chapter

Youth Sport Trust. "Tuning Your Mind." In *The Young Athlete's Handbook*, 77–96. Champaign, IL: Human Kinetics, 2001.

Online Articles

Dedekind, Brendon. "The Swimmer Is on the Starting Block." About.com. swimming.about.com/od/sportpsychology/a/pre_event_psych. This article by a South African Olympic swimmer provides a look into one swimmer's pre-race mental preparation.

The Nemours Foundation/KidsHealth. "Handling Sports Pressure & Competition." TeensHealth, reviewed October 2010. teenshealth.org/teen/food_fitness/sports/sports_pressure.html#.

Websites and Organizations

American Athlete Magazine (www.americanathletemag.com). According to the "About Us" page, "American Athlete Magazine is an innovative new interactive publication focusing on the American Athlete's inner life. . . . Our mission is to present readers with true portraits of what it's like, and what's required to compete at the most challenging levels." A section titled "Mental Toughness" features stories about athletes in various sports, many of whom have overcome adversity and still compete.

Competitive Advantage (www.competitivedge.com). Competitive Advantage is the website of Dr. Alan Goldberg, who specializes in sports psychology. Much of the website is about the services and products you can buy, but on the lower left side of the page there's a helpful section called "Free Online Resources." Here you'll find tips on getting mentally tough, advice on rebounding from an injury, and a blog in which Dr. Goldberg gives advice on staying calm under pressure, coping with failure, creating smart goals, and much more. On the right side of the page is a long list of sports; click on yours to find out how mental toughness relates to your sport in particular. Dr. Goldberg also offers a free mental toughness newsletter, which you can sign up for on his website.

Way of Champions (www.wayofchampions.com). Way of Champions is the website of sports psychologist Jerry Lynch. Dr. Lynch has a unique approach to teaching mental toughness, combining traditional psychology with spiritual lessons from various religions. His goal is to teach athletes mental skills that can be applied to the bigger game of life as well as specific sports situations. Dr. Lynch has written several articles on becoming a champion and developing mental toughness, which can be accessed through the "Articles" tab at the top. His website also has information on the books he's written and the famous professional athletes he's helped.

Notes

1. Alan Goldberg, "Getting Mentally Tough," Competitive Advantage, www.competitivedge .com/resources_getting_mentally_tough.htm (accessed January 5, 2012).
2. Francois Fortin, ed., *Sports: The Complete Visual Reference* (Willowdale, ON: Firefly Books, 2000), 152; Human Kinetics, with Thomas Hanlon, *The Sports Rules Book: Essential Rules, Terms, and Procedures for 54 Sports*, 3rd ed. (Champaign, IL: Human Kinetics, 2009), 122; Golf Europe, "A History of Golf since 1497," www.golfeurope.com/almanac/history/ history1.htm (accessed March 19, 2012).
3. "Famous False Starts in Olympic Sports: Usain Bolt," *SI.com*, sportsillustrated.cnn.com/ multimedia/photo_gallery/1108/famous.false.starts/content.1.html (accessed March 7, 2012).
4. "Women's World Cup: U.S. vs. Japan: Victory on Penalty Kicks Earns Japan the Title," *Los Angeles Times*, July 17, 2011, latimesblogs.latimes.com/sports_blog/2011/07/womens-world-cup -us-vs-japan-victory-on-penalty-kicks-earns-japan-world-title.html (accessed March 7, 2012).
5. Michael Jordan, "Michael Jordan Quotes," BrainyQuote, www.brainyquote.com/quotes/ authors/m/michael_jordan.html (accessed March 7, 2012).
6. Associated Press, "Jacobellis Loses Shot at Gold with Stumble," NBC Sports, February 17, 2006, nbcsports.msnbc.com/id/11403461/ns/sports-winter_olympics/ (accessed March 7, 2012).
7. Bob Holt, "A-Rod's Strikeout to End Yankees' Season Goes Down in MLB History," *New JerseyNewsRoom.com*, October 7, 2011, www.newjerseynewsroom.com/professional/a-rods -strikeout-to-end-to-yankees-season-goes-down-in-mlb-history (accessed March 7, 2012).
8. Quoted in David Yukelson, "What Is Mental Toughness and How to Develop It?" www .mascsa.psu.edu/dave/Mental-Toughness.pdf (accessed January 3, 2012), 1.
9. Graham Jones, Sheldon Hanton, and Declan Conhaughton, "What Is This Thing Called Mental Toughness? An Investigation of Elite Sport Performers," *Journal of Applied Sport Psychology* 14 (2002): 205, cited in Yukelson, "What Is Mental Toughness?," 1.
10. Quoted in Yukelson, "What Is Mental Toughness?," 2.
11. Goldberg, "Getting Mentally Tough."
12. Quoted in *Maurice Jones-Drew's Outdoor Cardio Routine* (video), Yahoo! Sports, sports.yahoo .com/elite-athlete-workouts/maurice-jones-drew (accessed January 9, 2012).
13. Quoted in *Allyson Felix's Intense Workout* (video), Yahoo! Sports, sports.yahoo.com/elite -athlete-workouts/allyson-felix (accessed January 9, 2012).
14. Youth Sport Trust (Great Britain), *The Young Athlete's Handbook* (Champaign, IL: Human Kinetics, 2001), 84.
15. Yukelson, "What Is Mental Toughness?," 2.
16. Brendon Dedekind, "The Swimmer Is on the Starting Block," About.com, swimming.about .com/od/sportpsychology/a/pre_event_psych.htm (accessed January 6, 2012).

17. Exercise is adapted from Youth Sport Trust, *Young Athlete's Handbook*, 87.

18. Karie Meltzer, "Thinking about Baseball? Michigan Kicker Brendan Gibbons Scores by Thinking about Brunettes," *The Post Game* (blog), January 4, 2012, www.thepostgame.com/blog/style-points/201201/think-about-baseball-michigan-kicker-brendan-gibbons-scores-thinking-about- (accessed March 7, 2012).

19. Yukelson, "What Is Mental Toughness?," 2.

20. Mike Doyle, interview with author, January 4, 2012.

21. Lenny Neslin, "Stanley Cup 101," *The Globe*, May 25, 2011, retrieved from Boston.com, www.boston.com/sports/hockey/bruins/articles/2011/05/25/stanley_cup_101_facts_sheet/ (accessed November 12, 2011).

22. Jacque Davisson, author's sports survey, October 21, 2011.

23. Kirsten Frame, author's sports survey, November 30, 2011.

24. Derek Ort, author's sports survey, July 23, 2011.

25. David Schuster, author's sports survey, September 7, 2011.

26. Davisson, author's sports survey.

27. Youth Sport Trust, *Young Athlete's Handbook*, 93–95.

28. Quoted in *Learning from a Loss* (video), TeensHealth, teenshealth.org/teen/food_fitness/sports/sports_pressure.html (accessed December 24, 2011).

29. Jordan, "Michael Jordan Quotes."

30. Billy Shepherd Sports Inc., "Student-Athlete Tip of the Week (11-28-11)," National Federation of State High School Associations, www.nfhs.org (accessed November 30, 2011).

31. *The Sports Book: The Games, the Rules, the Tactics, the Techniques* (London: Dorling Kindersley, 2007), 189.

EAT TO WIN

··

During the off-season, NFL running back Maurice Jones-Drew follows the Bommarito Performance Systems program run by Pete Bommarito. The program involves intense strength and conditioning, weight training, and instruction in proper nutrition. When asked how important the nutrition part is in the whole training package, Bommarito said, "In my opinion, it's probably the most important thing."[1]

Have you ever considered that eating is part of your training program—by some accounts, the most important part? Food is your primary source of carbohydrate, protein, fat, vitamins, and minerals—all the things you need to perform at your best. Your body breaks down food and turns it into energy. If you don't eat enough of the right kinds of food, you can run out of energy at inconvenient times—like in the middle of a game or race. You won't have the strength to pin your opponent or the power to jump and make that touchdown catch. When you're fatigued, skills such as dribbling (with your hands or feet) become sloppy, and you don't think as clearly. You're also more likely to get injured when your body is tired. Read on to learn what to eat and when to eat it in order to have the energy you need in the middle of practice and competition.

Food Is Fuel

Remember this basic fact: food is fuel. It's your basic source of energy. Everything you eat or drink (except water) has energy stored in it, and this energy is measured in terms of calories. Your body needs this energy to perform any action, both conscious and unconscious. It takes energy to breathe and to make your heart beat. In reality, you are burning calories every second of every day. Every time you blink, think, or smile, your body is burning calories. When you exercise, you need even more energy since your muscles, lungs, and heart are all working harder.

How many calories does your body need to accomplish all these tasks? That depends on many factors, including your age, height, current weight, physical fitness, and activity level. Teenagers generally require more calories than adults because they're still growing, and growth requires a lot of energy. Your calorie

Daily Calorie Needs

The number of calories each person needs varies by body type, height, weight, age, gender, and activity level. Athletes need more calories than nonathletes, and guys need more calories than girls. Even among athletes there's a big range, with some football players eating more in one day than a gymnast eats in two. Compare the average calories needs for teens aged fourteen to eighteen.

Nonathletes

Girls	1,800–2,200 calories
Guys	2,000–2,500 calories

Athletes

Girls	2,200–3,200 calories
Guys	2,500–5,000 calories

Chances are that you're not going to go around counting calories; I don't. So, how do you know if you're eating enough? One way is to compare what you're eating with the recommended daily servings provided in table 4.1. Another way is to do a self-evaluation: Do you find it hard to maintain a steady weight, especially during the season? Do you tire out more easily than your teammates? If the answer is yes to these questions, you might need to take in more calories so you have the energy to perform at your best.

needs also depend on your metabolism rate, or the rate at which your body breaks down food so it can be used as energy. Metabolism is affected by several factors, including genetics and activity level. More activity leads to faster food breakdown because the body is using more fuel. High school athletes, who often practice two to three hours every day after school in addition to competitions, need more calories than teenagers who go home after school and sit on the couch.

Energy in the form of calories is stored in three basic "units," or types, of food: carbohydrate, protein, and fat. Each gram of carbohydrate contains four calories, each gram of protein contains four calories, and each gram of fat contains nine calories. Judging from these numbers, you might think that eating a lot of fat will give you the most energy, but it's not quite that simple. Read on to find out the roles that carbohydrate, protein, and fat all play in terms of fueling athletic activity.

Carbohydrate

Repeat after me: "Carbohydrates are good." Since the early 2000s, some popular diets have been giving carbohydrates a bad rap (see the sidebar on low-carb diets). If you're an athlete, however, carbohydrates are your friend. They're the body's energy source of choice, making them a key part of any athlete's diet. Most sports nutrition specialists agree that at least 50 to 60 percent of an athlete's daily calories should come from carbohydrates.[2]

What makes carbohydrates so special? Carbs are your body's primary source of both immediate and long-term energy. Your body breaks down carbs into glycogen (a form of the sugar glucose), which is absorbed into the bloodstream and used to fuel action. Some glycogen is used right away to perform unconscious (blinking, breathing, etc.) and everyday (writing, talking, etc.) activities as well as exercise. Whatever glycogen is not used right away is stored in your muscles and liver. The glycogen stored in muscles is what athletes use to sprint, lift, throw, row, or kick; in particular, athletes rely on carbs for endurance, or the ability to keep on going. If you don't have enough glycogen in your muscles, you're going to burn out or "hit the wall" a lot sooner. You might know the hit-the-wall feeling—your legs turn into lead weights, you get lightheaded during a workout, or you "lock up" in the middle of your kick to the finish line or end zone.

! Low-Carb Diets

In the early twenty-first century, a new diet fad started that basically knocked out the bottom level of the food pyramid (see figure 4.1). These so-called low-carb (and even no-carb) diets emphasize cutting out carbohydrates and eating more protein and fat. The Zone Diet and Atkins are two popular examples. These diets do work for people who are trying to lose weight. However, for athletes—especially high school athletes—low-carb diets are not the answer. Carbohydrates are your most important source of energy. As an athlete, cutting back on carbs can leave you weak, fatigued, and more susceptible to injury.

Figure 4.1 The food pyramid created by the U.S. Department of Agriculture in 1992. The bottom tier (which should make up most of your daily diet) is complex carbs, the next level is fruits and vegetables, next is protein and dairy, and at the top is fats and sweets. This pyramid design was changed to a plate in 2011. *Image courtesy of Dynamic Graphics/Thinkstock.*

Keep It Complex

Carbohydrates come in two forms: complex and simple. Complex carbohydrates are sometimes called starches and include pasta, legumes (beans), bread, rice, cereal, and some vegetables (e.g., potatoes, green beans, corn). Simple carbohydrates, on the other hand, taste sweet; examples include fruit, soda, and candy bars.

Most carbohydrates in an athlete's diet should be complex. This is because, in general, complex carbohydrates are higher in fiber, minerals, and vitamins. Basically, they're better for you nutritionally speaking. In addition, complex carbohydrates are digested more slowly and, as a result, provide a longer-lasting supply of energy.[3]

Sports drinks are another source of carbs for athletes. Though not a food, drinks such as Gatorade, All Sport, and Powerade are a key source of energy (more on sports drinks later).

Alcohol and Athletes

Let's just start with the obvious: if you're under the legal drinking age, you shouldn't be drinking alcohol. If that's not a good enough reason to avoid it, here's another one: alcohol and sports don't mix. Alcohol is high in calories that your muscles can't use. Technically, alcohol is a source of carbohydrate, but it is not converted into glycogen like bread or pasta. Instead, the sugars from alcohol are converted to fatty acids and stored as fat, particularly around the stomach. Ever hear of the terms *beer belly* or *spare tire*? Not exactly what you want when you're trying to glide over the high jump bar or dive into the water without a splash. In addition, alcohol can affect your ability to learn and remember plays, slow muscle recovery and growth, and reduce your energy and endurance levels. Consuming alcohol can basically negate all the hard work you put in at practice, in the weight room, and in learning new strategies.[4]

All Complex Carbs Are Not Created Equal

In general, complex carbohydrates will give you longer-lasting energy, but if you really want to get the most from your carbs, choose whole grain/whole wheat over white when you can. White bread, white rice, and so on have gone through more processing and have lost some of their nutrients.

The following whole-grain complex carbs will give you a better supply of energy and nutrition than the white versions:[5]

- Brown rice
- Whole-grain cereal
- Whole-wheat bread, bagels, English muffins
- Whole-wheat pasta
- Whole-wheat tortillas

Too Much of a Good Thing

If more glycogen in your muscles means more long-lasting energy, the more carbs you eat, the better, right? Unfortunately, no. It is possible to get too much of a good thing. Your muscles have a limit as to how much glycogen they can store. The rest will be eliminated from the body or stored as fat (the latter is what the low-carb diets are designed to avoid). One way to increase the amount of glycogen your muscles can store is to increase the amount of muscle, or muscle mass.[6] (See chapter 7 for tips on weight and resistance training.)

Protein

In addition to carbohydrates, your body needs protein to perform at its best, but for different reasons. Protein doesn't provide immediate energy the way carbs do. When the body breaks down protein, the energy released mainly goes toward building and repairing muscles and other tissues. So, the more protein you eat, the bigger your muscles will get, right? Wrong. Your body can only break down and use so much protein. It's not stored for later use like carbohydrates. If you overload on protein, your body is going to use what it needs to build and repair muscles and then eliminate the rest. Some of the extra may be stored as fat, but this has not been proven conclusively.[7] Good sources of protein include lean meat, chicken, fish, eggs, nuts, milk, yogurt, and cheese.

How Much Protein?

Sports nutritionists have different opinions on exactly how much protein athletes should eat. Some say around 20 to 25 percent of your daily calories should come from protein; some say as little as 15 percent.[8] Most nutritionists agree that strength and power athletes (e.g., football players, wrestlers, sprinters) benefit

Check the Label

In your search for whole-grain snacks and foods, check the labels. According to WebMD, "Foods labeled with the words 'multi-grain,' 'stone-ground,' '100% wheat,' 'cracked wheat,' 'seven-grain,' or 'bran' are usually *not* whole-grain products." In truly whole-grain products, ingredients such as whole wheat, whole oats, oatmeal, and brown rice will be listed *first* on the label.[9]

Protein for Vegetarians and Vegans

If you're a vegetarian or vegan, you need to make sure you eat enough calories in general and protein in particular. If you don't, you'll get fatigued more easily than your competitors. (For those of you who don't know the difference, a *vegetarian* doesn't eat meat; a *vegan* doesn't eat meat or any meat by-products, including eggs, milk, and cheese.)

The best sources of meat-free protein for vegetarians include eggs, tofu, soy, milk, yogurt, and cheese. The dairy products in particular provide all the essential amino acids that make up proteins. The best protein sources for vegans fall into four categories:

1. Legumes (beans, peas, lentils)
2. Nuts and seeds (peanuts, cashews, almonds, sunflower seeds)
3. Grains (bread, pasta, rice, oats, cereal)
4. Soy products (tofu, soy milk, soybeans)

These nonmeat by-products are good sources of protein, but they are incomplete by themselves; that is, eaten alone, they each lack some of the important amino acids that make up proteins. You'll need to combine sources from at least two of the four categories in order to get a complete protein. For example, you could eat the following combinations:

- Bean burrito (legumes, grains)
- Peanut butter sandwich (nuts, grains)
- Tofu burger on a bun (soy, grains)
- Lentil soup and a roll (legumes, grains)[10]

from increased protein consumption more than endurance athletes (e.g., cross-country runners, long-distance swimmers). Football linemen, for example, focus on muscle building, and they need the extra protein to support their training. But there's still a limit as to how much protein the body can use. Though a lineman's body might use more protein than, say, a cross-country runner's body, there is still a point at which the body stops converting protein into muscle. Think of it this way: the recommended daily servings of protein is two to four; a cross-country runner probably needs two or three and a football player probably needs four or five—not nine or ten. That extra is not going to add muscle or increase strength.[11] (For a summary of the recommended number of daily servings of carbohydrates, proteins, and fats, see table 4.1.)

Also, protein is only going to do its job as a muscle builder if you're eating enough calories overall. Remember, your body needs energy from food for basic functioning. If you don't take in enough carbohydrates for energy, your body will start using protein for energy, which means protein is not being used to build and repair muscle. Bottom line: Even if you want to build muscle mass, you have to eat a lot more than just protein.

Protein Supplements

Protein powder, protein shakes, and protein bars are probably the most common supplements among teen athletes. You can mix the powder into a glass of milk or a fruit smoothie; shakes and bars are ready to drink/eat. Protein supplements are readily available at the store, and the bars are easy to carry around for a snack before games. Unlike some supplements (see chapter 5), protein bars and shakes seem safe to take as a *supplement*; they're not intended to replace the protein you get from food. Also, protein supplements should be part of a diet that consists of enough overall calories, or else the extra protein will be used for energy, not muscle building.

As mentioned, athletes in strength and power sports may benefit from a little extra protein, but there's a limit to that benefit. As a result, some nutritionists question whether protein supplements are worth it. Why pay for extra protein when your body is going to either eliminate the extra or possibly store it as fat? Also, the quality of protein found in supplements is not better than the protein found in food. The bars can be handy, but for the most part, you're probably better off saving your money. Eat your protein as part of a balanced diet.[12]

Fat

If you think of your day's calories as a plate, at least half your plate should be filled with carbs (mostly complex); the other half should be divided about evenly between protein and fat. Like protein, fat should make up about 20 to 25 percent of your daily calorie intake; some nutrition specialists say fat should make up 30 percent of an athlete's diet.[13]

"I eat very healthy and never eat the school food consisting of fries, tater tots, pizza bread, cupcakes, ice cream, chips, etc."—Mikalla, 15, soccer

That probably sounds like a lot of fat, right? In elementary or middle school, you may have learned that fats are in the smallest triangle at the top of the food pyramid (figure 4.1), meaning they should make up the smallest part of your daily food choices. But that old pyramid didn't distinguish between good and bad fats.[14] Yes, you should limit the number of Cheetos and Snickers and gummy worms you consume. But your body needs the good fats that are found in dairy products, nuts and seeds, meat, and oily fish (e.g., salmon and trout). Good fats protect your organs and provide energy for exercise—especially exercise over

Table 4.1 Recommended Daily Servings

Food Group	Servings per Day*
Complex carbs (pasta, bread, rice, cereal)	4–6
Fruit	2–4
Vegetable	3–5
Dairy (milk, cheese, yogurt)	2–4
Protein (meat, chicken, eggs, beans, tofu)	2–4
Healthy fats (oily fish, nuts, seeds)	2–4

Source: Data from "The Fitness Food Pyramid," in Anita Bean, *The Complete Guide to Sports Nutrition* (Guilford, CT: The Lyons Press, 2004), x–xi.

*These numbers are based on the nutrition needs of an athlete; they are slightly different than those found in the original USDA food pyramid.

Serving Size

So what does one serving look like? Here's a practical guide to give you an idea of what equals one portion:[15]

Food Group	Size of One Serving	Examples
Complex carbs	palm of your hand	rice, pasta, cereal
	your fist	baked potato
	two slices	bread (or one bagel)
Fruit	tennis ball	medium apple, cup of berries, orange
Vegetable	palm of your hand	carrot cut into sticks, cooked broccoli
Dairy	four dice	cheese
	one carton	yogurt
	one cup	milk
Protein	deck of cards	meat, chicken, fish, tofu
	palm of your hand	legumes (beans, lentils), two eggs
Healthy fats	deck of cards	oily fish
	palm of your hand	nuts or seeds

long periods of time. Nordic skiers, cross-country runners, and soccer players, for example, depend on fat energy so they can conserve carbohydrate energy for later in the race or match. No matter what your sport, low- and nonfat diets are not a good idea for athletes.[16]

Drink Up!

In addition to food, your body needs plenty of fluids in order to perform at its best. If you don't drink enough, you can become dehydrated and fatigued. Combined with prolonged exercise in hot weather, dehydration (severe loss of body fluids) can lead to heat exhaustion, heatstroke, and even death.

Fluid Loss

Whether or not you're exercising, your body loses fluids on a daily basis. Every time you exhale, you breathe out water vapor; every time you go to the bathroom, you're losing water. If you live in the desert or in a humid area, you probably sweat on a daily basis, and again you're losing water. Add the sweat you produce during practice, intervals, or weight training in addition to games or races, and you can see how much water you lose every day. If you don't replenish that water, your body becomes dehydrated.

As you exercise, your muscles start working and they produce extra heat. Sweating is the body's method of cooling itself off. As sweat evaporates, the body cools down and keeps its core temperature within a normal range.[17]

Dehydration Symptoms

Your body's loss of fluids can reach the level of dehydration before you feel thirsty. Some nutritionists think many people walk around in a state of mild dehydration on a daily basis. Pay attention to the following symptoms, especially if they occur during a workout:

- Headache
- Sluggishness
- Fatigue
- Loss of appetite
- Nausea
- Feeling lightheaded or dizzy
- Fainting

If you start feeling these symptoms while training, you need to replenish your fluids as soon as possible. Listen to your body. Everyone sweats at different rates, and you may become dehydrated sooner than your teammates or before your coach gives you a water break.[18]

Foods That Prevent Dehydration

In addition to drinking water, you can eat foods with high water content to help your body stay hydrated. Here are some examples:

- Plum
- Peach
- Orange
- Mango[19]

Everyone sweats at a different rate. How much you sweat depends on several factors, including

- how hard you're exercising,
- how long your workout (or game or race) lasts,
- the outside temperature and humidity level,
- your height and weight (smaller people tend to sweat less),
- your fitness level (fitter people tend to start sweating sooner), and
- your gender (women tend to sweat less).[20]

Genetics can also cause some people to sweat more than others, and some sports tend to cause more sweating. Marathon runners, for example, can lose up to two liters (as in the large bottle of soda) of fluid *an hour!*[21] The bottom line is the more you sweat, the more careful you have to be about replacing the fluids you have lost. Hydration should begin long before your practice or game; you should be drinking water all day, every day, whether or not you'll be exercising and whether or not you're thirsty.

Dehydration is cumulative. When you play in a tournament or doubleheader or when you race in an invitational, you have multiple competitions in one day. If you don't replenish enough after the first game or heat, then you start the next one partially dehydrated and at greater risk of heat-related illness. Partial dehydration can even be carried over from one day to the next.

If possible, drink cold water or sports drinks during and after practice and competition. Your body absorbs cold liquids faster; a side benefit is that cold drinks are much more refreshing on a hot day. Pouring cold water over your head may feel good, but it doesn't replenish your fluids; you need to drink it. Those of you who live in hot climates—especially hot, humid areas—need to be even more careful about staying hydrated.

If you compete in the pool or in an ice rink, you might not feel like you're losing fluids through sweat, but you are. To avoid dehydration, you need to replenish fluids just like everyone else. *Photo courtesy of Thinkstock.*

What to Drink

Good old-fashioned water is the cheapest and most readily available source of fluids. It's also the best all-around fluid for your body. Get your own water bottle (I like the sport-top kind, but I've seen people carry a plastic one-gallon jug), and carry it with you. Many doctors recommend that people drink eight 8-ounce

Check the Bowl

Are you drinking enough water? Besides counting glasses, there's one way to find out: check the toilet bowl. If your urine is clear or pale yellow, you're doing great. If it's dark yellow, you need to start drinking more water, even on days you don't have competition or practice. Dark-colored urine is actually a sign that your body is dehydrated. Try carrying a sport-top water bottle with you wherever you go, and get in the habit of drinking throughout out the day, even when you're not thirsty.[22]

glasses per day (if you carry a typical twenty-four-ounce sport-top bottle, drink three bottles' worth and you'll be at nine glasses). But that doesn't take into consideration the amount of fluid that athletes lose during workouts and games. You'll most likely need to drink more than eight or nine glasses to avoid becoming dehydrated.

While water should be your first choice, fruit juice, sports drinks, and even an occasional soda count as fluid replenishment. However, you should avoid soda and fruit juice immediately before and after you work out since they don't effectively fuel your body for exercise, and they can actually hinder your recovery (more on what to drink and when later in the chapter).[23]

Three Wrestlers Die Trying to Make Weight

Nineteen-year-old Billy Saylor was trying to lose six pounds. Twenty-two-year-old Joseph LaRosa was trying to lose four and a half pounds. Twenty-one-year-old Jeff Reese was trying to lose seventeen pounds. All three were trying to lose this weight in a couple days or less so they could wrestle at a lower weight class. To "make weight," all three wrestlers used intentional dehydration methods—exercising for prolonged periods of time in rubber wet suits and refusing fluids.

Sadly, within six weeks of each other in 1997, all three wrestlers died in their attempts to lose weight. Billy, a freshman at Campbell University in North Carolina, died of cardiac arrest. Joseph, a senior at the University of Wisconsin, La Crosse, died of heatstroke. Jeff, a junior at the University of Michigan, died of kidney failure and heart malfunction. In each case, severe dehydration led to the malfunction or complete shutdown of bodily functions.

It seems at least one of these wrestlers was taking creatine, a legal, over-the-counter protein supplement. Wrestlers use creatine to recover more quickly from workouts and to help develop muscle bulk. However, creatine must be used according to the directions, which includes drinking plenty of water. One of the side effects of creatine is dehydration; in combination with intentionally depriving the body of fluids, the consumption of creatine can be life threatening.[24]

Heat-Related Illnesses

Dehydration alone is bad; in conjunction with exercise in extremely hot weather, it can be deadly. When you train in hot weather, your body has to work overtime to cool off. Sweating is part of your body's natural cooling system. In addition, blood rushes to the surface of your skin, meaning less blood is flowing to your muscles, brain, and other organs; as a result, you can experience a decrease in physical strength and mental alertness.[25] If you keep exercising in an overheated, dehydrated state, you are likely to experience heat-related illness.

Unfortunately, heat-related illnesses such as heat exhaustion, heat cramps, and heatstroke hit high school athletes every year. Heatstroke (also known as sunstroke) is the most serious heat-related illness. Between 1995 and 2005, more than twenty-four high school football players died of heatstroke. In almost every case, these deaths occurred during a preseason practice at the end of summer, when outside temps were very high and players were still getting back in shape.[26]

Heatstroke occurs when the brain's temperature regulating feature malfunctions. Blood stops flowing to the brain, and the body stops sweating. Football players are at greater risk because not only are they performing strenuous exercise in crazy hot weather, but they're doing so in full or partial pads and helmets. The pads add extra weight, making players work harder and sweat more. Helmets make it more difficult for the body to cool itself off. Football players can lose an incredible amount of fluid during practice, and they often have two-a-days during

Heatstroke Symptoms

If you're training or playing in excessive heat, it's a good idea to use the buddy system to watch for heatstroke symptoms. You and a teammate can look out for each other and say something to a coach if you notice the following changes in appearance or performance:[27]

- Red, dry skin
- Lack of sweating
- Dizziness
- Nausea or vomiting
- Confusion or disorientation
- Rapid, shallow breathing

the hottest part of summer. Soccer and tennis are other sports where heatstroke is a bigger threat, partly because players often compete in tournaments involving multiple matches in one day.[28]

Timing Is Everything

> *"The right combination of fluid and nutrients consumed within the Performance Zone will help you improve your athletic performance far more than the latest high-tech equipment or training device."*
> —*John Ivy and Robert Portman, authors of* The Performance Zone[29]

Now you have the basics of what you need to eat and drink on a daily basis: carbs for energy, protein for muscle, fats for organ protection and energy, and fluids to keep your body hydrated and functioning properly. How do all those elements fit into a game-day schedule? In other words, what should you eat and drink, and when? Here are general guidelines on what to eat and drink before, during, and after practice and competition, along with reasons why and practical examples (see table 4.2 for a summary). Specific, sport-by-sport tips are provided a little later in the chapter.

Table 4.2 Game-Day Nutrition Summary

	Goals	What to Eat	What to Drink
Before	Fuel and hydrate	Lots of complex carbs Moderate amount of protein Limit fat and fiber Last meal should be 3–4 hours before game/race	Water Sip sports drink in the hour before
During	Replenish	Starchy, easy-to-digest carbs (only if you need something)	Sip sports drink during breaks (time-outs, between innings, at halftime)
After	Recover	Carbohydrate and protein snack as soon as possible	Sports drink within forty-five minutes

Pregame Summary

- Eat foods that are high in carbohydrates. Limit protein, fat, and fiber before you play.
- Give yourself plenty of time to digest a pregame meal; three to four hours is recommended.
- Try eating different foods on practice days to make sure they sit well while you're training. Don't try anything new on game day.
- If you feel nervous, you might want to sip a carbohydrate sports drink and eat crackers instead of having a full meal.
- Bring starchy carbohydrate snacks with you in case you need a little something closer to game time. Cereal bars, fruit, and dry cereal are good options (but remember to try them on training days first).
- Stay hydrated! Try to drink sixteen to twenty ounces an hour before game time, and then sip fluids during the half hour before you start.[30]

Before: Fill the Tank

Let's use the analogy of a car: you need fuel in the tank before you can go anywhere. The same principle applies to your body (the car) and food/drink (fuel). In terms of eating and drinking, you have two main goals before any training or competition: (1) fuel your body with usable energy and (2) fully hydrate your body with fluids. At this stage, carbohydrates are your most important source of energy. You need to fill up your muscles' store of glycogen so you can avoid fatigue as long as possible. Your last meal—whether it's the night before an early morning practice or at lunch before an afternoon game—should consist mainly of complex (starchy) carbohydrates.

Has your coach ever told you to eat spaghetti the night before a race or game? That's because pasta is a complex carb that breaks down slowly and puts a good supply of glycogen in your muscles, preparing you for the next day's competition. Each person digests food at a different rate, but in general, your last big meal should be at least three to four hours before competition.

"The girls on the track team host pasta parties the night before to load up on carbs and get pumped for the meet the next morning."—Anna, 19, track and field

Breakfast of Champions

If you skip a meal, it's probably breakfast, right? The whole house is rushing around, taking showers, making lunches, and trying to get out the door. Some of you probably don't feel hungry in the morning anyway. I'm sure you've heard this before: breakfast is the most important meal of the day. And it's true, especially on game days. Here are some fairly quick breakfast ideas (remember: give yourself three to four hours to digest before competition): [31]

- Hot or cold cereal (not high fiber), milk, fruit
- Bagel with juice or milk
- Yogurt and toast
- Frozen waffles and juice or milk

On nongame days, some of you may have before-school practices. If you're supposed to be in the pool at six in the morning, there's no way you're eating a meal three hours earlier! Instead, try to drink a glass of orange juice with a cereal bar or eat some fruit on the way to the pool—just something to give your body a carbohydrate boost. When you're done with practice, eat a breakfast that's easy to carry with you; for example, a bagel with cream cheese or a peanut butter sandwich and fruit.

Your body needs time to break down the food into glycogen. You also want your stomach to be empty so you don't get cramps.

About thirty minutes before your match or race time, top off your fuel supply by sipping eight to sixteen ounces of a sports drink that contains carbohydrates. It's better to use a sports drink that contains the sugar *sucrose*—not fructose—since sucrose is absorbed more quickly and is less likely to cause an

"Because I live in such a hot climate I have to start drinking water early in the morning before any practice or game. I make sure to drink at least three bottles of water before practice, then a jug during practice and Gatorade during a game."—Caitlin, 16, tennis

> ### ❗ Game-Day Meals You Can Bring to School
>
> Many high schools schedule games, matches, and meets after school or in the evening. This means you're probably not going home between school and competition, so you need to bring high-carb pregame meals with you. Here are some ideas:[32]
>
> - Chicken sandwich on whole-wheat bread, fruit or juice
> - Tuna fish in pita, fruit or juice
> - Thick-crust slice of pizza, fruit or juice
> - Sliced turkey wrap, fruit or juice

upset stomach; Gatorade is an example of a sports drink containing sucrose.[33] It's also a good idea to take small sips over the whole half hour. If you gulp it all at once, you are more likely to feel full and uncomfortable when you start your game or race. Also, sipping helps you maintain a constant inflow of carbs right up to game time.[34]

Sipping a sports drink also fills your tank with fluids, the second pregame goal. In addition to your day-by-day practice of drinking water, you need to add extra fluid to your body in the hours before practice and competition, especially if it's hot and humid. In the last hour before you compete, try to drink around sixteen to twenty ounces of water (about two-thirds to three-fourths of a regular sports bottle). If it's really hot, keep sipping right up to game time, but not so much that you get a sloshy stomach.

You need protein and fat in your sports nutrition plan, but don't eat too much of either right before you exercise. Protein and fat take longer to digest and can leave you feeling heavy and full at game time. On game days, it's best to limit the dairy, eggs, tofu, and meat you eat before you play, and you should probably avoid fried foods, chips, and candy altogether. It's also best to avoid high-fiber foods (beans, lentils) before a game, as they can cause gas and other intestinal issues.

During: Replenish Glycogen and Fluids

Once practice or competition begins, you have two goals: avoid dehydration and delay fatigue. As already mentioned, your body becomes dehydrated when you lose fluids faster than you're replacing them. Your best strategy during exercise is to drink small amounts of fluid frequently. If you wait until you're thirsty, you're

> ## ! Electrolytes
>
> You've probably noticed that sweat is salty. That's because you lose a lot of sodium (salt) and other electrolytes when you sweat. Electrolytes carry electrical impulses between cells so that the body's systems (e.g., digestive, nervous, muscular) all function properly. Among other things, losing a lot of electrolytes can result in muscle cramping—not a good thing if you're in the middle of a competition. It's important to replenish the electrolytes as soon as possible. Sports drinks add electrolytes such as sodium chloride and potassium—another reason to keep a bottle of Gatorade or Powerade close at hand during practice or competition.[35]

more likely to gulp down too much at one time, resulting in an upset stomach or feeling uncomfortably full.

When you exercise for long periods of time, fatigue is going to set in sooner or later, since your muscles can only store so much glycogen. Your goal is to delay fatigue as long as possible; the best way to do that is consuming small amounts of carbs throughout exercise. Your body will use this immediate energy source first, and then go back to using the stored glycogen. The longer the stored glycogen lasts, the longer you delay that hit-the-wall feeling of exhaustion.

What's the best way to get carbs in the middle of a game? Most of you probably don't feel like eating anything, even if it's an easily digestible carbs (e.g., a sports bar), so your best bet is a sports drink with carbohydrates. Try to sip seven to ten ounces of sports drink every ten to twenty minutes. It might be easier to keep track of mouthfuls: one mouthful is approximately one ounce.[36]

Some sports have built-in opportunities to rehydrate and replenish carbs—during time-outs, during changes in offense/defense, or in between innings, quarters, or periods. In sports like soccer or field hockey, however, it's not as easy because play is basically continuous. In these sports, make sure you drink plenty before the match starts and then sip a sports drink during halftime.

After: It's All about Recovery

After your game, race, or practice, you really only have one goal: help your body recover so you're ready for next time. Specifically, you're trying to put energy (glycogen) back into your muscles so you're ready to perform. You're also try-

> ## Energy Drinks Are Not the Same as Sports Drinks
>
> NOS, Monster, Red Bull, Rockstar—these drinks have become popular among athletes, especially teen athletes, who are looking for a little energy boost. The boost comes from the high amounts of sugar and caffeine contained in each can. The problem is that some teens use these energy drinks as fluid replacement before and after exercise.
>
> Caffeine is a diuretic that can aggravate dehydration. When you use energy drinks as part of your nutrition game plan, you're not replacing the fluids you sweat off; you're actually making the dehydration worse. *Energy drinks are not the same as sports drinks.* Before, during, and after exercise you need the carbohydrates and electrolytes contained in sports drinks such as Gatorade, Accelerade, and Powerade. As you'll read in chapter 5, energy drinks can actually be dangerous for young athletes and should be avoided.[37]

ing to replenish fluids. Remember, dehydration is cumulative. That means if you don't recover fully after your morning practice or after the first match in the tournament, you'll start the next practice or match dehydrated and you'll probably feel fatigued more quickly.[38]

Recovery should start as soon as possible after exercise ends. You probably don't feel like eating right after you finish, so start your recovery with fluids—water as well as a sports drink with carbohydrates and electrolytes. Your body needs the carbohydrates to replenish the glycogen you just used up. Immediately after exercise—that is, in the first forty-five minutes after you stop—your muscles are primed for rebuilding and repairing. During this "metabolic window," your cells absorb carbohydrates *three to four times faster* than they do three hours after exercise, which means you get a lot more stored energy out of the carbs you drink. Let's say you drink one bottle of Gatorade fifteen minutes after playing a tennis match, and you drink another bottle two hours later. Your body will produce and store twice as much glycogen from the first bottle, just because of when you consumed it. According to some sports nutritionists, a sports drink that has a little protein in addition to carbs (e.g., Accelerade) aids the recovery process even more.[39]

How much should you drink? At least twenty-four ounces right away, but most experts agree that you should drink as much as you can as soon as you can. If you're playing in a tournament, you need to gauge how much to drink based on when your next game is so your body has time to digest the fluids.

Postgame Snacks

Here are some easy-to-carry postgame snacks:[40]

- Fruit and string cheese
- Sports bar (e.g., Cliff, Luna, Balance)
- Crackers and peanut butter
- Bagel with juice
- Fruit smoothie with protein (store-bought brands include Naked Juice and Odwalla)

It is important to carry foods like these with you, especially when you go to tournaments or away games. Remember: These are just snacks. Unless you're playing in a tournament or have a doubleheader, you should also eat a full meal within a couple hours.

Even though you may not feel like eating, your body needs food to recover and rebuild. The sooner you eat a snack after strenuous exercise, the better—definitely within an hour and preferably high-carb foods with a little protein. Carbs will put more glycogen in your muscles, and the protein will help with muscle repair and recovery. Remember the goal: Refuel the body for next time, whether that's a few hours or a few days away.

Sport-by-Sport Nutrition Tips

Now it's time to get specific. How do the specific energy needs of your sport affect what and when you should eat? As stated in the first section, athletes' diets

Bad Recovery Foods

When your body is in recovery mode, try to avoid soda, as well as fast food, potato chips, and other high-fat foods. Carbonated beverages make you feel full, so you may not drink as much as you need to for recovery. Foods that are full of bad fat can slow down the process of repairing muscles.[41]

in general should consist of approximately 50–60 percent carbohydrates, 20–25 percent protein, and 20–25 percent fat; in addition, sports nutritionists have sport-specific recommendations based on the energy needs and training goals involved.

There are three general categories of sports:

> "In water polo [you] burn so many calories you can eat whatever you really want."
> —Samantha, 17, water polo

1. Those that involve short, high-intensity bursts of speed, power, and strength followed by rest (*power sports*)
2. Those that involve less-than-maximum activity over a longer period of time (*endurance sports*)
3. Those that involve both all-out bursts and continual activity over a long period of time (*power and endurance sports*)

Table 4.3 summarizes the characteristics and nutrition needs of each and gives examples of which sports fall into each category. The tips that follow build on this table by highlighting sport-specific factors that influence the timing, type, and amount of food and drink consumed. Not all high school sports are covered here. If your sports isn't listed, look at the suggestions for a sport with similar features; for example, field hockey and lacrosse are similar to soccer in that they all involve power, endurance, and nonstop action, and diving is similar to gymnastics in the emphasis on power, control, and body image.

Power Sports

These sports involve short, high-intensity bursts of speed, power, and strength followed by rest.

Baseball/Softball[42]

1. Both sports require mental sharpness in the field. When you become fatigued, your ability to make quick decisions suffers and errors are often the result. For example, you might forget the number of outs and throw to first instead of turning a double play to end the inning. To prevent dehydration and mental sluggishness, drink plenty of fluids—particularly sports drinks with electrolytes and carbohydrates. Get into the habit of taking a few sips from your sports drink every time you come into the dugout. Then take a few more before you take the

Table 4.3 Summary of Different Types of Sports and Nutrition Needs

	Power Sports	Endurance Sports	Power and Endurance Sports
Characteristics	- Involve short bursts of all-out effort followed by periods of "rest"; muscles work without oxygen since high-intensity bursts usually last ninety seconds or less (called *anaerobic metabolism*) - Need energy to be fastest over short distance - Not concerned with being able to sustain speed for long distances - Focus on building muscle mass to provide explosive strength, power, speed	- Involve performing exercise at less-than-maximum speed over a long period of time; muscles need oxygen to do the endurance activity (called *aerobic metabolism*) - Focus on building aerobic capacity - Focus on resistance training to increase muscles' glycogen storage capacity	- Involve short bursts of power/ speed followed by lower intensity exercise over a long game (aerobic and anaerobic metabolism) - Need speed and the ability sustain activity over long distance/time - Focus on building aerobic capacity and increasing muscle mass

Nutrition Needs	- Phosphocreatine (from protein) and glycogen (from complex carbohydrates) to fuel anaerobic activity - High overall calorie intake for energy and muscle growth - High complex carbohydrate intake for muscle energy (glycogen) - Slightly higher protein intake to sustain muscle growth and repair - Moderate fat intake	- Glycogen (from complex carbohydrates) and fat to fuel aerobic exercise - High overall calorie intake for energy - High complex carbohydrate intake for maximum glycogen storage in muscles - Moderate protein intake - Slightly higher fat intake to help conserve glycogen	- Phosphocreatine (from protein) to fuel the power bursts and glycogen (from complex carbohydrates) to fuel the long-lasting exercise - High overall calorie intake for energy and muscle growth - Very high complex carbohydrate intake to delay fatigue - Moderate protein intake - Moderate fat intake
Nutrition Breakdown*	- Daily calorie needs = 2,000–5,000 - Carbohydrates = 60–65 percent of daily calories - Protein = 20 percent of daily calories - Fat = 15–20 percent of daily calories	- Daily calorie needs = 2,500–4,000 - Carbohydrates = 60–65 percent of daily calories - Protein = 15 percent of daily calories - Fat = 20–25 percent of daily calories	- Daily calorie needs = 2,000–4,500 - Carbohydrates = 65 percent of daily calories - Protein = 15 percent of daily calories - Fat = 20 percent of daily calories

(continued)

Table 4.3 (continued)

	Power Sports	Endurance Sports	Power and Endurance Sports
Example Activities	- 100-meter race - Stealing second base - Gymnastics floor exercise	- Three-mile cross-country race - 1500-meter freestyle - Triathlon	- Sprint for ball, shot on goal, then jog back to defense - Fast-break to the basket, jump shot, then jog back to defense - Swim to ball, shoot, then back to egg beating
Sports	- Alpine skiing - Baseball - Crew - Diving - Football - Gymnastics - Ice hockey - Snowboarding - Softball - Swimming (sprints) - Track and field (sprints, jumps, throws) - Volleyball - Wrestling	- Cross-country - Nordic skiing - Swimming (distance) - Track and field (distance)	- Basketball - Field hockey - Lacrosse - Soccer - Tennis - Water polo

Source: Data from Benardot, *Advanced Sports Nutrition*, 234–37, 263–71, 282–86.

*Factors that affect overall calorie needs include an athlete's height, weight, gender, and sport. Breakdown of carbohydrate, protein, and fat percentages is

field. This constant influx of glucose will help keep you alert. Some of you might need a snack midgame in order to stay focused; raisins or an energy bar are some options, but try them on a practice day first to make sure they don't give you an upset stomach.

2. *Teams play multiple games each week and sometimes twice in one day.* This means recovery from each game is very important. Drink plenty of sports drink immediately after, and have a carb/protein snack as soon as possible. As mentioned already, dehydration and fatigue are cumulative. If you don't recover fully after each game, you are likely to start the next game with less energy.

3. *Pitchers and catchers are involved in every play.* While all players need to make sure they eat enough before a game, pitchers and catchers are probably burning the most calories. Don't skimp on your pregame meal! Make sure you get enough complex carbs and protein, and limit the fat and fiber. Sip your sports drink right up to game time, as well as during breaks. Pitchers: If you're pulled from the game before it's over, start your recovery right away—drink at least twenty-four ounces of sports drink and have a carb/protein snack if possible.

Football

Football is a classic example of a power sport. As soon as the ball is snapped, every player on the field—on offense and defense—explodes into all-out effort. Then the teams stop, huddle, and explode into action again. Each play lasts around fifteen seconds, but players are usually breathing hard when it is over.

Here are some specific training and diet concerns for football players:[43]

1. *Some players want to be really big and agile at the same time.* Linemen, both offensive and defensive, are generally the biggest guys on the team. They work out to build muscle mass, and they need to eat more protein than most athletes. However, linemen also need to make sure they're eating enough carbohydrates and fats for overall energy. If they don't, the protein they eat will be used for energy and not muscle building. At the same time, linemen need to make sure they're not eating too much fat. Even though fat will increase overall size, it will not increase muscle mass. Too much fat will slow you down. To get enough energy, linemen may need to eat around 5,000 calories a day (compared to the average nonathlete

"I tried to eat a lot of meat and vegetables. I love fruit so I would eat that anyway. I was more strict during the summer when I tried to gain muscle and speed and wanted my diet matching my workouts."
—David, 23, football

> ## ! What Does Five Thousand Calories Look Like?
>
> If you're a football player, you need a lot of calories; if you're still growing, you need to eat even more. Nutrition expert Ann Litt suggests the following sample menu for a freshman three-sport athlete who wants to bulk up for football (total calories is over 5,300):[44]
>
> Breakfast: orange juice (twelve ounces), two cups cereal with two cups milk (skim or 1 percent), two slices toast with butter/margarine and jelly
>
> Midmorning snack: one cup of granola (in baggie), one juice box
>
> Lunch: sandwich (four slices deli meat on large roll), juice or milk, fruit, large chocolate chip cookie
>
> Before practice: banana, sports drink (sixteen ounces)
>
> During practice: water, sports drink (sixteen ounces)
>
> After practice: two string cheese, two mini bagels, juice box
>
> Dinner: three cups spaghetti with three meatballs, large slice garlic bread, salad, milk (eight ounces), large scoop of ice cream

teenage guy who eats around 2,500), with approximately 60 percent being carbs, less than 25 percent being fat, and around 15–20 percent being protein.

2. Some players want to be strong, agile, and fast. Receivers and running backs, for example, want to be able to shake off a defender and sprint for the end zone. Defensive backs want to be able to beat the receiver to the ball, or at least out-jump him once the ball arrives. If you play one of these positions, you need a lot of glycogen stored up in your muscles to support your juking, sprinting, and jumping. You also want to maintain lean muscle mass. This means a diet high in carbs and low in fats. Also, you might do better eating six smaller meals rather than three large ones.

3. Football players lose a lot of fluids. The combination of intense bursts, pads and helmets, and hot weather (at least at the beginning of the season) means football players sweat a lot. Because they lose so many electrolytes through sweat, football players in particular are susceptible to leg cramps. They are also prone to heat exhaustion and dehydration. Make sure you drink plenty of fluids before the game, and sip a sports drink during time-outs, when you're on the sidelines, and between quarters. Use halftime to drink more than just a sip or two.

4. The stop-and-start action requires a lot of muscle glycogen. No matter what position you play, you are required to go all out and then stop, over and over and

Foods That Prevent Leg Cramps

Cramps are those sudden, painful muscle contractions—usually in your calf, thigh, or foot—that may wake you up in the middle of the night or seize your leg in the middle of a game. Some people call them charley horses. Watch almost any football game played in hot conditions, and you're likely to see at least one player being treated for cramps. Leg cramps are caused by muscle fatigue, dehydration, and salt loss from excessive sweating.[45]

Your first line of defense is to drink plenty of fluids before and during exercise, particularly sports drinks with electrolytes to replace salt and water loss. Foods that are high in potassium, calcium, and magnesium can also help prevent leg cramps:[46]

- Banana
- Grapefruit
- Apricot
- Poultry (chicken or turkey)
- Dairy (milk, yogurt, cheese)

over. These intense bursts require a lot of energy from muscle glycogen, which means you need a high-carb diet in addition to the protein for muscle building. Three to four hours before kickoff, have a high-carb meal that's relatively low in protein and fat; on game day, you really need the carbs, not the protein. After your last meal, sip a carbohydrate sports drink right up to game time. And then keep sipping it throughout the game.

What Does Maurice Jones-Drew Eat?

The usual pregame meal for Maurice Jones-Drew, running back for the Jacksonville Jaguars, consists of chicken and rice soup, turkey sausage, and hash browns. He says, "Right before games I don't eat much. . . . I want to be at my lightest point before games. If I'm at my lightest point, I'll be able to perform pretty well."[47]

Gymnastics

The suggestions provided here also apply to diving.[48]

1. Part of a gymnast's success is in the hands of a judge. In lacrosse, the number of goals determines the score; in softball, it's the number of runners that cross the plate. In track, the winner is the first one across the finish line. The victor in each of these sports is determined by clear, objective criteria—a time or a number of points. In gymnastics, however, scoring is more subjective; the winner is determined by a panel of judges that decides how many points a certain routine deserves. The score is at least partly based on aesthetics or appearance. As a result, gymnasts sometimes skip meals or eat very little, and they worry about body image more than, say, soccer or basketball players. This can lead to not consuming enough calories, carbohydrates in particular, which can in turn lead to fatigue, injuries, and more serious conditions such as eating disorders (more on eating disorders later in this chapter). Fatigue can also lead to mental fogginess, which can severely affect performance since most routines require focused concentration and precise movements. Gymnasts need to make sure they eat enough calories to support their energy needs—around 2,000 per day for teenage girls and 2,500 for teenage guys.

2. Gymnasts need lean muscle mass. In order to perform twists and flips while standing on a four-inch-wide balance beam or while hanging from two rings, gymnasts need incredible strength. In conjunction with weight training to build this lean muscle, gymnasts need a diet with sufficient protein—on the higher end of the day's recommended servings. However, if you eat more protein without eating enough calories overall, that protein is going to be used for energy instead of muscle building. If you don't eat enough overall, you're actually going to lose muscle and your performance will suffer as a result.

3. Gymnastics meets are often all-day events. This means a lot of sitting around in between your events, but not enough time to actually have a full meal if you get hungry. You need to keep your glycogen levels up so that your muscles are ready to explode with power when it's time. If possible, eat a high-carb breakfast before your meet; something like a whole-wheat bagel and fruit rather than eggs. Then, bring plenty of complex-carb snacks and sports drinks with you. Sip the sports drink throughout the day, and have a snack in between events.

Ice Hockey

1. You can still get dehydrated in an ice rink. Despite the cold temperature in the rink, hockey players lose a lot of fluids through sweat. That's because they're constantly moving and because they're wearing some heavy-duty padding. As a result, players need to drink up whenever they get the chance—between periods, after subbing out of the game, and so on. A sports drink is better during a game since it will also put carbs back in your system for some quick energy.

2. Hockey players burn a lot of calories. Male hockey players in particular often find it hard to keep their weight up during the season. While training and competition is in full swing, guys should aim for eating around four to five thousand calories a day, and girls three to four thousand. Around 60 percent of those daily calories should be complex carbohydrates since hockey demands a lot of muscle glycogen to explode down the ice. Around 20 to 25 percent should be protein, since the hard-hitting nature of hockey favors those with a solid, muscular build. Remember that more protein is only going to build more muscle to a certain point. Also, you need to eat enough calories overall or the protein will be used for energy, not muscle building. Some of you might find it necessary to eat six meals instead of three in order to eat enough calories.[49]

3. Fatigue in the third period often leads to mistakes and injuries. Fatigue affects reaction time, speed, and the ability to think clearly. A tired, dehydrated team is going to allow more goals in the final minutes than a team that has been replenishing its glycogen supply. A tired team is also more likely to get hurt. A study by the U.S. Hockey League found that game-related injuries were more common in the third period, when players were tired. The best way to fight fatigue is to eat and drink plenty of carbohydrates, starting with a high-carb pregame meal and continuing with a sports drink to replenish glycogen and electrolytes. A study

Have You Ever Heard of Bandy?

- Bandy is also called banty, Russian hockey, and winter football.
- The game is over two hundred years old and is mainly played in Sweden and Russia.
- Bandy is played on an ice rink the size of a soccer field. As in soccer, bandy teams consist of eleven players and a game consists of two 45-minute halves. The object is to hit an orange ball (about the size of a tennis ball) into a seven-by-eleven-foot goal using a four-foot-long curved stick.
- There is only one full-size outdoor bandy rink in the United States; it's in Roseville, Minnesota.
- As of 2010, approximately three hundred men, fifty women, and two hundred youth played bandy in the United States—and they all lived in Minnesota.[50]

done at the University of South Carolina showed that "athletes who consumed a sports drink during a high-intensity hockey game were able to continue playing 45 percent longer than athletes who drank only water."[51]

Swimming

For the most part, swimming is a power sport. Most races last less than two minutes and consist of all-out effort followed by rest until the next heat or event. Here are some suggestions for swimmers:[52]

1. Swimmers often have practice before school. For some, these practices may start as early as 5:30 or 6 in the morning. Not many people feel like eating at that hour, but to have energy for a productive practice, your body needs a little carbohydrate boost. A glass of orange juice, a banana, a fruit shake, some toast, or even just a sports drink will give your muscles some immediate energy. After practice, have your real breakfast—something with carbohydrates and protein to refuel and repair your muscles, as well as prepare your body for the afternoon workout.

2. Swimmers can still become dehydrated in the water. You might not feel like you're sweating, but you are, which means you're losing fluids and you need to replace them. On practice days, start putting a water bottle at the end of your lane. When you get a break, take a few sips—not gulps, since that will probably result in cramps and an uncomfortable workout. You can fill your bottle with water or sports drink. A sports drink will give you a little carbo boost, but some people find it causes burping or cramps during a swimming workout. The important part is to stay hydrated. During swim meets, drink some sports drink between races.

3. Swimmers usually have several races during a meet. If you don't refuel properly after each race, chances are you'll be fatigued by the time you get to your last event. How much you eat and drink between races depends on how much time you have. Definitely have sports drink with carbs after each race. If you have a longer break—say, a couple hours—have an easily digestible carbohydrate snack such as a banana or a whole-wheat bagel. You should experiment on practice days

What Does Michael Phelps Eat?

On the day of a big race, U.S. Olympian Michael Phelps has a high-carb breakfast: fruit, bagel with cream cheese, and oatmeal. He says, "I never eat protein before I race just because it's not immediate energy. I just try to get as many carbs into my system as I can because it's easier for me to use that as energy."[53]

to see what gives you the most energy and how much time you need to digest what you eat.

4. *Some swimmers are concerned about looking good in a bathing suit.* Others might want to reduce drag in the water by losing a little weight. However, swimmers burn a lot of calories. If you limit your calorie intake in an effort to slim down, you might lose some muscle mass in the process and negatively affect your performance in the pool. Before you start a weight-loss program, talk to your doctor or trainer so you can do it without compromising your speed and power.

Track and Field (sprints, jumps, throws)

By definition sprints involve going as fast as possible over a short distance. The suggestions here apply to events lasting around ninety seconds or less (for longer track races, see the suggestions in the Cross-Country section):[54]

1. *Like swimmers, track and field athletes often compete in several events and/or heats in one meet.* This means recovery after each race, jump, or throw is crucial, or your performance in the last event or two will be negatively affected by fatigue. After each event or heat, sip a carbohydrate drink right up until your next race. If your break is two hours or more, you might need to eat some carbs for an energy boost. Most sprinters like racing on an empty stomach, so pick foods that your body will digest quickly, such as a banana, whole-wheat bagel, or energy bar.

2. *Like football players and other power athletes, sprinters benefit from extra protein more than endurance athletes.* The creatine in protein is converted into phosphocreatine and stored in the muscles; along with glycogen, this phosphocreatine fuels short bursts of all-out effort lasting around ninety seconds or less—for example, sprints such as the 100 or 200 meters. (When exercise lasts longer than ninety seconds, the body switches to a different energy system that uses mainly glycogen from carbs.) Beef, chicken, turkey, pork, and fish all contain creatine, which the

? What Does Allyson Felix Eat?

U.S. Olympic sprinter Allyson Felix has a regular schedule as far as eating goes. She says, "I'm not big on supplements so I like to get my nutrients through food." In the morning before practice, she usually has oatmeal; immediately after practice she has a recovery drink followed by a small lunch—a sandwich or salad. Then Felix has a weight room workout, after which she eats a full meal of grilled chicken or fish. "It's really important to get a lot of protein in. I run a lot and so to keep weight on is sometimes difficult."[55]

Creatine and Power Athletes

In theory, more phosphocreatine stored in your muscles means more energy available for short, repetitive bursts of all-out effort. This means your muscles need less time to recover between sprints, and you can also perform more sprints at high intensity—something you definitely want at track meets that consist of several heats and a final. In an effort to put more phosphocreatine into their muscles, some sprinters turn to protein supplements such as creatine, and studies seem to indicate that creatine does extend the time before fatigue sets in.

However, those studies don't evaluate overall calorie intake of the athlete *before* he or she started taking creatine. It could be that the athlete wasn't eating enough calories overall; the protein consumed was being used for basic energy needs instead of being converted to phosphocreatine, and the athlete's power was suffering as a result. It could be that just taking in more carbs would have had the same result as taking the creatine supplement. Before you try creatine, make sure you're getting enough calories in your diet. Though creatine might help you, increasing your carb intake is a much easier and cheaper solution.[56]

body converts into phosphocreatine and uses to fuel sprints. The recommended protein servings for all athletes is two to four, so aim for three or four per day. Just don't forget to eat enough calories overall (mainly from carbs) so protein is used for its intended purpose.

Volleyball[57]

1. Volleyball players burn a lot of calories, both through weight training and during matches. In addition to overall fitness, volleyball players rely on strong legs, arms, and shoulders. Weight training to build muscle mass in these areas needs to be supported by a diet that is high in complex carbs and slightly higher in protein. Girls in particular may be guilty of skimping on calories because they are self-conscious about wearing the form-fitting shorts. However, not eating enough will lower your energy level and prevent protein from doing its muscle-building job.

History of Volleyball

Like basketball, volleyball was invented by a Massachusetts YMCA teacher who was looking for an indoor game for the men to play. In 1895, William G. Morgan decided to blend aspects of basketball and tennis into a game that involved less physical contact than basketball. He raised the tennis net so that it was just above the head of an average man, and the players hit the ball back and forth over the net. Morgan originally called the game mintonette, but after watching the players volley the ball back and forth, someone suggested changing the name to volleyball and it stuck.[58]

A female volleyball player should eat at least 2,500 calories a day, most of them complex carbs. Guys will probably need around 3,500 to keep weight on during the season.

2. Matches do not last a set amount of time. Some high schools play best two out of three games; some play best three out of five. Either way, there's no way to know how long you'll be playing when you step out onto the court. It could be thirty minutes of intense, stop-and-start activity, or it could be two hours. You need to start your game day with a high-carb meal, and then bring enough fluids to last a long match—sports drinks in particular since (1) you lose a lot of salt through sweating and you need to replace electrolytes as well as fluids, and (2) you need the carbs to ward off fatigue. If you become tired and unfocused in a volleyball match, it's easy to roll an ankle or miss a dig.

Wrestling

1. Many wrestlers try to "make weight" before each match. In order to cut this weight, some wrestlers use potentially life-threatening methods such as refusing fluids, vomiting after eating, exercising in rubber suits, and simply not eating.

If you wrestle, you know the pressure to make weight. If you don't make it, you can't wrestle, you lose points, and the whole team suffers as a result. However, be aware that although these drastic measures work, they also put your body under great stress that can cause long-term digestive issues and even death. Athletes who go through weight loss and gain cycles are at greater risk of becoming obese when they're older. In addition, denying your body food can have an interesting

Did You Know?

During the 1997–1998 wrestling season, three college wrestlers died of heatstroke that resulted from their attempts to make weight (see page 102 for more details on their deaths). As a result, in 1999 the NCAA (National Collegiate Athletic Association) implemented weight loss guidelines for wrestlers. Seven years later the National Federation of State High School Associations (NFHS) made changes to its own rules regarding weight loss management. Now high school wrestlers must weigh in before their first match of the season; their body weight and body fat percentage are both recorded. Based on these figures, a "safe minimum weight" is determined for each athlete, and for the rest of the season, the wrestler must stay at or above this safe minimum weight. The new rule also puts a limit on the amount of weight that can be lost at one time.[59]

Losing Weight Safely

Derek, age eighteen, only had to cut weight a few times during his wrestling career—usually just after Christmas break—and when he did, he made sure he took precautions to do so safely. He followed two basic methods:

1. Derek started eating six smaller meals a day instead of three big ones. This caused his metabolism to increase since he was eating and burning calories all day. Eating more often is by far the safest method since your body does the work itself.
2. Derek worked out on the elliptical machine wearing many layers of clothing. He made sure a trainer was in the office before he started his workout, just in case he needed help.[60]

There might be times when you need to shed a few pounds to make weight. Just make sure you stay within guidelines set by the NFHS rule: don't lose more than 1.5 percent of body weight per seven days. And never intentionally refuse fluids.

effect: you start thinking about food all the time. Such obsession can lead to eating disorders such as anorexia or bulimia. Wrestlers are among the athletes most susceptible to developing eating disorders (the last section of this chapter deals with athletes and eating disorders).[61]

2. Wrestling is a power sport, and protein provides power. If you're restricting food intake, you're probably not getting enough protein or enough calories overall, limiting the amount of creatine that's being converted to phosphocreatine and stored in your muscles. Less phosphocreatine means less power when you need it. If you're limiting calories, you're probably not getting carbohydrates either, which means you might find yourself tired and unfocused—both on the mat and in the classroom. It's hard to compete at your best without enough (or any) fuel in your tank.

Endurance Sports

These sports involve less-than-maximum activity over a longer period of time.

Cross-Country

Cross-country runners, as well as those who run marathons and triathlons, depend on fat for energy more than athletes in other sports. Glycogen is still the main source of energy, but athletes perform better if their bodies use fat for most of the race and tap into glycogen when extra energy is needed to pass another runner, run up a hill, or kick at the end of a race.[62] Here are some specific issues that distance runners (including track athletes who run the 1,500 or 3,000 meters) face:[63]

1. Distance runners put in a lot of miles each week. As a result, they can develop stress fractures in their feet or lower legs from all the pounding. To prevent stress fractures, runners should eat plenty of calcium, which is primarily found in dairy

Foods That Heal Blisters

If you run or play a sport that involves running, you've probably had a blister on some part of your foot. Blisters form when a loose-fitting sock or shoe rubs repeatedly against your toe or heel. A fluid-filled sack appears at the point of friction. Blisters are the body's attempt to protect the inner layers of skin. Eating *eggs* and *oats* can help heal your blisters more quickly.[64]

> ### Foods That Prevent Osteoporosis
>
> Osteoporosis is more common in women, particularly women who are not having their periods. The best prevention is to eat lots of calcium, phosphorous, and magnesium. Also, a little sunshine every day will give you vitamin D, which helps the body turn calcium into bone.
>
> Here are some calcium-rich foods to prevent osteoporosis: [65]
>
> - Milk
> - Yogurt
> - Cheese
> - Tofu

products such as milk, cheese, and yogurt. However, these foods should not be eaten close to race time as it takes your body a while to digest them.

2. Distance runners usually have low body fat. While this is true for guys and girls, low body fat can have more negative effects in girls. For example, girls can develop amenorrhea—a condition in which they stop having a monthly period. This may seem like a good thing, but it can lead to more serious problems such as osteoporosis (brittle bones) and greater risk of stress fractures. Male and female distance runners need to make sure they take in enough calories overall to support the energy they expend on long runs. Girls especially need to make sure they're getting enough calcium as well.

3. Distance runners need fluids and carbs. To perform at their best, distance runners need to stay hydrated, which can be difficult during a run. Be sure to drink plenty of fluids an hour or two before—at least twenty-four ounces. Then sip a carbohydrate-containing sports drink in the half hour or so before your race. If you're running a 10K (6.2 miles) or longer, you should make use of the drink stations along the route or carry your own bottle or hydration backpack filled with sports drink. Remember to sip, not gulp, during a race. Replenish your fluids as soon as possible after you finish.

Cycling

The following tips apply to distance swimmers and triathletes as well:[66]

1. Cycling races usually involve long distances. The cycling leg in triathlons can be anywhere from 12.4 miles to 112 miles; the longer the ride, the more important continual hydration becomes. You might not feel like you're sweating as much as when you run, but you're still losing fluids. It's important to drink water in the hours before your race and to start with a full bottle of water or sports drink on your bike. It's better to sip your drink more frequently than to wait until you're really thirsty and then gulp it all down. If you're drinking sports drink, you get a continual source of carbs/energy as well as continual hydration; you're also less likely to get cramps or a sloshy feeling in your stomach. If you happen to be riding in cold weather, don't forget to drink—you still need to replace lost fluids.

2. *Cyclists sometimes have decreases in bone density.* Cycling is a low-impact sport, which is good for your feet and legs, but if that's your only form of exercise, you're susceptible to decreased bone density. Decreased bone density can lead to osteoporosis later in life. One way to fight these issues is by including some weight-bearing exercise (exercise you perform on your feet) in your training program—running and jumping rope, for example. Also, make sure you eat enough calcium and vitamin D. You can get calcium from fortified orange juice, milk, cheese, and other dairy products. If you do a lot of cycling in the sun, you probably get enough vitamin D.

3. *Cyclists need lots of carbohydrates for energy.* To have energy for the whole race, you need to consume carbohydrates as you ride. Sports drinks, bars, and gels with carbohydrates are all good sources, but you have to find out which brands, flavors, and forms work for you. Don't wait until a big race to try out a new kind of carb gel. The last thing you want is an upset stomach halfway through a fifty-mile race.

Nordic Skiing

1. *Like distance runners and swimmers, Nordic skiers have high energy needs.* This is partly because of the distances covered and partly because races often occur at higher altitudes and your lungs are working overtime to get enough oxygen to the muscles. High energy needs means meals that are at least 60 percent carbohydrates, especially right before a race. Always have a sports drink ready so you can replenish glycogen as soon as possible after a workout or race. If you're doing an especially long workout, you might consider taking some carbohydrate gel packs with you.

2. *Despite the snow and cold weather, Nordic skiers lose a lot of fluids.* Like hockey players, skiers shouldn't be fooled by their icy surroundings. Nordic skiing is hard work, and your body sweats and loses electrolytes as you work. Electrolytes need to be replaced so you can stay focused and cramp-free. It's best to carry a bottle of water or sports drink with you at all times so that you never allow your body to become dehydrated and so that you know you're starting each race on a full tank.

Alpine vs. Nordic Skiing

If you're on an alpine or Nordic ski team, then you know the difference between these skiing styles, but what about the rest of you? Alpine skiing is also known as downhill skiing because, well, the skier is traveling downhill. The skier's entire boot is attached to the ski, and the skier's forward movement largely depends on the downward steepness of the slope. Events in the alpine/downhill category include downhill, slalom, and giant slalom. Alpine skiing is mostly a power sport since the events involve bursts of energy for two minutes or less.

Nordic skiing is more commonly known as cross-country skiing and involves traveling on various inclines—not just downhill. The skier's boot is only attached to the ski at the toe, leaving the heel free so the skier can climb a hill or traverse flat terrain in more of a walk/run motion. Other Nordic sports include ski jumping and biathlon (combined cross-country skiing and riflery). Nordic skiing is an endurance event.[67]

Power and Endurance Sports

These sports involve both all-out bursts and continual activity over a long period of time.

Basketball

1. Basketball games are often won by the team that's the least fatigued in the final quarter. Fatigue affects your ability to jump, run, shoot, slam, pass—basically every aspect of the game. To be sharp at the end of the game, you have to fill up on carbs long before the game even begins. Try to eat a full meal three to four hours before tip-off, and then have a quick-energy carb snack (fruit, sports drink, energy bar) about an hour before. During the game, sip a sports drink with carbs every chance you get—time-outs, period breaks, anytime you're sitting on the bench—so you continually fill your tank with energy. Aim for drinking seven to ten ounces (mouthfuls) every fifteen minutes. Also, use halftime to fill up on carbs; sip a car-

❓ What Does Chris Paul Eat?

Los Angeles Clippers point guard Chris Paul had to learn what to eat in order to keep his body in top condition for the long haul. He says, "As soon as we got on the road my first few years in the NBA, I was calling room service and I wanted chicken fingers and French fries to my room as fast as physically possible. . . . And now it's salmon, it's greens, it's different things like that." Paul's trainer also has him take a recovery drink within twenty minutes of finishing practice in order to replenish the fluids and calories lost. These drinks all have a 4:1 ratio of carbs to protein.[68]

bohydrate sports drink and perhaps eat some plain crackers—nothing with a lot of fat or fiber. With this constant influx of carbs, you are less likely to burn out before the end of the game.[69]

2. Teams often play several games a week. In order to be ready for the next game or practice, you need to begin recovery as soon as the first game is over. Drink at least twenty-four ounces of fluid immediately after, and then have a carb/protein snack as soon as possible. You might need to bring something with you if you're playing an away game. Remember: Your cells convert more carbs to glycogen in the first forty-five minutes after exercise, so the sooner you eat, the better.

Soccer

The following hints also apply to lacrosse, field hockey, and, in some ways, water polo players:

1. Fatigue at the end of the game can lead to mistakes and injuries. Fatigue affects every aspect of your performance, including your speed, endurance, reaction time, and skills such as dribbling. Don Kirkendall and his colleagues conducted a three-year study of youth soccer injuries. They found that almost 25 percent of all game-related injuries happen in the last ten to fifteen minutes of games, when players are the most fatigued. The last part of the game is also when about 30 percent of goals are scored—again, the period in which tired defenders get burned by strikers and when tired keepers don't react as quickly.[70] The key to fatigue prevention is carbohydrate consumption, both before and during the game. Soccer is a nonstop sport, which makes it difficult to drink sports beverages during a game, so it is very important to fill up before the game and at halftime.

2. Soccer is definitely about both endurance and power. Like an endurance athlete, you need energy to keep running up and down the field for ninety minutes; like a power athlete, you need energy to sprint, jump, and kick with explosive power. To give your muscles a full supply of glycogen to perform both kinds of activity, eat a high-carb meal three to four hours before game time; avoid fats and high-fiber foods on game day since they may give you cramps. An hour or so before a game, start sipping a sports drink to keep your muscles primed and ready. At halftime, sip (don't gulp) at least eight ounces of sports drink.

3. If you're playing in a tournament, make sure you recover fully after each game. In tournaments, you have multiple games over a one- or two-day period. That means you have to replenish fluids and glycogen after each game so that you're ready for the next. How much you drink and eat afterward depends partially on how soon you play again, but you should at least drink ten to sixteen ounces of sports drink as soon as the game is over. Then try to eat a carbohydrate and protein snack like a sports bar or crackers and peanut butter—no candy or soda.

Tennis

1. When tennis players step on the court, they don't know how long they will be playing. It could be anywhere from ninety minutes to five hours. That's a huge difference!

Foods That Heal Athlete's Foot

Athlete's foot is a fungal infection that is highly contagious. It usually forms between the toes and causes the skin to become dry, itchy, and sometimes cracked. You can catch athlete's foot from locker room floors or from the floors in public showers, so it is best to not go barefoot whenever you're in these areas; keep a pair of flip-flops in your workout bag.

To help heal your athlete's foot, avoid foods that are high in yeast, such as bread, at least until the infection is under control. Also, add the following foods to your diet:

- Yogurt
- Eggplant
- Garlic
- Cinnamon[71]

You need to be ready for the worst, and that preparation starts long before the day of competition. As a tennis player, you need a daily high-carb diet to make sure muscles are fully loaded with glycogen on game day. You also need to drink water all day, every day to make sure they are fully hydrated when the match starts. On the day of competition, switch to sports drink for added carbo boost in addition to fluids.[72]

> "When I'm doing any of my sports I have to make sure that I double the amount of calories that I usually eat because I'm burning so much."
> —Caitlin, 16, tennis

2. Tennis players burn a lot of calories. If you play tennis, you already know that you have to be in excellent shape to succeed on the tennis court. You need cardio training for endurance, weight training for strength, and practice on the court for skills. All this means you need a lot of energy from food—at least three thousand calories a day. Without sufficient calorie intake, you will become fatigued more quickly and your performance will suffer. Also, to try to make up for the deficit, your body will start using protein for energy, meaning protein will not be used to build and repair muscle.

3. Tennis matches often take place in hot weather. This is yet another reason to drink water all day, every day. The combination of fluid loss and high temperature can lead to heat-related illness such as cramps and heat exhaustion. The best defense is to start your match fully hydrated and then sip some sports drink during every changeover. Be aware of the symptoms of dehydration and heatstroke (see

What Does Three Thousand Calories Look Like?

According to nutrition expert Ann Litt, a five-foot-three, fourteen-year-old elite female tennis player needs at least three thousand calories a day to have enough energy and to build muscle. Here's an example of what that looks like in terms of meals:[73]

Breakfast: egg white omelet, two packs of instant oatmeal, bagel, chocolate milk
Lunch: cheese pasta, salad, apple, milk
Before practice: orange, lemonade, bagel
After practice: energy bar, sports drink
Dinner: chicken, rice, vegetables, baked potato, salad, water

the sidebars on pages 99 and 103, respectively). Speak up if you think one of your teammates is showing signs of either, and also know when it's time for you to get out of the sun for a bit.

When Food Becomes the Enemy: Athletes and Eating Disorders

By now it should be clear that eating is an important part of your athletic success. Consuming the right amount of food at the right time can make a big difference in your energy level, mental alertness, and skills execution. For some teen athletes, however, this positive relationship with food becomes distorted by the pressures of competition, troubles at home, emotional problems, and other psychological issues. These athletes can develop a serious condition called an eating disorder.

What Are Eating Disorders?

The Mayo Clinic defines eating disorders as "a group of serious conditions in which you're so preoccupied with food and weight that you can often focus on little else."[74] The National Eating Disorder Association (NEDA) states that eating disorders "include extreme emotions, attitudes, and behaviors surrounding weight and food issues."[75] And according to the National Institute of Mental Health (NIMH), eating disorders are illnesses that cause "serious disturbances to your everyday diet, such as eating extremely small amounts of food or severely overeating."[76]

It's a Fact

According to the "National Comorbidity Survey—Adolescent Supplement," girls are two and a half times as likely as boys to develop an eating disorder (survey results are for adolescents aged thirteen to seventeen).[77] Why do you think that is? Here are a few possible reasons:[78]

- The media presents the "ideal" body type for women as being thin and trim. For guys the emphasis is more on having muscles and being fit.
- Guys already have more lean body weight than girls.
- There's less pressure on guys to be a certain size and shape. The "desirable" guys in the magazines and movies are both thin/trim and big/buff.

In short, eating disorders are potentially life-threatening conditions that involve a person's distorted relationship with food. For some people that relationship involves self-starvation; for others it involves eating huge amounts of food at one time and then eliminating it from the body through self-induced vomiting, laxatives, or excessive exercise. Like most medical illnesses, these disorders will not go away without treatment. Unfortunately, most people—teens and adults alike—suffering from eating disorders have a hard time admitting they're sick and need help.

What Causes Eating Disorders?

Eating disorders do not have one cause; they result from a complex combination of psychological, emotional, and interpersonal (relationships with others) factors. Health professionals also have different opinions on what causes the development of eating disorders. According to NEDA, people who develop eating disorders may suffer from the following psychological and interpersonal issues:[79]

- Low self-esteem
- Feelings of inadequacy or lack of control
- Depression
- Anxiety
- Anger
- Loneliness
- Difficulty expressing emotions
- History of being teased about size or weight
- History of physical or sexual abuse

In the sports context, eating disorders can arise out of psychological and emotional pressures related to performance. Imagine a situation in which a high school starter becomes a benchwarmer at the college level; it happens all the time. That athlete might become angry and depressed, especially if the athlete's identity and sense of self-worth in high school was closely tied to his or her athletic performance. In some way not completely understood, these feelings of low self-esteem

"[One girl] compared herself too much to the other girls on our team, and eventually it became too much for her. In her mind, it was better to be super skinny and therefore 'have less weight to carry.' She was a fast runner because she was average in weight and had muscle. She wasn't a stick, but in track, being a stick skinny girl doesn't always mean the best runner."—Anonymous

and lack of control can cause an athlete to unconsciously look for something he or she can control, and the result can be a distorted relationship with food.

The media can also contribute to the development of eating disorders. This is especially true for girls. From the dolls girls play with to the mannequins in stores to the models in magazines, girls are taught that the perfect body type is thin and trim. Girls who don't fit this type may suffer from low self-esteem and develop eating disorders in their efforts to fit in. In general, guys are less likely than girls to develop an eating disorder over body image, partly because the media doesn't glorify male thinness to the same degree. Guys can and do develop eating disorders, but it's usually not because they want to be thin.[80]

What Is the Connection between Athletes and Eating Disorders?

People who develop eating disorders often have certain personality traits. They tend to be hardworking perfectionists who demand a lot from themselves and have

Barbie in Real Life

If we were to take a Barbie doll and make her life size, her body proportions would be way out of whack; in fact, they're anatomically impossible without surgical intervention. To prove this point, model Katie Halchishick posed for a photograph that was then outlined to show the extensive plastic surgery required to give her a Barbie figure. Here's a summary of what Halchishick would need to have done: "a brow lift, a jaw line shave, rhinoplasty, a cheek and neck reduction, a chin implant, scooped-out shoulders, a breast lift, liposuction on her arms, and tummy tuck." And that's just the top half of her! (To see the photograph of Halchishick, go to the website provided in note 81.)

Halchishick doesn't want or need any of these procedures. She's actually started a website called Healthy Is the New Skinny to encourage girls to rethink the skinny Barbie image of beauty. She also runs a modeling agency that features women with more natural figures.

The fact is that unlike Barbie (or Ken, for that matter), real people come in all shapes and sizes and curves.[81]

> ## It's a Fact
>
> By some estimates, one million guys (athletes and nonathletes) will develop an eating disorder at some point. One source says that around one in ten men suffers from anorexia, a specific type of eating disorder that involves self-starvation. However, these numbers are probably higher because men and boys are less likely to go the doctor and get diagnosed.[82]

a strong desire to please others. Successful athletes often have these same characteristics. They are disciplined, focused, and driven to succeed—positive traits that can become distorted and cause an athlete to develop an unhealthy relationship with food.[83]

If a coach tells a highly competitive diver that she can improve her scores by losing a few pounds, she will most likely take the coach's advice. Then some combination of psychological and emotional issues might cause such a diver to become obsessed with losing weight, especially if her scores do improve. Perhaps the diver already suffers from loneliness or low self-esteem, or perhaps she has an abusive boyfriend or out-of-control home life. Losing weight might become something she can control. The drive to keep weight off could turn into a full-blown eating disorder with serious health implications.

For a wrestler, an eating disorder could start as repeated food restriction in order to make weight. For a cross-country runner, it could start as increased weekly mileage in order to build endurance. Both of these goals are part of the sport. But somewhere along the way, the dieting or the extra cardio becomes a psychological issue that the athlete can't control. The wrestler might become obsessed with counting calories and avoiding food, even during his off-season. The runner might punish herself with extra miles when she eats "too much" for dinner. At this point, athletes need help. Unfortunately, many eating disorders among athletes go unnoticed. Teammates, coaches, and parents see a highly motivated, physically fit individual, not someone with an eating disorder. The athlete probably tries to hide his or her eating habits, so no one else knows what is really going on.[84]

Which Sports?

Eating disorders are more common among athletes in sports where weight and appearance play a bigger role. Wrestling, for example, is a sport that requires athletes to make weight, and some competitors go through extreme measures to get there, including skipping meals, using laxatives, and wearing rubber sweat suits.

In sports such as crew, cross-country, and pole vault, light weight is considered an advantage, so athletes pay close attention to how much they eat, and some struggle with distorted body image. In contrast, athletes in sports such as football, basketball, soccer, and ice hockey do not struggle as much with eating disorders. In these sports, light weight and a trim figure have no advantage; in fact, lighter weight could be a disadvantage in some cases.

Eating disorders are also more common in sports such as diving, gymnastics, and skating, where athletes' success is partially based on their ability to please the judges. These athletes are more conscious of their appearance, knowing that their

Athlete Bio: Christy Henrich, Gymnastics

Christy Henrich was a world-class gymnast. She missed making the 1988 Olympic team by .118 points. In 1989, at age seventeen, she won fourth place in the uneven parallel bars at the world championships, and she won second place in the all-around competition at the U.S. national championships. Next stop: the 1992 Olympics.

But Christy never made it to those Olympics; she was forced to retire from gymnastics in 1991 because she was suffering from an eating disorder.

In March 1988, at a team critique session in Budapest, Hungary, a judge told Christy she needed to watch her weight if she wanted to go far in gymnastics. Being the hardworking athlete that she was, Christy took the judge's words to heart. She went home and started changing her diet. She lost around seven pounds in the next few months, and her performance started improving.

But Christy didn't stop losing weight. It became an obsession. She couldn't shake the feeling that she was fat, even though that's not what the judge had said or meant. Over the next several years, Christy developed a life-threatening case of anorexia and bulimia. She would skip meals or make herself throw up if she did eat. She went from one hundred pounds to weighing less than fifty.

Christy was in and out of treatment for her eating disorders. At one point she started improving and gained about fifteen pounds. But then she relapsed and never recovered. Without food, she just kept getting weaker, and her organs started shutting down.

Christy died of multiple organ failure in July 1994, about a week after she turned twenty-two.[85]

score is at least partly based on how they look. In contrast, eating disorders are not as common in sports such as baseball or lacrosse, where the winner is determined by runs or goals, or in track or swimming, where the outcome is based on time.

Types of Eating Disorders

There are three types of eating disorders: anorexia nervosa, bulimia nervosa, and binge eating disorder; the two most common among athletes are anorexia and bulimia and will be discussed here. See the Find Out More section at the end of this chapter for more information on binge eating disorder.

Anorexia Nervosa

Anorexia nervosa literally means "loss of appetite for nervous reasons."[86] In reality, anorexia is more like self-starvation. The person feels hungry but chooses to eat very little or nothing at all, and as a result, she loses an excessive amount of weight. Though it may be obvious to others, the anorexic person does not view herself as being too thin; in fact, she may see herself as fat and thus keep avoiding food in an effort to lose weight. Anorexia isn't just dieting that has become a little extreme; it's a combination of emotional and psychological issues manifested in a person's control of what she eats.

How do you know if someone has anorexia? Here are some *warning signs* to be aware of:[87]

- Dramatic weight loss
- Eating only "safe" foods, for example, foods low in fat or sugar
- Making frequent comments about feeling fat or overweight despite weight loss
- Developing odd food rituals (e.g., eating foods in certain orders, excessive chewing, rearranging food on a plate)

> "She just stopped eating. . . . We would go out for dinner and she would pick the two tomatoes off the top of the salad that she ordered and eat that and say that she just wasn't hungry because she didn't work out hard in practice or blah, blah, blah. There was always an excuse for her to not have to eat."—Anonymous

Anorexia typically starts in adolescence and is more common in girls than guys. About 90–95 percent of all anorexics are female, with teenage female athletes such as divers having the highest risk. *Photo courtesy of Black 100/ Thinkstock.*

- Having consistent excuses to avoid mealtimes or situations involving food
- Following a strict and excessive exercise program
- Wearing extra layers of clothes to hide weight loss
- Withdrawing from family, friends, and activities

If someone you know is displaying some of these signs, talk to an adult who can help. Anorexia is not something that will go away on its own, and the lack of vitamins, minerals, and other nutrients from food will start harming the body. As

"When someone has anorexia to that extent [this athlete lost thirty-five pounds in around six months], it becomes pretty obvious to almost everyone around. It's obvious in the weight room especially. She was doing like twenty-nine chin-ups our sophomore year and then could barely do like five or six within six months. It was a huge drop in things she was able to do physically."—Anonymous

mentioned earlier, everyone needs food for the body to perform basic functions, and athletes need even more food for energy to train and compete. Athletes with anorexia won't have enough glycogen in their muscles for fuel or enough protein to build up and repair muscle. Their bodies will actually start breaking down the very muscle they're trying to build. At some point, anorexic athletes will have to stop competing due to weakness and fatigue.

"She skipped meals every day and would not eat on game day, and her plan backfired. She did lose weight but she got sick, had to stop running, quit the team, and lost a lot of friends. . . . Because she starved herself during high school, she caused damage to her digestive organs and has to monitor her weight very carefully."—Anonymous

Anorexia has serious *physical consequences*, especially for young adults whose bodies are still growing. Without enough food, the body has minimal energy resources to use for normal body functioning. To conserve what energy it does have, the body slows all processes way down. According to the NEDA, this slowdown can have severe medical consequences:[88]

- Increased risk of heart failure as heart rate slows and blood pressure drops
- Decreased bone density (a condition called osteoporosis), which can lead to fractures
- Loss of muscle strength
- Severe dehydration, which can lead to kidney failure

"I did have one friend that wasn't eating and . . . had to be pulled out by her doctor. She was later cleared to come back. She struggled with anorexia."
—Anonymous

If the self-starvation goes on long enough, the body can start shutting down completely, ultimately resulting in death. Sadly, the death rate for women age fifteen to twenty-four is twelve times higher for anorexia than any for other cause.[89]

Bulimia Nervosa

Bulimia nervosa is characterized by cycles of bingeing (eating large amounts of food at one sitting) and purging (eliminating the food eaten by making oneself throw up, taking laxatives or diet pills, or exercising excessively). The number of binge-purge cycles varies from person to person. Some bulimics binge once a day, while others binge twenty times a day, each time purging food afterward. (Technically exercise isn't purging, but it is a way for people to "run off" or get rid of the calories they just ate.) In a single binge, some people can eat up to five thousand calories *at one sitting*; most young adult athletes don't eat more than four thousand calories *in a whole day*.[90]

Bulimia affects more women than men (80 percent of bulimics are female) and is more common than anorexia, affecting approximately 1–2 percent of all adolescent and young adult women (anorexia affects around .5–1 percent).[91] Unlike anorexics, those with bulimia realize their eating habits are not normal; they may feel ashamed or depressed over their inability to stop the binge-purge cycle. In some ways, bulimia is harder to diagnose than anorexia because sufferers are often average weight or even overweight. Nonetheless, bulimia does have certain *warning signs*:[92]

- Evidence of bingeing (e.g., wrappers and containers left over from large quantities of food eaten)
- Evidence of purging (e.g., frequent trips to the bathroom after eating)
- Cuts on knuckles from scraping teeth when making oneself throw up
- Obsession with exercising to burn off calories (e.g., needing to run even when sick or when it's snowing)
- Discolored or stained teeth
- Swelling of cheeks or jaw area

Many *physical consequences* of bulimia are related to the repeated vomiting that takes place. Bulimics can develop gum disease, and they often need expensive dental work to repair the damage stomach acid has done to their teeth. Some develop an inflamed or even ruptured esophagus. Those who abuse laxatives can also develop chronic constipation and irregular bowel movements. In addition, the repeated binge-purge cycles results in a loss of electrolytes, which can cause chemical imbalances that result in an irregular heartbeat, heart failure, and even death.[93]

Do You Have an Eating Disorder?

If you answer yes to one or more of the following questions, consider talking to an adult so you can get help. Remember, eating disorders are medical conditions and need to be treated. They don't go away on their own:[94]

1. Do you have secret food rituals (e.g., what you eat or how you eat it) that are too weird to explain to someone else?
2. Do you get mad when someone makes suggestions regarding your eating habits?
3. Do you buy, cook, and eat food all by yourself?
4. Do you think your life will be ruined if you stop your current eating habits?
5. Do you obsess about what and/or how much you've eaten?
6. Do food and thoughts of food dominate your daily routine?
7. Do you think of yourself as being fat or as needing to lose a few pounds even though others tell you that you're getting too thin?

Find Out More

Books

Benardot, Dan. *Advanced Sports Nutrition: Fine-Tune Your Food and Fluid Intake for Optimal Training and Performance.* Champaign, IL: Human Kinetics, 2006.

Ivy, John, and Robert Portman. *The Performance Zone: Your Nutrition Action Plan for Greater Endurance & Sports Performance.* North Bergen, NJ: Basic Health Publications, 2004.

Jones, William. *Performance Eating: The High Performance High School Athlete Nutrition Guide.* Lincoln, NE: iUniverse, 2006.

Litt, Ann. *Fuel for Young Athletes: Essential Foods and Fluids for Future Champions.* Champaign, IL: Human Kinetics, 2004.

Owen, Sarah. *The Top 100 Fitness Foods: 100 Ways to Turbocharge Your Life.* London: Duncan Baird, 2009.

Zahensky, Barbara A. *Frequently Asked Questions about Athletes and Eating Disorders.* New York: Rosen Publishing, 2009.

Online Articles

The Nemours Foundation/KidsHealth. "Female Athlete Triad." TeensHealth, reviewed February 2010. kidshealth.org/teen/food_fitness/sports/triad .html#cat20134.

———. "The Food Guide Pyramid Becomes a Plate." TeensHealth, reviewed May 2009. kidshealth.org/teen/food_fitness/nutrition/pyramid.html#.

———. "A Guide to Eating for Sports." TeensHealth, reviewed November 2011. kidshealth.org/teen/food_fitness/nutrition/eatnrun.html?tracking=T_Related Article.

Websites and Organizations

Eating Disorders: Resources for Recovery since 1980 (www.bulimia.com). This website has a variety of resources related to eating disorders and treatment. You can look at articles on a specific disorder, search for therapists and treatment centers in your state, or shop for related books in the online store.

National Eating Disorders Association (www.nationaleatingdisorders.org/ information-resources/index.php). NEDA's website has links to general information on eating disorders, information specifically for girls and specifically for guys, stories of people who have successfully beat eating disorders, and much more.

National Institute of Mental Health (www.nimh.nih.gov/health/publications/eating -disorders/complete-index.shtml). The NIMH website has a helpful online booklet on the symptoms, causes, and treatment options for eating disorders.

Notes

1. Quoted in *What Maurice Jones-Drew Eats* (video), Yahoo! Sports, sports.yahoo.com/elite -athlete-workouts/maurice-jones-drew (accessed March 12, 2012).
2. See, for example, Ann Litt, *Fuel for Young Athletes: Essential Foods and Fluids for Future Champions* (Champaign, IL: Human Kinetics, 2004), 8; John Ivy and Robert Portman, *The Performance Zone: Your Nutrition Action Plan for Greater Endurance & Sports Performance* (North Bergen, NJ: Basic Health Publications, 2004), 70.
3. Litt, *Fuel for Young Athletes*, 8.
4. Office of Alcohol and Drug Education, "Alcohol and Athletes," oade.nd.edu/educate -yourself-alcohol/alcohol-and-athletes/#Nutrition (accessed April 4, 2012).
5. Jennifer Warner, "Whole Grains Fight Belly Fat," WebMD, February 25, 2008, www .webmd.com/heart-disease/news/20080225/whole-grains-fight-belly-fat (accessed August 18, 2011).

6. Anita Bean, *The Complete Guide to Sports Nutrition: How to Eat for Maximum Performance* (Guilford, CT: The Lyons Press, 2004), 3.

7. Bean, *Complete Guide*, 43.

8. Bean, *Complete Guide*, 4; Litt, *Fuel for Young Athletes*, 10–11.

9. Warner, "Whole Grains."

10. Litt, *Fuel for Young Athletes*, 37, 42; Bean, *Complete Guide*, 44.

11. Bean, *Complete Guide*, 43.

12. Bean, *Complete Guide*, 46; Litt, *Fuel for Young Athletes*, 36.

13. Litt, *Fuel for Young Athletes*, 11; Ivy and Portman, *Performance Zone*, 70.

14. In 2011, the USDA changed the pyramid to a plate; see The Nemours Foundation/KidsHealth, "Food Guide Pyramid Becomes a Plate," TeensHealth, reviewed May 2009, kidshealth.org/teen/food_fitness/nutrition/pyramid.html# (accessed August 19, 2011). Keep in mind that the plate, like the pyramid, represents nutrition guidelines for everyone; the amount needed from each food group is slightly different for athletes because of their increased need for energy and muscle repair.

15. Bean, *Complete Guide*, xii.

16. Bean, *Complete Guide*, 8–9.

17. Litt, *Fuel for Young Athletes*, 23.

18. Bean, *Complete Guide*, 85.

19. Sarah Owen, *The Top 100 Fitness Foods: 100 Ways to Turbocharge Your Life* (London: Duncan Baird, 2009), 121.

20. Bean, *Complete Guide*, 83–84.

21. Bean, *Complete Guide*, 83–84.

22. Litt, *Fuel for Young Athletes*, 26.

23. Litt, *Fuel for Young Athletes*, 30.

24. Frank Litsky, "Wrestling: Collegiate Wrestling Deaths Raise Fears about Training," *New York Times*, December 19, 1997, www.nytimes.com/1997/12/19/sports/wrestling-collegiate-wrestling-deaths-raise-fears-about-training.html?pagewanted=all&src=pm (accessed March 9, 2012).

25. WebMD, "Understanding Heat-Related Illness—the Basics," reviewed November 4, 2010, firstaid.webmd.com/understanding-heat-related-illness-basics (accessed August 23, 2011).

26. Jane E. Brody, "Surviving the Playing Field When It's Too Darn Hot," *New York Times*, September 20, 2005.

27. WebMD, "Heat Stroke: Symptoms and Treatment," reviewed July 22, 2010, firstaid.webmd.com/heat-stroke-symptoms-and-treatment (accessed August 23, 2011).

28. Brody, "Surviving the Playing Field."

29. Ivy and Portman, *Performance Zone*, 8.

30. Litt, *Fuel for Young Athletes*, 102.

31. Litt, *Fuel for Young Athletes*, 102.

32. Litt, *Fuel for Young Athletes*, 102.

33. Dan Benardot, *Advanced Sports Nutrition: Fine-Tune Your Food and Fluid Intake for Optimal Training and Performance* (Champaign, IL: Human Kinetics, 2006), 283.

34. Benardot, *Advanced Sports Nutrition*, 131.

35. "What Are Electrolytes?" HowStuffWorks.com, January 21, 2008, health.howstuffworks.com/wellness/diet-fitness/information/question565.htm (accessed March 11, 2012); Steve Born, "Electrolyte Replenishment—Why It's So Important and How to Do It Right,"

Hammer Nutrition, updated June 2011, www.hammernutrition.com/knowledge/electrolyte -replenishment.1274.html (accessed March 11, 2012).

36. Litt, *Fuel for Young Athletes*, 30.
37. Robyn Norwood, "Young Athletes, Energy Drinks: Bad Mix?" *Florida Today*, December 4, 2011.
38. Ivy and Portman, *Performance Zone*, 52.
39. Ivy and Portman, *Performance Zone*, 40, 42.
40. Litt, *Fuel for Young Athletes*, 105.
41. Ivy and Portman, *Performance Zone*, 38–39.
42. Litt, *Fuel for Young Athletes*, 74; Benardot, *Advanced Sports Nutrition*, 237–40.
43. Benardot, *Advanced Sports Nutrition*, 246–47; Ivy and Portman, *Performance Zone*, 80.
44. Litt, *Fuel for Young Athletes*, 77–78.
45. Scott Anderson and E. Randy Eichner, "Preventing Muscle Cramps in Football," CBS Interactive Resource Library, May 2001, findarticles.com/p/articles/mi_m0FIH/is_10_70/ ai_n18611880/?tag=mantle_skin;content (accessed September 8, 2011).
46. Lisa Porter, "Foods to Prevent Leg Cramps," Livestrong.com, updated May, 4, 2010, www .livestrong.com/article/116308-foods-prevent-leg-cramps/ (accessed September 8, 2011).
47. Quoted in *What Maurice Jones-Drew Eats* (video), Yahoo! Sports, sports.yahoo.com/elite -athlete-workouts/maurice-jones-drew (accessed March 12, 2012).
48. Litt, *Fuel for Young Athletes*, 92–93.
49. Benardot, *Advanced Sports Nutrition*, 251–52.
50. Jeff Z. Klein, "It's Not Hockey, It's Bandy," *NYTimes.com*, January 28, 2010, www .nytimes.com/2010/01/29/sports/olympics/29bandy.html?pagewanted=all (accessed October 11, 2011); "What Is Bandy?" American Bandy Association, www.usabandy.com/home .php?pg=about (accessed October 11, 2011).
51. John Seifert, "For Hockey Players," in Ivy and Portman, *Performance Zone*, 82.
52. Benardot, *Advanced Sports Nutrition*, 257–58; Litt, *Fuel for Young Athletes*, 84–85.
53. Quoted in *Race-Day Eats* (video), TeensHealth, kidshealth.org/teen/food_fitness/nutrition/ eatnrun.html?tracking=T_RelatedArticle (accessed September 21, 2011).
54. Benardot, *Advanced Sports Nutrition*, 254–55; Ivy and Portman, *Performance Zone*, 94.
55. Quoted in *Allyson Felix's Olympic Diet* (video), Yahoo! Sports, sports.yahoo.com/elite-athlete -workouts/allyson-felix (accessed March 12, 2012).
56. Benardot, *Advanced Sports Nutrition*, 254–55.
57. Litt, *Fuel for Young Athletes*, 93–94.
58. Francois Fortin, ed., *Sports: The Complete Visual Reference* (Willowdale, ON: Firefly Books, 2000), 270; Volleyball.org, "History of Volleyball," www.volleyball.org/history.html (accessed April 1, 2012).
59. Abigail Funk, "Wrestling with Regulations," *Training & Conditioning* 16, no. 2 (March 2006), www.momentummedia.com/articles/tc/tc1602/wrestling.htm (accessed February 13, 2012).
60. Derek Ort, interview with author, December 3, 2011.
61. Litt, *Fuel for Young Athletes*, 87.
62. Benardot, *Advanced Sports Nutrition*, 272.
63. Benardot, *Advanced Sports Nutrition*, 272–74.
64. Owen, *Top 100 Fitness Foods*, 120.
65. Owen, *Top 100 Fitness Foods*, 123.
66. Andrew Pruitt, "For Cyclists," in Ivy and Portman, *Performance Zone*, 78–79; Benardot, *Advanced Sports Nutrition*, 278.

67. "What Is Cross Country Skiing?" XCSkiWorld.com, www.xcskiworld.com/beginners.htm (accessed October 24, 2011).

68. Quoted in *Chris Paul's Diet* (video), Yahoo! Sports, sports.yahoo.com/elite-athlete-workouts/chris-paul (accessed March 12, 2012).

69. Benardot, *Advanced Sports Nutrition*, 288–89; Litt, *Fuel for Young Athletes*, 76.

70. Don Kirkendall, "For Soccer Players," in Ivy and Portman, *Performance Zone*, 90.

71. Owen, *Top 100 Fitness Foods*, 120.

72. Litt, *Fuel for Young Athletes*, 90.

73. Litt, *Fuel for Young Athletes*, 91.

74. Mayo Clinic staff, "Eating Disorders: Definition," Mayo Clinic, January 15, 2010, www.mayoclinic.com/health/eating-disorders/DS00294 (accessed August 24, 2011).

75. National Eating Disorder Association (NEDA), "What Is an Eating Disorder? Some Basic Facts," 2005, www.nationaleatingdisorders.org/nedaDir/files/documents/handouts/WhatIsEd.pdf (accessed August 24, 2011).

76. National Institute of Mental Health (NIMH), "Eating Disorders," NIH Publication No. 11-4901, revised 2011, www.nimh.nih.gov/health/publications/eating-disorders/complete-index.shtml (accessed August 24, 2011).

77. National Comorbidity Survey, "National Comorbidity Survey—Adolescent Supplement," accessed from NIMH, "Eating Disorders among Children," www.nimh.nih.gov/statistics/1EAT_CHILD.shtml (accessed April 5, 2012).

78. Anita Bean, "Body Image and Eating Disorders," in *Sports Nutrition for Women*, ed. Anita Bean and Peggy Wellington (London: Hunter House, 2001), 118–19.

79. NEDA, "Factors That May Contribute to Eating Disorders," 2004, www.nationaleatingdisorders.org/uploads/file/information-resources/Factors%20that%20may%20Contribute%20to%20Eating%20Disorders.pdf (accessed August 24, 2011).

80. Bean, "Body Image," 118–19.

81. Piper Weiss, "The Plastic Surgery a Model Needs to Look Like Barbie," Shine, October 14, 2011, shine.yahoo.com/fashion/the-plastic-surgery-a-model-needs-to-look-like-barbie-2584798.html (accessed March 13, 2012).

82. Zahensky, *Frequently Asked Questions*.

83. Barbara A. Zahensky, *Frequently Asked Questions about Athletes and Eating Disorders* (New York: Rosen Publishing, 2009), 17–18; Bean, "Body Image," 118.

84. Zahensky, *Frequently Asked Questions*, 24.

85. M. DeArmond, "Ex-Star Gymnast Is Dead at 22," *Kansas City Star*, July 27, 1994, p. A1, edresources.pbworks.com/w/page/9788158/Christy%27s%20Death#ChristysDeathJuly261994 (accessed August 25, 2011).

86. Bean, "Body Image," 120.

87. NEDA, "Anorexia Nervosa," 2005, p. 1, www.nationaleatingdisorders.org/nedaDir/files/documents/handouts/Anorexia.pdf (accessed August 26, 2011); Arthur Schoenstadt, "Warning Signs of Anorexia," MedTV, anorexia.emedtv.com/anorexia/warning-signs-of-anorexia.html (accessed August 26, 2011).

88. NEDA, "Anorexia Nervosa," 2.

89. Zahensky, *Frequently Asked Questions*, 7.

90. Zahensky, *Frequently Asked Questions*, 39.

91. NEDA, "Bulimia Nervosa," 2005, p. 2, www.nationaleatingdisorders.org/nedaDir/files/documents/handouts/Bulimia.pdf (accessed August 26, 2011); NEDA, "Anorexia Nervosa," 2.

92. NEDA, "Bulimia Nervosa," 1.

93. Michael Myers, "What Are Electrolytes?" *Eating Disorders Today* 2, no. 4 (Summer 2004), reprinted at www.bulimia.com/client/client_pages/newsletteredt17.cfm (accessed August 26, 2011); NEDA, "Bulimia Nervosa," 2.

94. Zahensky, *Frequently Asked Questions*, 29–30.

STEROIDS AND OTHER PERFORMANCE ENHANCERS

....

"If you're good but not quite good enough, you get all sorts of advice on how to get better. Kids work their tail off and still they're not in the mix. So they try whatever they can, because coaches and parents are telling them they're almost there."
—*Marc Sardakis, a character in* Boost *by Kathy Mackel*[1]

What do baseball player Barry Bonds, sprinter Marion Jones, and cyclist Floyd Landis have in common? At the height of their careers, all three were accused of using illegal performance-enhancing drugs, specifically steroids. So, what happened to these star athletes?

- After being formally accused of steroid use in 2007, Bonds went from being home run king to not having a team to play on. In 2011, Bonds was found guilty of misleading the jury about his steroid use; he was fined and sentenced to two years' probation, 250 hours of community service, and thirty days of house arrest. Even though Bonds holds the record for career home runs (as of 2012), his steroid scandal might prevent him from making it into the Baseball Hall of Fame.[2]
- After years of denying the accusations, in 2007 Jones finally admitted using steroids and she was convicted in 2008. Jones was then stripped of all five of her medals (three gold, two bronze) from the 2000 Olympics, and she spent six months in jail for lying to federal prosecutors.[3]
- Like Jones, Landis initially denied the accusations; in 2010, three years after he was found guilty of doping, Landis admitted that he had been using steroids for years. Following his 2007 conviction, Landis lost his "Tour [de France] title, his career, his life savings and his marriage."[4]

Do you think doping was worth the consequences for these athletes? Why do athletes use illegal performance-enhancing drugs when the risks seem pretty high?

This chapter takes a look at steroids and other performance-enhancing substances, both legal and illegal. Let's start with looking at what performance enhancers are and what they can possibly do for an athlete, followed by the risks and potential side effects.

Types of Performance Enhancers

Performance-enhancing drugs and supplements are substances used to improve athletic performance. Anything that reportedly increases muscle size, strength, speed, endurance, recovery rate, or any combination of these classifies as a

What Do You Think?

After she was convicted of steroid use, Marion Jones was forced to return the five medals she won in the 2000 Olympics. Two of those medals were earned in relays. On April 10, 2008, the International Olympic Committee (IOC) ruled that since Jones had been found guilty of doping, her relay teammates had to return their medals as well.

Chryste Gaines was one of those teammates, and she had this to say about being stripped of her 4x100 bronze medal: "We are being unfairly punished. If the drug testing agencies cannot determine if an athlete is taking performance enhancing drugs how are the teammates supposed to know? . . . It negates all the family functions, church functions, and social events we missed in the name of winning an Olympic medal."[5]

Gaines and her teammates appealed the IOC's decision, and in July 2010, they won the right to have their medals restored. However, the IOC said the ruling was "disappointing and especially unfortunate for the athletes of the other teams who competed according to the rules."[6]

What do you think? Is it fair to other competitors to let a team win if someone on that team was doping? On the other hand, should the whole team be disqualified for the actions of just one team member?

performance enhancer. Some are legal, widely used substances such as caffeine, sports drinks, and energy bars. Some are illegal drugs that are banned from athletic competitions at the high school, collegiate, and professional levels. Sports drinks and energy drinks aside, anabolic steroids, steroid precursors (also called steroidal supplements), and creatine are the most commonly used performance enhancers among teen athletes.[7]

Anabolic Steroids

Steroids are a group of hormones produced by your body. Among other things, they are important for controlling metabolism (the process of getting energy from food), regulating your immune system (which helps you to fight illness and heal from injuries), and developing sexual characteristics. The androgen hormone group is responsible for the development of male sex traits such as facial hair and a deep voice, and it also contributes to muscle growth. Testosterone is the most powerful androgen hormone, and both guys and girls produce it naturally, though most girls produce very small amounts.

"Several people in other sports at my school use steroids. I think there is more pressure for males to be muscled up and they feel the pressure to be bigger or meet their goal weight. I know quite a few kids that use steroids in football and wrestling but not in tennis."
—Caitlin, 16, tennis

Anabolic steroids are a man-made form of testosterone. They are more formally called androgenic-anabolic steroids—*androgenic* refers to the drugs' likeness to androgen hormones and their ability to produce male sex characteristics; *anabolic* refers to their muscle-building ability. There are over one hundred variations of anabolic steroids available in creams, pills, and injections—every one of them illegal

Slang Terms for Steroids[8]

Arnolds	Pumpers
Gym candy	Roids
Hype	Sauce
Juice	Slop
Product	Stackers
Pump	Weight trainers

without a prescription. And even if you somehow manage to get a prescription, you can't legally use the drugs to enhance athletic performance. If you test positive—even with a prescription—you'll suffer disciplinary consequences.

Man-made steroids are legally used to treat certain medical conditions. For example, doctors prescribe anabolic steroids to men who have hypogonadism, a condition in which the testes don't make enough testosterone. Steroids are also used to treat some forms of anemia (a condition in which the blood has an abnormally low number of red blood cells) and asthma. However, anabolic steroids are never prescribed to improve athletic performance.

Perhaps the biggest reason athletes turn to anabolic steroids is that steroids build muscle—lots of muscle. This is because the steroids cause muscle tissue

Timeline of Manufactured Steroid Use[9]

1930s: Man-made anabolic steroids are produced to treat hypogonadism.

1948: Doctors use cortisone steroids to treat rheumatoid arthritis.

1954: Soviet weight lifters use anabolic steroids at the World Weightlifting Championships in Vienna, Austria. As the story goes, the Soviet doctor went out for drinks with the U.S. team doctor, John Ziegler. The Soviet doctor got drunk and told Ziegler that the Soviets were using man-made testosterone.

1958: Dr. Ziegler and others create the oral anabolic steroid Dianabol for U.S. weight lifters.

1963: Use of anabolic steroids spreads to the NFL (National Football League).

1968: Drug testing is first used at the Winter and Summer Olympic Games. Because testing methods were still being developed, anabolic steroids were not included on the list of banned substances. Out of 753 tests performed in both Olympic Games, one athlete tested positive.

1970s: Every NFL team has some players using anabolic steroids. At this point, steroid use is not viewed as cheating.

1975: Anabolic steroids are added to the IOC's list of banned substances.

1976: The Montreal Summer Olympics marks the first time Olympic athletes are tested for anabolic steroids. Out of 786 tests performed, eleven athletes tested positive.

1987: The NFL starts testing for steroid use.

1989: Use of anabolic steroids officially becomes cheating in the NFL; players are fined and suspended for doping.

1990: Congress passes the Anabolic Steroids Control Act, officially making it illegal to use steroids without a prescription.

1990: The NCAA (National Collegiate Athletic Association) starts random drug testing.

1991: MLB (Major League Baseball) bans anabolic steroids.

2000: The U.S. Anti-Doping Agency forms and begins testing Olympic athletes for steroid use.

2003: BALCO (Bay Area Laboratory Co-Operative) is raided by federal investigators looking for evidence of banned substance use among several high-profile athletes, including Barry Bonds and Marion Jones.

2004: President Bush asks for funding to start a banned-substance testing program in U.S. high schools. The first schools start testing in 2005.

2005: MLB implements punishments for positive drug tests.

2006: The NCAA expands random drug testing to include summer months.

2007: The NFL announces stricter anti-doping policies.

to "bulk up" in response to training and weight lifting. As a result, steroids also increase an athlete's overall strength and endurance. Another reason anabolic steroids appeal to athletes is that they speed up the time muscles need to recover. According to the Mayo Clinic, "anabolic steroids may help athletes recover from a hard workout more quickly by reducing the muscle damage that occurs during the session. This enables athletes to workout harder and more frequently without overtraining."[10]

Though anabolic steroids build muscle, there are parts of sports performance that they won't improve—for example, agility, speed, hand-eye coordination, and sport-specific skills such as dribbling a soccer ball or throwing a curveball. Those all come from genetic makeup and hard work.

Steroid Precursors

Steroid precursors, also called steroidal supplements or pro-hormones, are another common performance-enhancing drug among teens. Examples include andro-stenedione (also called andro), a hormone that your body produces naturally, and dehydroepiandrosterone (DHEA). These man-made supplements are basically weaker forms of the hormones found in anabolic steroids. Like anabolic steroids, most steroid precursors are illegal without a prescription. DHEA can be purchased at some health food stores, but it's on the IOC's list of banned substances.

Young athletes use steroid precursors for the same reason they use anabolic steroids: to get bigger and stronger. In theory the supplements increase the body's testosterone levels as well as muscle mass and strength. In fact, however, there is little evidence to show that steroid precursors actually produce these results.[11]

Creatine

Creatine monohydrate is possibly the most commonly used performance enhancer among teenagers. Athletes mainly use it to build muscle mass and to speed muscle recovery. Like hormones, creatine is produced naturally by your body. Your liver makes about .07 ounces (two grams) of creatine each day, which is then stored in your muscles until you need it for energy bursts such as sprinting and jumping. You also get creatine from eating meat protein, especially beef and fish. Any excess creatine in your system is removed by your kidneys.[12]

Creatine is most commonly used as a powder that can be mixed into water or a fruit smoothie. You can buy it without a prescription. According to the Mayo Clinic, "scientific research indicates that creatine may have some athletic benefit by producing small gains in short-term bursts of power. Creatine appears to help muscles make more adenosine triphosphate (ATP), which stores and transports energy in cells, and is used for quick bursts of activity, such as weightlifting or sprinting. There's no evidence, however, that creatine enhances performance in aerobic or endurance sports."[13] In other words, creatine might benefit athletes in some power sports mentioned in chapter 4—for example, football, wrestling, and track and field (sprints, throws, jumps)—where repetitive explosive bursts are required. However, it's not likely to enhance the performance of cross-country runners, distance swimmers, Nordic skiers, and other athletes who need stamina not power.

There's some question as to how effective it is to take extra creatine as a supplement when the muscles apparently have enough to work with. If the kidneys are already removing excess that occurs from what the liver produces and from what you eat, it seems like most creatine taken as a supplement would also be eliminated as extra.

Stimulants

The term *stimulants* refers to a broad category of substances that stimulate the central nervous system and increase the heart rate. Athletes use stimulants to increase alertness, aggressiveness, concentration, and endurance. The most commonly used stimulants among athletes include

- caffeine, which is found in coffee, energy drinks (e.g., Red Bull, Monster, NOS), and some soda;
- ephedrine and pseudoephedrine (pseudoephedrine is a decongestant found in many allergy and cold medicines; e.g., Sudafed, Contact Cold); and
- illegal drugs such as cocaine, amphetamines, and methamphetamine.

Caffeine is the only stimulant that can be legally used to enhance performance, though it is banned by the NCAA and IOC in large doses. Research seems to indicate that athletes who need to keep a steady pace for a long period of time (e.g., cross-country runners, triathletes) benefit from caffeine more than power athletes who need energy for short bursts. Citing the website of the Sports Medicine Council of Manitoba, the *Sport Journal* reports that "endurance athletes might gain some advantage by exploiting caffeine to derive energy from fat early in a competition, thereby leaving more muscle glycogen available to provide energy later on."[14] Athletes have been disqualified for doping because they were taking allergy medicine that contained a banned stimulant such as pseudoephedrine. Make sure you know what you're taking and what is banned.

Risks and Side Effects

If you choose to use take illegal or banned performance-enhancing substances, you're putting yourself at risk in many ways. The most obvious risk is suspension or disqualification; remember what happened to Barry Bonds, Marion Jones, and Floyd Landis. At the high school level, penalties vary by state and school district. In California, for example, the CIF (California Interscholastic Federation) now requires student-athletes to sign a pledge saying they won't use steroids. If athletes violate this contract, they can be suspended for a number of days or expelled from school entirely. Some California school districts have taken the pledge even further. They've banned over-the-counter supplements (such as creatine) as well as steroids because of the potential health hazards.[15]

Beyond suspension, performance enhancers pose a more serious risk to your health. Even legal performance-enhancing substances can have serious physical side effects, including death. The rest of this section covers health-related risks. It's best to know what they are before you start injecting or ingesting any kind of performance enhancer.

Athlete Bio: Allyson Felix, Track and Field

When Allyson Felix tried out for the track team in ninth grade, she was wearing baggy shorts and clunky basketball shoes—not exactly the outfit of a sprinter. But when she ran, the coach took notice. He had her run the 60 meters twice because he couldn't believe her time was right.

That was in 2000. Three years later, Felix broke the world junior record at 200 meters and then she just kept going:

- At the 2004 Olympics, at the age of eighteen, Felix won silver in the 200 meters.
- At the 2008 Olympics, Felix won silver (200 meters) and gold (4x400 relay).
- Felix is the only woman to ever win gold in the 200 meters at three consecutive World Track and Field Championships (2005, 2007, 2009).
- In 2011, Felix won the 400 meters at the U.S. national championships. With this win she became the first woman in U.S. history to hold the U.S. title at 100, 200, and 400 meters.
- At the 2012 U.S. Olympic trials, Felix ran the fourth fastest time in history in the 200 meters.
- At the 2012 Olympics, Felix won three gold medals: 200 meters, 4x100 relay, and 4x400 relay. In the 4x100 relay, Felix and her teammates set a new world record.

The best part is that Felix has racked up this impressive list of accomplishments without the help of steroids. She is part of USA Track and Field's Win with Integrity program and goes to schools to speak to students about competing clean. She is also part of the U.S. Anti-Doping Agency's Project Believe, which started in 2008 after several track and field athletes were accused of doping. Through Project Believe, athletes such as Felix and decathlete Brian Clay are tested randomly and far more often than most athletes just to prove that athletes are competing clean. Felix says, "Whatever I can do to prove I'm clean, whatever it takes, I want to do it to show that I'm not taking drugs."[16]

Anabolic Steroids

Most people produce hormones naturally in amounts that are appropriate for normal sex trait development, muscle building, metabolism maintenance, and immune system functioning. Adding extra hormones in amounts much higher than those approved for any medical condition is bound to have negative consequences.

Anabolic steroids are drugs, and like any drug, they can be addictive. You can become psychologically dependent on steroids and believe you can't compete without them. Lyle Alzado, a former NFL player, said of his steroid use, "It was addicting, mentally addicting. . . . I just didn't feel strong unless I was taking something."[17] You can also suffer depression and other withdrawal symptoms if you stop using. In 2005, *USA Today* published a story about steroid use in high school

---

Athlete Bio: Lyle Alzado, Former NFL Player

At six foot three, 254 pounds, Lyle Alzado was a huge defensive end who played with the Denver Broncos, Cleveland Browns, and Los Angeles Raiders (before they moved to Oakland).

But he wasn't always that big. In high school he was actually on the small side, and he didn't get any scholarship offers to play in college. Alzado ended up at a tiny college in South Dakota, and that's where he started using steroids.

And they worked. Alzado grew in size and strength, so much so that he got drafted by the Broncos in 1971. From there he gained a reputation as a tough, even violent player. Alzado later said, "I outran, outhit, outanythinged everybody. All along I was taking steroids and I saw that they made me play better and better." Alzado estimated that he spent thirty thousand dollars a year on steroids!

Alzado played his last regular season game in 1985. Six years later, he was diagnosed with brain cancer. Although doctors didn't link his steroid use and brain lymphoma, Alzado was convinced the drugs caused his cancer. Three months after his diagnosis, he finally admitted to using steroids, something he had denied for years.

"It wasn't worth it," Alzado wrote in 1991, when he admitted to *Sports Illustrated* that he had been doping. "If you're on steroids or human growth hormone, stop. I should have."

Alzado died in 1992 at the age of forty-three.[18]

"He [an athlete on steroids] was always very calm and happy, then when something went wrong, he would freak out in scary and very dangerous ways."
—Jessica H., 20, golf

and gave examples of two young adults who committed suicide as a result of depression caused by steroid withdrawals.[19] Have you ever heard the term *roid rage*? It refers to the super-aggressive outbursts people on steroids sometimes experience. Users can flip out at relatively minor events. When Lyle Alzado was on roids, he chased some guy all over the neighborhood and "beat the hell out of him" after the guy accidentally sideswiped Alzado's car.[20]

Here's a long list of health risks and side effects associated with anabolic steroid use:[21]

- Severe acne
- Increased risk of tendinitis and tendon rupture
- Liver abnormalities and tumors
- Increased low-density lipoprotein (LDL) cholesterol (the "bad" cholesterol)
- Decreased high-density lipoprotein (HDL) cholesterol (the "good" cholesterol)
- Hypertension (high blood pressure)
- Heart and circulatory problems
- Prostate gland enlargement
- Aggressive behaviors, rage, or violence
- Psychiatric disorders, such as depression

"When I was thirteen, I was still the smallest guy in my class. All the other guys . . . treated me like a little kid, called me 'shrimp-o,' and were always picking on me. I was always the last to be picked for any sports team. I was so miserable that I had to do something. So I started taking steroids. . . . At first it seemed as if they were working. Suddenly, I shot up and bulked up a bit. But just when things got going, they stopped. Later, the doctor told me that the roids had forced my body into puberty before it was ready. My own hormones never kicked in. . . . So today I am 5'2" and my doctor says I won't ever grow any taller. I regret what I did to my body."—Bobby, 18[22]

- Drug dependence
- Infections or diseases such as HIV or hepatitis if you're injecting the drugs
- Inhibited growth and development, and risk of future health problems in teenagers

And that's not all. There are additional risks just for guys and just for girls. The risks for guys include

- shrinking of the testicles,
- pain when urinating,
- breast development,
- impotence (inability to get an erection), and
- sterility (inability to have children).[23]

The risks for girls include

- increased facial hair growth;
- development of masculine traits, such as deepening of the voice, and loss of feminine body characteristics, such as shrinking of the breasts;
- enlargement of the clitoris; and
- menstrual cycle changes.[24]

Before you use anabolic steroids, take a long look at these three lists of health risks and side effects and decide if doping is worth it. Also remember that as a teenager, your body is still developing and growing. Your hormones are going crazy as it is. Adding more hormones in the form of steroids can be especially risky. Sure, you might gain twenty pounds of pure muscle, get an awesome-looking body, or get into the college of your dreams on an athletic scholarship. But what if you get caught doping and no college wants to take the risk of signing you? What if you develop a heart condition as a result of steroids and need to quit the team so you don't have a heart attack?

"I really believed that I was a goddess or something. . . . I could lift so much weight. I looked great in the mirror. The other girls on the track team, they seemed to be jealous of how I looked. I would never have thought that steroids would one day turn against me—that I would be constantly shaking, that I'd tear the tendons in my leg and not be able to run, that I'd start doing all this crazy stuff like beating up my little brother in a sudden rage for no reason at all."—Jackie, 14 [25]

"The guys who all used them [steroids] had some horrible injuries happen to them late in the year because their body couldn't handle that much extra testosterone and it wore their body down as the season progressed. It was almost always several torn muscles and a few ligaments that ripped because of the added stress on the muscles, especially late in the year. None of them were ever the same again on the field either."—David, 23, football

Steroid Precursors

Because steroid precursors are hormones like anabolic steroids, the risks involved in taking them are basically the same as those just listed. Guys run the risk of developing more feminine attributes, such as bigger breasts. They can also experience shrinking of the testicles. Girls, on the other hand, tend to have increased masculine characteristics: deeper voice and baldness. All teens taking steroid supplements are likely to increase their bad cholesterol and decrease their good cholesterol, which increases their risk of heart attack. They are also likely to develop severe acne.[26]

Creatine

Ironically, though teens take creatine to enhance performance, several side effects can actually decrease athletic performance, for example, stomach cramps, muscle cramps, nausea, diarrhea, and weight gain. In some cases, creatine causes the muscles to retain more water, and other organs suffer from a lack of water as a result. This can lead to dehydration. As mentioned in chapter 4, taking creatine without replacing lost fluids can be extremely dangerous, even deadly. High doses of creatine can also cause kidney and liver damage.[27]

Stimulants

Like steroids, many stimulants are drugs and can be addictive, both physically and psychologically; even caffeine is considered a drug because it stimulates the central nervous system and people can become addicted to its energy rush. In addition, the body can become tolerant so that it takes larger doses of the drugs to achieve the desired effect.

As with creatine, stimulants can cause side effects that actually hinder athletic performance rather than enhance it. Too much caffeine, for example, can cause nervousness, an inability to concentrate, and insomnia—not good if you're already a little nervous about a big game and need a good night's sleep. Other side effects from stimulant use include

- irritability,
- dehydration,
- heatstroke,
- heart palpitations (feeling like your heart is racing or pounding),
- hallucinations,
- stroke, and
- heart attack.[28]

During the 2010 football season, at least four high school football players in California had to go to the emergency room with persistent rapid heartbeats caused by caffeinated energy drinks. Also in 2010, Dakota Sailor, a seventeen-year-old football player from Missouri, drank two 16-ounce NOS energy drinks in one day. His stepfather found him lying on the couch and had to perform CPR because Dakota wasn't breathing. Dakota's doctors think he suffered a seizure, and he ended up in the hospital for five days. Because of incidents like these, in October 2011, the National Federation of High School Associations issued a warning about the use of caffeinated energy drinks (NOS, Monster, Red Bull, etc.) before, during, or after athletic competition because of the increased risk of dehydration and heatstroke. Michael Shepard, a team doctor from California, says that if you combine these energy drinks with dehydration (whether from having the flu or from exercising in hot weather) or with supplements such as creatine, there's a high risk of fatal cardiac arrhythmia, or irregular heartbeat. In other words, the super jolt of caffeine in conjunction with fluid and electrolyte loss can overwhelm the heart muscle.[29]

Reasons Athletes Take Performance-Enhancing Substances

Given the risks and side effects just described, why do athletes take performance enhancers? There are several reasons, and in some way, they all stem from the pressures athletes feel—pressure to perform, to win, to impress the coach or college scouts, even to look good in a bathing suit.

Good Read: Boost by Kathy Mackel

Sport: Basketball

Life apps: Steroid use, sibling rivalry, moving to new state/school, importance of practice

Summary: Savannah "Savvy" Christopher is a six-foot-two, fourteen-year-old basketball player. After her family moves from New Mexico to Rhode Island, Savvy tries out for the 18U club team—an elite team dominated by older, more experienced players. She makes the team, but she has to practice hard to prove herself and earn a starting position. Then someone accuses Savvy of taking steroids in order to "boost" her game, and she is forced to sit on the sidelines until the truth is uncovered.

If you're a female athlete, you'll probably relate to Savvy's struggles on and off the court—practicing to improve skills, dealing with competition, having a crush on the good-looking wide receiver, arguing with your sister. Told from Savvy's viewpoint, *Boost* allows the reader into the main character's thoughts and feelings. Author Kathy Mackel played multiple sports in high school (varsity field hockey, basketball, softball), so the game descriptions and teammate interactions are realistic. If you're familiar with women's college basketball, you'll recognize the player names and teams the author weaves into the plot.

Dial Books, 2008

248 pages

To Get Bigger

This is a common reason given by guys in particular. Some of you know exactly what I'm talking about. You have teammates who are six foot three, 220 pounds of pure muscle. You are barely five foot ten, and you're lucky if you weigh 160. And no matter what you do—no matter how much you eat, how much you lift, how much training you put in—you don't gain the muscle and weight like your teammates.

Sometimes the pressure to get bigger is not all in your head. You might hear it from your coach: "If you want to make varsity, you need to get bigger." Increasing muscle mass the good old-fashioned way takes time, and for some teen guys it seems nearly impossible. Enter anabolic steroids—since they speed muscle recovery time, you don't need as much rest in between workouts so you can work the same group of muscles every day. A guy on steroids is going build muscle mass in a much shorter time than a nonuser. That's a big reason to risk the side effects (and getting caught; remember, steroid use in sports is illegal) and start doping to get bigger.

> "A few people I know from wrestling used steroids and they all wanted to get bigger faster."—Corey, 20, wrestling

But here's the thing about getting bigger on steroids: it only lasts as long as you're on the drugs. It's not a natural strength; it's a synthetic, or man-made, strength. Sure you worked out at the gym and lifted weights. But it was the steroids that enabled you to make such huge gains in such short time. Mark Schlereth, a former NFL player, says, "You won't be able to quit steroids and hang on to those gains [in muscle size and strength]. . . . I'd rather keep the strength gains that I've worked so hard for. . . . It's natural strength, and I want to keep it."[30]

> "I was definitely curious [about steroids]. We had a super stud linebacker my sophomore and junior year in high school and I wanted to be like him, and he took steroids."
> —David, 23, football

To Improve Performance

A big part of the reason guys want to get bigger is to improve athletic performance. Girls can fall into this thinking too: more leg muscle equals higher jumping, which means more rebounds and more blocks at the basket; more arm, shoulder, and back muscle equals stronger throwing arm and farther throws from

> "When it comes down to it, either a person has heart or they don't have heart. Steroids can't build heart. . . . A lot of people who take steroids are trying to compensate for something they don't have."—Marshall, 18[31]

> "They felt they did not have the natural talent of others so they thought steroids would make them faster and stronger and not need natural talent."
> —Jessica H., 20, golf

> "Boys on the baseball team used steroids to hit more home runs."—Kirsten, 20, softball

the outfield; and so on. Teens are also drawn to steroids' ability to increase muscle endurance (the ability to perform an action over and over); the guy or girl on steroids might be the one who can swim harder for a longer period of time. Remember: Though steroids can improve muscle performance, they haven't been proven to improve specific skills or speed. Those come from natural ability and practice.

As you play at higher levels of competition, the pressure to win, to be the best, also increases. You might demand a lot from yourself, but sometimes your teammates, your coaches, and your parents demand even more. Without intending to, others can cause you to feel that the training you're putting in isn't enough. Or that winning really is the only thing that matters. Some teens turn to performance-enhancing drugs as a result.

Which Sports Have the Most Steroid Abuse?

Weight lifters and bodybuilders are the main users of steroids, but other athletes have joined them. Here's a short list of sports with the most common steroid use:[32]

Sports in which size is important:

- Football
- Wrestling
- Baseball

Sports in which muscle endurance is important:

- Swimming
- Cycling
- Track and field

History of Baseball

For many years, General Abner Doubleday was credited with inventing the game in Cooperstown, New York, in 1839. The story goes that Doubleday and his troops were stationed in Cooperstown, and the general came up with the game as a way for his troops to relax. There's just one problem with that story: General Doubleday wasn't stationed in New York in 1839. Also, he never referred to baseball in his lifetime and never claimed to have invented it. There is no mention of baseball in Doubleday's *New York Times* obituary from 1893.

It appears that a group of baseball bigwigs decided to name Doubleday the father of baseball; they just wanted someone they could declare the creator so they could distinguish baseball from the English game of rounders. These leaders apparently picked Doubleday based on a letter from one of his schoolmates. The schoolmate claimed that Doubleday had devised rules for the game in 1839. By some accounts, however, this schoolmate was also a patient at a hospital for the criminally insane. Nonetheless, the myth that General Doubleday was the father of baseball stuck until 1953, when the U.S. Supreme Court officially recognized Alexander Cartwright as the inventor of baseball.[33]

Even this recognition, however, is probably not 100 percent accurate. According to a plaque on the wall in the Baseball Hall of Fame, Cartwright is the one who put the bases ninety feet apart, decided games would last nine innings, and established nine players as a team. However, author John Thorn says Cartwright "did none of these things, and every other word of substance on his plaque is false." Thorn claims three other men—Daniel Lucius Adams, William Rufus Wheaton, and Louis Fenn Wadsworth—should receive credit for establishing these baseball rules.[34]

No one knows for sure who invented baseball, but by the 1840s it was being played according to the rules we know today. The first baseball club, the New York Knickerbockers, formed in 1845. The National League formed in 1876, the American League followed in 1901, and the leagues faced off in the first World Series in 1903.[35]

"At first [steroids] were used to help heal a couple guys' previous injuries, but they abused it and used it to get huge muscles and a starting spot. And it worked."—David, 23, football

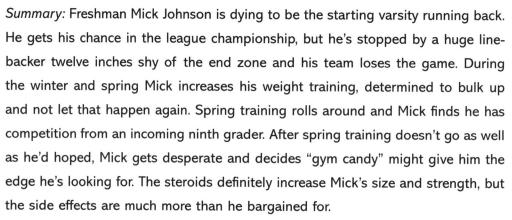

Good Read: Gym Candy *by Carl Deuker*

Sport: Football

Life apps: Steroid use/addiction, wanting to be the best, friendship, father-son relationship

Summary: Freshman Mick Johnson is dying to be the starting varsity running back. He gets his chance in the league championship, but he's stopped by a huge linebacker twelve inches shy of the end zone and his team loses the game. During the winter and spring Mick increases his weight training, determined to bulk up and not let that happen again. Spring training rolls around and Mick finds he has competition from an incoming ninth grader. After spring training doesn't go as well as he'd hoped, Mick gets desperate and decides "gym candy" might give him the edge he's looking for. The steroids definitely increase Mick's size and strength, but the side effects are much more than he bargained for.

Gym Candy gives a realistic, balanced picture of the struggles some teen athletes experience: wanting so badly to be the best and willing to do anything to get there. The story is told from Mick's viewpoint, giving the reader a glimpse into his inner conflict: knowing steroids are illegal and knowing that he's cheating, but not being able to stop himself once he sees the results. The author keeps the reader guessing as to how Mick's situation will resolve; the ending definitely wasn't what I expected.

Graphia, 2007

313 pages

To Get to the Next Level

A major reason behind wanting to improve performance is that teens want to move to the next level in their sport, whether that's making the varsity team or playing at the college level. Most of you already know this: competition for playing time is fierce. Some coaches play everyone, but as you move to the higher levels in high school sports, coaches tend to play the best players and the others sit on the bench. Some teen athletes see steroids as the key to making themselves stand out to the coach. The main character of *Gym Candy* (summary on page 164) falls to this temptation.

Competition for athletic scholarships is also tough. Colleges only have so many scholarships for each sport, and only a few of those are "full ride." Unfortunately, since some teen athletes vying for those scholarships are on steroids, others feel they need to level the playing field by doping.

For teens whose families can't afford to pay for college, an athletic scholarship might be their only ticket to an education. Parents might pressure their kids to succeed in sports in order to get that free ride. With these high expectations, some teen athletes might use steroids so they get noticed, even though they know the risks to their body and their future if they get caught.

> "A lot of parents put pressure on kids to perform at this combine [where college scouts can see you perform] and do this to get in college for free. Be that star. A lot of parents thrive off that, probably more than the kid does."
> —Marshall, 18[36]

How Many Teens Have Tried Steroids?

That's a tough question. In 2007, one newspaper reporter claimed that "depending on which national studies you read, estimates of usage among kids in 8th through 12th grade ranges between 4 and 11 percent."[37] That's a pretty big range. Let's say six million eighth through twelfth graders in the United States play sports. If 4 percent are taking steroids, that equals 240,000 athletes. If 11 percent are doping, that equals 660,000 athletes. Big difference! Studies come up with different numbers based on which teens they interview and how honest those teens are about their usage. Here are the results from various studies completed since 1991:

- According to a study done by the Centers for Disease Control and Prevention, the number of high school steroid users more than doubled between 1991 and 2003.[38]
- A study by the National Institute on Drug Abuse shows that 3.4 percent of U.S. high school seniors admitted to using steroids in 2005.[39]
- Independent surveys (from 2005) suggest that 1.5 to 2 percent of high school athletes in Florida might be using steroids; that means potentially 4,000 out of 215,000 student-athletes are doping.[40]
- In 2005, the CIF estimated that 20,000 to 30,000 out of 700,000 California student-athletes were using steroids; that's approximately 3.6 percent of high school athletes in grades 9–12.[41]
- A 2009 study by the National Institute on Drug Abuse found that 1.3 percent of eighth and tenth graders and 2.2 percent of seniors admitted to trying steroids at least once.[42]

Win with Integrity

Win with Integrity is a program sponsored by USA Track and Field. Members of the U.S. track team visit schools and talk to students about competing drug-free. Participants in the program are encouraged to make the following pledge:

I pledge to make good decisions in my life.
I will be an enthusiastic and positive person.
I will live with integrity every day.
I will lead a healthy, active lifestyle.
I will take pride in my successes on the playing field and in the classroom.
I will be honest and drug-free, knowing cheaters never win.
I am a Champion![43]

To Look Good

The pressure to be thin, toned, and muscular is everywhere—movies, magazines, television, billboards. Though most teen users are athletes trying to build muscle and perform better, some just want to look like a model or bodybuilder. According to a study done in 1997, 38 percent of American teens tried steroids to improve their appearance.[44] Do you think that percentage has gone up or down since then? My guess is that it's gone up or at least stayed the same since the pressure to have chiseled abs and well-defined pecs is still everywhere. The desire to look good also leads some athletes to develop eating disorders, which are discussed in chapter 4.

So, you have a choice—to use or not to use. Only you can make that decision. As a competitive high school athlete, you face real, intense pressures to perform and to win. Coaches, parents, teammates, college scouts, and others may be asking a lot of you, possibly too much. Will you train and compete on your own skill and guts, or will you give yourself a man-made edge? If you choose steroids, just remember there are risks involved—physical and psychological. Also remember that you will be cheating yourself out of the opportunity to compete solely on your own talents and what you have gained through hard work and practice.

What Do You Think?

Teen steroid use is concerning for several reasons. Yes, it's cheating. Yes, it's illegal. But more important for athletes your age are the health risks. Doctors, coaches, parents, school counselors, and others are all trying to find ways to cut down on steroid use by teens. The most effective way they've come up with is random drug testing, just like professional athletes get. But drug testing is not cheap (up to $250 per test!), and there are arguments about who should pay for it and even who should get tested. Should it be athletes only? All students? Athletes plus any student who parks his or her car on school property? And what should the punishment be for students who are "dirty"?

In 2005, the governor of New Jersey signed an order that required drug testing for athletes competing in state championships. This order went into effect during the 2006–2007 school year, making New Jersey the first state to require such testing. The punishment in New Jersey is a one-year ban from competition if a test comes back positive. [45]

According to a follow-up article in January 2012, the New Jersey testing program has been a successful deterrent. There were four positive tests in 2011 and at least eight in the previous four years. Dave Ryden, president of one of the state's athletic conferences, says, "For me, it's not about catching the kids. It's about making the playing field level and keeping the kids safe. . . . If you save one kid, great. If you have zero taking steroids, that's even better." The executive director of the New Jersey State Interscholastic Athletic Association agrees: "If we can save just one kid from going off the deep end or from further damage through our testing policy then I think the program is truly a success."[46]

However, some people, including teens, don't think random drug testing works. Ron, an eighteen-year-old who was part of a round-table discussion on steroids, said part of the reason it won't work is that some trainers help kids avoid getting caught: "In high school, through word of mouth there's always a way around it. . . . Like for drugs, our trainers are like, 'OK, the doctors are coming next week.' They'll tell you how to wash it all away or make it so it doesn't show up. It's not going to make a difference."[47] Also, studies have shown that the percentages of students who report using illegal drugs (steroids, as well as marijuana, cocaine, etc.) do not go down once drug testing starts. In fact, in some studies show the percentage of teens using illegal drugs is higher in schools with random testing than in schools without testing.[48]

What do you think?

Find Out More

Book

Spring, Albert. *Steroids and Your Muscles: The Incredibly Disgusting Story.* New York: Rosen, 2001.

Chapters

Kern, Jennifer. "Testing Student Athletes for Drugs Is Not Appropriate." In *Sports and Athletes: Opposing Viewpoints*, 197–201. Detroit: Greenhaven Press, 2009.

McMahon, Regan. "Young Athletes Use Steroids." In *Sports and Athletes: Opposing Viewpoints*, 182–86. Detroit: Greenhaven Press, 2009.

Rains, B. J. "Testing Student Athletes for Drugs Is Appropriate." In *Sports and Athletes: Opposing Viewpoints*, 192–96. Detroit: Greenhaven Press, 2009.

Smith, Marcia C. "Steroid Use among Youth Is Declining." In *Sports and Athletes: Opposing Viewpoints*, 187–91. Detroit: Greenhaven Press, 2009.

Online Articles

KG Investments. "Q&A Articles: Steroids." TeenGrowth.com, updated February 14, 2012. www.teengrowth.com/index.cfm?action=info_sub&SubCategory=sports_Steroids&CatDesc=Sports&SubDesc=Steroids&Category=sports.

Mayo Clinic staff. "Performance-Enhancing Drugs and Teen Athletes." Mayo Clinic, December 22, 2010. www.mayoclinic.com/health/performance-enhancing-drugs/SM00045.

———. "Performance-Enhancing Drugs: Know the Risks." Mayo Clinic, December 23, 2010. www.mayoclinic.com/health/performance-enhancing-drugs/HQ01105.

The Nemours Foundation/KidsHealth. "Are Steroids Worth the Risk?" Teens Health, reviewed April 2009. kidshealth.org/teen/drug_alcohol/drugs/steroids.html.

Websites and Organizations

NIDA for Teens (teens.drugabuse.gov). The National Institute on Drug Abuse (NIDA) has a division just for teens.

United States Anti-Doping Agency (www.usantidoping.org). This is the organization that promotes and regulates drug-free competition among U.S. athletes on the national teams.

Win with Integrity Program (www.usatf.org/about/programs/WinWithIntegrity). This is the program sponsored by USA Track and Field that encourages young athletes to compete drug-free.

Notes

1. Kathy Mackel, *Boost* (New York: Dial Books, 2008), 244–45.
2. Associated Press, "Judge Stays Barry Bonds' Sentence," ESPN.com, December 18, 2011, espn.go.com/mlb/story/_/id/7360235/barry-bonds-sentenced-two-years-probation-30-days -house-arrest (accessed March 14, 2012).
3. Associated Press, "Jones Pleads Guilty, Admits Lying about Steroids," NBC Sports, nbc sports.msnbc.com/id/21138883/ (accessed March 14, 2012).
4. Bonnie D. Ford, "Landis Admits Doping, Accuses Lance," ESPN.com, May 21, 2010, sports .espn.go.com/oly/cycling/news/story?id=5203604 (accessed March 14, 2012).
5. ProCon.org, "Sports and Drugs: Should the Teammates of Athletes Who Are Found Guilty of Using Performance-Enhancing Drugs in the Olympics Also Return Their Medals?" updated July 22, 2010, sportsanddrugs.procon.org/view.answers.php?questionID=001303#answer -id-006828 (accessed March 15, 2012).
6. "Marion Jones' Relay Teammates Win Back 2000 Olympic Medals," *Aol News*, July 16, 2010, www.aolnews.com/2010/07/16/marion-jones-relay-teammates-win-back-2000-olympic -medals/ (accessed March 15, 2012).
7. Mayo Clinic staff, "Performance-Enhancing Drugs and Teen Athletes," Mayo Clinic, December 22, 2010, p. 1, www.mayoclinic.com/health/performance-enhancing-drugs/SM00045 (accessed March 7, 2011).
8. "Slang Names for Anabolic Steroids," Anabolics Mall, www.anabolicsmall.com/Steroid_ Slang.html (accessed March 5, 2011); The Nemours Foundation/KidsHealth "Are Steroids Worth the Risk?" TeensHealth, April 2009, kidshealth.org/teen/drug_alcohol/drugs/steroids .html (accessed March 6, 2011).
9. Albert Spring, *Steroids and Your Muscles: The Incredibly Disgusting Story* (New York: Rosen, 2001), 7, 9; Steve Courson, "Performance-Enhancing Drugs Should Be Banned from Sports," in *Sports and Athletes: Opposing Viewpoints*, ed. Christine Watkins (Detroit: Greenhaven Press, 2009), 170–72; ProCon.org, "Sports and Drugs: Historical Timeline," sportsanddrugs .procon.org/view.resource.php?resourceID=002366 (accessed March 15, 2012); Shaun Assael, "High School Testing Losing Momentum," *ESPN: The Magazine*, March 5, 2009, sports.espn.go.com/espn/otl/news/story?id=3951039 (accessed March 15, 2012); Drug Free Sport, "NCAA Summer Drug Testing," *Insight Newsletter*, 2006, www.drugfreesport.com/ newsroom/insight.asp?VolID=35&TopicID=7 (accessed March 15, 2012).
10. Mayo Clinic staff, "Performance-Enhancing Drugs: Know the Risks," Mayo Clinic, December 23, 2010, p. 1, www.mayoclinic.com/health/performance-enhancing-drugs/HQ01105 (accessed March 7, 2011).
11. Anita Bean, *The Complete Guide to Sports Nutrition: How to Eat for Maximum Performance* (Guilford, CT: The Lyons Press, 2004), 77.
12. Mayo Clinic staff, "Know the Risks," 2.
13. Mayo Clinic staff, "Know the Risks," 2.
14. Russ Paddock, "Energy Drinks' Effect on Student-Athletes and Implications for Athletic Departments," *Sport Journal* 11, no. 4 (2008), www.thesportjournal.org/article/energy -drinks-effects-student-athletes-and-implications-athletic-departments (accessed March 16, 2012).
15. Seema Mehta, "CIF Tosses Penalty Flag at Steroids," *Los Angeles Times*, September 26, 2005, articles.latimes.com/2005/sep/26/local/me-steroids26 (accessed March 19, 2012).

16. "U.S. Sports Stars Try to Dim Doping Fears with 'Project Believe,'" AFP, April 16, 2008.

17. Mike Puma, "Not the Size of the Dog in the Fight," ESPN.com, espn.go.com/classic/biography/s/Alzado_Lyle.html (accessed March 7, 2011).

18. Puma, "Not the Size."

19. Seth Livingstone, "Fight against Steroids Gaining Muscle in High School Athletics," *USA Today*, June 8, 2005, www.usatoday.com/sports/preps/2005-06-08-sports-weekly-steroids-report_x.htm (accessed March 7, 2011).

20. "Lyle Martin Alzado," Find a Grave, www.findagrave.com/cgi-bin/fg.cgi?page=gr&GRid=4672 (accessed March 10, 2011).

21. Mayo Clinic staff, "Know the Risks," 1.

22. Spring, *Steroids and Your Muscles*, 27–28.

23. The Nemours Foundation/KidsHealth, "Are Steroids Worth the Risk?," 3.

24. The Nemours Foundation/KidsHealth, "Are Steroids Worth the Risk?," 3.

25. Spring, *Steroids and Your Muscles*, 29.

26. Mayo Clinic staff, "Know the Risks," 2.

27. Mayo Clinic staff, "Know the Risks," 2.

28. Mayo Clinic staff, "Know the Risks," 2.

29. Robyn Norwood, "Young Athletes, Energy Drinks: Bad Mix?" *Florida Today*, December 4, 2011.

30. Mark Schlereth, "The Steroid Danger You Can't Ignore," *Men's Health*, September 26, 2007, www.menshealth.com/best-life/steroids-addiction (accessed March 10, 2011).

31. "'Roids Are All the Rage," *USA Today*, June 8, 2005, www.usatoday.com/sports/preps/2005-06-08-sw-special-report-steroids-roundtable_x.htm?loc=interstitialskip (accessed March 10, 2011).

32. Spring, *Steroids and Your Muscles*, 15.

33. "Abner Doubleday," Tulane.edu, www.tulane.edu/~latner/Doubleday.html (accessed October 30, 2011); "Abner Doubleday Didn't Invent Baseball," Who-Invented-Baseball.com, who-invented-baseball.com/abner-doubleday-didnt-invent-baseball/ (accessed October 30, 2011).

34. "Historian Disputes Who Created Baseball," FoxSports, March 13, 2011, msn.foxsports.com/mlb/story/official-major-league-baseball-historian-disputes-who-invented-game-031311 (accessed October 30, 2011).

35. Francois Fortin, ed., *Sports: The Complete Visual Reference* (Willowdale, ON: Firefly Books, 2000), 220.

36. "'Roids Are All the Rage."

37. Regan McMahon, "Young Athletes Use Steroids," in *Sports and Athletes: Opposing Viewpoints*, ed. Christine Watkins (Detroit: Greenhaven Press, 2009), 183.

38. McMahon, "Young Athletes Use Steroids," 183.

39. McMahon, "Young Athletes Use Steroids," 183.

40. Livingstone, "Fight against Steroids."

41. Mehta, "CIF Tosses Penalty Flag."

42. NIDA for Teens, "Anabolic Steroids," teens.drugabuse.gov/facts/facts_ster1.php (accessed March 6, 2011).

43. USA Track & Field, "The 'Win with Integrity' Pledge," www.usatf.org/about/programs/WinWithIntegrity/ (accessed March 6, 2011).

44. Spring, *Steroids and Your Muscles*, 19.

45. McMahon, "Young Athletes Use Steroids," 186.

46. Kevine Minnick, "NJ Sees Success in Fighting Steroids in Schools," *Greenwich Time .com*, January 22, 2012, www.greenwichtime.com/sports/article/NJ-sees-success-in-fighting -steroids-in-schools-2673959.php (accessed April 5, 2012).

47. "'Roids Are All the Rage."

48. The results are from a 2003 University of Michigan Drug Testing Study cited in Jennifer Kern, "Testing Student Athletes for Drugs Is Not Appropriate," in *Sports and Athletes: Opposing Viewpoints*, ed. Christine Watkins (Detroit: Greenhaven Press, 2009), 199.

STAYING OFF THE INJURED LIST

··

"I believe injuries are most often the hardest thing to deal with. . . . Not being able
to compete is devastating when you have put in so much work doing your sport."
—*Lauren, 22, track and field*

Disclaimer: I'm not a doctor. I'm a sports fanatic just like you, which means I understand what a bummer it is to be injured. Like some of you, I've played through pain instead of going to the doctor because I didn't want to find out what I had done. I've had my share of sprained ankles (thanks to volleyball, softball, and football), and I know the agony of watching from the sidelines while on the injured list. I've also had shoulder surgery (too much softball), and I know what it's like to go through rehab and wonder if you're ever going to play the same. So, you can believe me when I say that I understand if you're reluctant to get that pain checked out. But please do. As you read this chapter, if you suspect that you have a concussion or some other sports injury, please go to the doctor and let a professional diagnose your injury and help you get better. In almost every case, the longer you wait, the worse it's going to get.

The good news is that there's a lot you can do to avoid sports-related injuries, so we'll start this chapter with prevention tips.

The Best Defense Is a Good Offense

Have you heard the saying that the best defense is a good offense? It definitely applies to injury prevention. By their very nature, sports put a strain on muscles, joints, tendons, and ligaments. However, that strain doesn't have to end in injury. By taking action long before you step onto the court or dive into the pool, you can greatly decrease the chance of injury.

> "Build a good strength-training program, even if your school doesn't include it as part of the training for your sport. If I had been lifting in high school, I might not have had the same problems with my shoulder."
> —Noah, 20, volleyball

1. Don't wait until the season starts to work on strength training. If you strengthen your joints, tendons, ligaments, and muscles all year long, you're less likely to sprain or tear something once your season starts. A strong body is more resilient; it is less affected by the twists, teaks, and awkward landings that happen in the course of a game. In this chapter you'll find sidebars with strengthening exercises for your ankles, core (abdomen, lower back, and butt), knees, and shoulders. These joints and/or muscle groups are involved in almost every sport. See chapter 7 for more information on resistance training in general.

2. Don't skip warm-ups. Laura Atkinson is a licensed massage therapist who works with a lot of injured high school athletes as part of their rehabilitation. She

Muscles

This may be a review for most of you, but just in case, here's a rundown of the main muscle groups used in athletic activity (I added the more common slang term in parentheses). To prevent injuries, your pre-exercise warm-up should include stretching all muscles used in your sport.

Abdominals (abs)—six muscles on your abdomen; hence the term *six-pack*

Biceps—muscles on the front side of the upper arm

Gastrocnemius—calf muscles

Gluteus maximus and minimus (glutes)—butt muscles

Hamstrings—muscles that run down the back of your thigh

Hip flexors—muscles on the front of your upper thighs, just below the hip bone

Obliques—muscles on the sides of your abdomen

Pectorals (pecs)—chest muscles

Quadriceps (quads)—muscle group in the front of your thigh

Rotator cuff—group of muscles and tendons that stabilizes the shoulder

Triceps—muscles on the back side of the upper arm

says there's one cause that's at the root of most injuries she sees: practicing or playing without a proper warm-up.[1]

A proper warm-up includes the following steps, performed in this order:

- *Slowly jog, swim, or skip to get the muscles warm.* This stage should take around five to ten minutes.
- *Stretch.* Never stretch cold muscles! That's another way to injure yourself. After your slow jog, stretch each muscle group slowly and without bouncing; this stage should take about five to ten minutes. Atkinson says another problem is that athletes don't stretch all of their muscles; for example, they might stretch their quadriceps in the front of their thighs but not the hamstrings in back.[2] Make sure you get all the key muscles and joints—hamstrings, quadriceps, calves, hips, groin, ankles, shoulders, neck, triceps, biceps, chest, and wrists. (See chapter 7 for more information on stretching and increasing flexibility.)
- *Perform sport-specific actions.* Depending on your sport, this will involve light throwing, passing, hitting, or kicking. Start off slow and controlled, maybe at half speed/strength. Concentrate on technique and work your way up to full speed/strength. This stage often moves right into game or the hard part of the workout.

3. Wear the appropriate protective gear. This gear differs for each sport, but it's likely to include a mouth guard, shin guards, pads, and more. Also make sure your equipment, including your shoes, fits correctly.

4. Learn and use proper form. Many injuries result from incorrect technique. You put unnecessary or unnatural strain on muscles or joints if you don't perform the throw, put, swing, or jump correctly. Talk to your coach to find out if there's anything you should change to avoid injury.

5. Stay hydrated. Loss of fluids and electrolytes can lead to dehydration and fatigue, and tired athletes are more likely to get injured. Drink plenty of water and sports drink before, during, and after every practice and competition.

Because guys play a more physical game of lacrosse, helmets with full face guards, shoulder pads, padded gloves, and mouth guards are all mandatory. In the girls' game, only goggles and mouth guards are required since intentional player-to-player contact is illegal. *Photo courtesy of Jupiterimages/ Thinkstock.*

! Most Common and Most Preventable

Between 2005 and 2009, the Scripps Howard News Service analyzed 99,793 high school sports injuries treated in emergency rooms at one hundred U.S. hospitals that were participating in a U.S. Consumer Product Safety Commission surveillance program. Of the 99,793 injuries analyzed, nearly one-third (32,765) were categorized as a sprain or strain. The next closest category was a fracture, with 18,811.[3] The good news about those numbers is that sprains and strains are also among the most preventable injuries. Take a mere *fifteen minutes* to warm up and stretch before every practice or game, and you could avoid being out for weeks or even months.

Sports drinks in particular can help replenish glycogen and reduce the effects of fatigue. If your coach doesn't call for regular water breaks, ask him or her to start doing so.

6. *Take breaks from your sport.* More and more teenage athletes are playing their sport year-round. As a result, their joints and muscles don't get a rest from the repetitive activities involved, whether it's throwing or swinging or jumping. If you want to stay healthy, you might need to take a season off from one of your teams.

Injuries Happen

Even if you wear all the right protective gear, use proper technique, warm up diligently, and strengthen all your muscles, ligaments, and tendons, you might still get injured. It's just part of the risk involved in sports. It's best to be aware of potential injuries for your sport, their causes, and their symptoms. The sooner you find out what happened, the sooner you can start the healing and recovery process and return to the game at 100 percent.

There are basically two types of sports injuries: acute and chronic. *Acute* injuries happen suddenly while playing your sport. They can usually be pinpointed to a single event—sliding into second, getting an elbow in the eye, and so on. *Chronic* injuries happen gradually. They usually result from overusing one joint or muscle group over a long period of time.

What follows is a general overview of the most common high school sports injuries, both acute and chronic. The discussion of each injury answers five questions:

1. What is it?
2. How does it happen?

Playing Hurt Is Not Smart

You played a game of touch football over the weekend, which was fun until you twisted your ankle. You know if you tell your coach, he's going to make you sit out, so you tape it up and try to practice on Monday.

Sound familiar? The fact is, your coach is going to notice even if you don't say anything because you can't perform at 100 percent with a sprained ankle. Just ask Ben Roethlisberger, quarterback for the Pittsburgh Steelers. Prior to spraining his ankle on December 9, 2011, Roethlisberger had a passer rating of 95.1 for the season. With a sprained ankle, his rating dropped to 69.9, primarily because he couldn't put weight on the injured left ankle—the stepping foot for a right-handed thrower—and thus he wasn't getting enough power and accuracy in his passes.[4]

As much as you don't want to admit when you're injured, here are five good reasons to do so:

1. If you keep playing while injured, you're likely to make it worse. This is exactly what happened to Roethlisberger. He aggravated his ankle injury the weekend before the 2011 AFC wild-card playoff game.
2. You might hurt something else trying to compensate for the injured limb. I don't want to pick on Big Ben (well, maybe just a little), but he experienced this side effect as well. Because Roethlisberger couldn't step into his throw, his passes lacked sufficient power. He tried compensating by throwing harder with his arm, but this put more stress on his shoulder, which was apparently already suffering.[5]
3. You'll delay full recovery. If you keep playing and make it worse, you could be out for the rest of the season instead of just a week or two.
4. You could cause permanent damage and end your sports career. If you love sports as much as I do, that's a really depressing thought.
5. You could cause permanent damage that will negatively affect the rest of your life. This is especially a concern if your injury involves your head or neck. Repeated concussions can permanently affect your memory, ability to concentrate, and other mental capacities. Repeated neck injuries could result in paralysis.

3. What are the best ways to prevent it?
4. What are the symptoms?
5. It happened; now what?

Remember: There is no surefire way to prevent a sports injury, other than staying off the playing field. The suggestions provided for each injury can increase the likelihood that you avoid injury, or at least lessen the severity of your injury. In a later section, you'll find a discussion of sport-specific injuries, with common causes and what you can do to prevent them from happening.

Acute Injuries

Concussion

What is it? A concussion is a temporary loss of brain function that results from the brain shifting suddenly inside the skull. The cause can be a direct hit to the head (e.g., hitting the gym floor or another player's helmet) or a violent hit to the upper body that also jars the head (e.g., slamming a shoulder into the boards in an ice rink). Your brain is a mass of soft tissue encased inside your skull and cushioned by spinal fluid. A violent shaking can cause the brain to shift, resulting in temporary loss of mental capacities such as memory and the ability to concentrate. The impact can also cause bleeding and swelling in the brain, which is a far more serious condition. A second hit to the head before the first concussion is fully healed can result in permanent damage, even death.

How does it happen? Most people associate concussions with football because of the repeated head-to-head and head-to-body hits—and rightly so. According to a study of nearly 11 million student-athletes in twelve different sports, football accounted for over half of all concussions reported between the 1997–1998 and 2007–2008 school years. But concussions are not limited to football; they can happen in *any sport* in which a player might receive a jolt to the head or a blow to the body that causes the head to move rapidly back and forth—for example, basketball (hitting the gym floor) and soccer (slamming into another player while jumping to head the ball). In fact, that same study found that after football, girls' soccer had the highest number of concussions.[6]

What are the best ways to prevent it? The best way to prevent a concussion is by wearing the proper protective gear for your sport. Most important, of course, is a properly conditioned and certified helmet. Some mouth guard manufacturers and dentists claim that wearing a properly fitted mouth guard can lessen the severity of concussions. Also, try to keep your head physically out of the play; for example, don't lead with your head when you tackle an opponent. The key

Postconcussion Syndrome

After suffering a concussion, some people experience postconcussion syndrome—they have concussion-like symptoms long after the injury itself takes place. The most common symptoms of postconcussion syndrome are headaches and dizziness. Other symptoms include

insomnia,

fatigue,

depression,

anxiety,

irritability,

personality changes (becoming more argumentative, stubborn, or suspicious), and

loss of concentration and memory.

Postconcussion syndrome often starts around seven to ten days after the injury happened, and the symptoms can continue for three to six months; some people experience symptoms for a year or more. Researchers aren't sure why some people develop postconcussion syndrome and others don't. There doesn't seem to be any link between the severity of the concussion and the risk of experiencing postconcussion syndrome.[7]

Unlike breaking your arm or spraining your ankle, postconcussion syndrome is often invisible to other people. Your closest friends and family might notice that you're more irritable or stubborn, but to most people, you look normal. Kate Pellin, a basketball player who missed half of her junior year after her fourth concussion, says, "My teachers couldn't understand why I couldn't do my homework. . . . I didn't have crutches, where everyone can see you're hurt. It's a hidden injury. Boys would tell me, 'You should wear a head brace!' like ha-ha, and I was like, 'Maybe that's what I should do for you to take me seriously.'"[8]

For a fictional picture of a teenage athlete struggling with postconcussion syndrome, read *Open Ice* by Pat Hughes (summary included on page 214 in the Ice Hockey section).

to preventing permanent damage from a concussion is making sure you're fully healed before returning to action. To do this, you (and your teammates, coaches, athletic trainers, and parents) have to know and recognize concussion and post-concussion symptoms in the first place.

What are the symptoms? You can't see a concussion, but you might experience one or more of the following symptoms:

- Dizziness
- Headache or pressure in your head
- Nausea and/or vomiting
- Loss of balance
- Sensitivity to light or noise
- Feeling sluggish or foggy
- Difficulty remembering
- Trouble concentrating
- Double vision

You might also just feel like something is not quite right. *Don't ignore any of these symptoms* in the hours, days, and even weeks after you bump your head.[9] Notice that loss of consciousness is not on this list. It's possible to have a concussion without blacking out; in fact, most athletes don't lose consciousness.

It happened; now what? Robert Cantu, a neurosurgeon and concussion expert, says a player should not return to practice or competition until he or she has been

Rule Change

To underscore the seriousness of any concussion, the National Federation of State High School Associations (NFHS) changed its rule regarding concussions. The rule used to state that officials had to remove from the game any player that was unconscious or apparently unconscious, which makes sense. However, by some accounts, 90 percent of athletes with concussions never lose consciousness. The new NFHS rule, which went into effect for all sports during the 2010–2011 school year, takes this stat into consideration. Now officials and/or coaches must remove from a practice or game "any player who exhibits signs, symptoms or behaviors consistent with a concussion (such as loss of consciousness, headache, dizziness, confusion or balance problems)." The rule also says that athletes showing concussions symptoms "shall not return to play until cleared by an appropriate health-care professional."[10]

Second-Impact Syndrome

In September 2009, sixteen-year-old Jaquan Waller suffered a concussion during football practice. The person who examined Jaquan cleared him to play in a game two days later. During the game Jaquan was tackled—nothing bell-ringing, just an ordinary tackle. Jaquan went to the sidelines, where he suddenly collapsed. He died the next day.[11]

In October 2011, sixteen-year-old defensive tackle Ridge Barden was having an ordinary football game. During the third quarter, he collided with an opposing player at the line of scrimmage the way he had done dozens, if not hundreds, of times before. Ridge didn't emerge from the collision shaking his head or looking dazed or doing anything else that would suggest something was wrong. Then Ridge just collapsed as he and his teammates prepared for the next play, and he died a few hours later.[12]

What happened? In both cases, the football players died from something called second-impact syndrome. The first hit that each player received—for Jaquan, the concussion a few days earlier; for Ridge, a tackle that happened sometime during the first three quarters or possibly earlier in the week at practice—injured the brain and possibly caused some bleeding or swelling. Then the second hit caused the rapid decline and death. A medical examiner in Jaquan's case noted that with second-impact syndrome, neither hit would be enough to cause death; it's the combination of the two.[13]

These sad stories illustrate the importance of making sure you and your teammates fully recover from a concussion before playing again. According to one study, high school baseball has the worst record for allowing players back into the game too soon after a concussion. Football is actually the best about making players wait, probably because there is more general awareness about concussions in football. No matter how the concussion happens, it's important to stay out of the game until all symptoms are gone. Because young adult brains are still developing, teen athletes have a higher risk of second-impact syndrome if they suffer a second concussion before the first has healed.[14]

These stories also illustrate the importance of doing everything you can to keep your head out of the game—at least the physical impact part of it. No one knows which first hit made Ridge vulnerable to second-impact syndrome; it could have been the accumulation of several hits. See pages 210–211 in the Football section for specific suggestions regarding football safety.

symptom-free (both while resting and while exercising) for *at least a week*—even if it was the athlete's first concussion and even if it was a mild one. Returning to action too soon has many risks. Because the brain is a bit sluggish, reaction time is slower and coordination is impaired, which means the athlete is very susceptible to other injuries, including a second concussion. In addition, if an athlete hasn't fully recovered from the first concussion, he or she has a lower concussion threshold. In other words, it doesn't take as much force to cause a sudden shifting of the brain. If this happens before the first concussion has healed, the consequences can be deadly.[15] (For more information on the dangers of returning too soon, read about second-impact syndrome on page 181.)

Dislocation

What is it? A dislocation is a separation of two bones where they meet at a joint (e.g., shoulder, finger, ankle).

How does it happen? A dislocation results from a sudden blow to the joint. In contact sports such as football or hockey, a player might dislocate a knee or hip after being hit by an opposing player. In sports such as volleyball or alpine skiing, an athlete might dislocate a wrist or elbow while breaking a fall. A baseball or softball player might dislocate a shoulder while diving to make a catch.

What are the best ways to prevent it? General resistance training to strengthen muscles and ligaments is the best way to prevent a dislocation. After you've dislocated a certain joint, you are more likely to dislocate it again because you've stretched the surrounding ligaments. It's very important to follow your doctor's orders in terms of physical therapy and strengthening exercises in order to prevent a second dislocation.

What are the symptoms? If you dislocate a bone, you'll probably feel sudden and severe pain as well as swelling and bruising in the joint. The area will also look deformed since there's a bone out of its socket. Most likely, you won't be able to move the joint where the dislocation occurred.

It happened; now what? It's important to get to a doctor or the emergency room as soon as possible so the doctor can put your bone back in place. Don't try to do it

What Is the Most Serious Injury You Have Suffered While Playing?

"Sprained wrist. I was playing from trees and hit a root in the ground on my follow-through."—Rachel, 18, golf

"My collarbone cracked during a game. I was pitching the hardest I could and my coach kept forcing me to pitch harder."—Yamil, 14, baseball

"In soccer, I fractured my middle finger playing keeper. In softball, I got hit in my arm by a bat while catching."—Alyssa, 15, softball

"Breaking the growth plate in my left ankle. I dropped back for a pass, threw it, and then was tackled. As I was falling, I landed on my ankle wrong."—Austin, 15, football

yourself! You might damage surrounding nerves, blood vessels, and ligaments. In the meantime, put ice on the dislocated area and don't move it. If possible, have someone splint the joint to keep it from moving.[16]

Fracture

What is it? A fracture is a break or crack in a bone. There are different types of fractures:[17]

- Closed fracture: fracture that doesn't break the skin
- Compound (open) fracture: fracture in which end of the bone breaks through the skin
- Greenstick fracture: bone cracks on one side only
- Hairline fracture: thin break in the bone
- Single fracture: bone is broken in one place
- Segmented fracture: bone is broken in more than one place
- Comminuted fracture: bone is broken is crushed or broken in several places

How does it happen? Like a dislocation, a fracture results from a hard blow or fall. Fractures can happen in any sport, though they are more common in contact sports such as football or rugby. Dr. Michael Magee, a sports medicine orthopedic surgeon, says he's seen a lot football-related breaks: "They are always having finger and clavicle [collarbone] fractures. It happens all the time."[18]

What are the best ways to prevent it? There are three main ways to prevent a fracture:

1. Always wear properly fitted protective equipment for your sport—helmet, pads, and so on.
2. Strengthen your bones through strength and conditioning (see chapter 7 for specific resistance-training ideas). Weight-bearing exercise, or exercise you perform while on your feet, is especially good for building strong bones—running, playing tennis, or jumping rope, for example. Swimming and cycling are excellent cardio workouts, but they're not as effective at strengthening bone.
3. Include enough calcium and vitamin D in your diet, both of which help build strong bones. Milk, cheese, yogurt, broccoli, and fortified orange juice are good sources of calcium. You can also get vitamin D from good old-fashioned sunshine. If you practice or play your sport outside, you probably do this without even thinking about it.

What are the symptoms? Most people experience a lot of pain! Breaking a bone really hurts; your body might go into shock, causing you to feel dizzy, cold, or nauseous. Some people even pass out. You most likely won't be able to move the injured area, and you shouldn't try. The symptoms for a dislocation, fracture, and sprain are very similar. Unless your limb is hanging at an unnatural angle or you see a bone sticking out, you might not know whether you broke a bone until you get an X-ray.[19]

It happened; now what? As with a dislocation, you should get to the emergency room as soon as possible. If an X-ray confirms you have a fracture, the doctor will set your bones back in line. With more serious breaks, this might involve inserting a metal pin into the bone. Then the broken limb is put in a cast, which you'll probably have to wear for one to three months.

Sprain

What is it? A sprain is a stretch or tear of a ligament; ligaments are the bands of tissue that connect the end of one bone to another.

How does it happen? The most commonly sprained area is the ankle: baseball or softball players jam an ankle sliding into a base, basketball or volleyball players jump and land on the side of their foot, football or soccer players plant and roll their foot. Knees and wrists are also commonly sprained joints—knees as a result

Diagnostic Tests

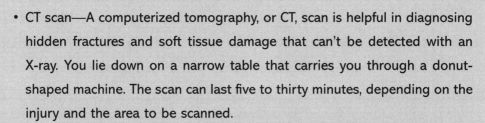

There are different ways that doctors determine exactly what you did to yourself. Here are some of the tests you might undergo as the doctor diagnoses your injury:[20]

- CT scan—A computerized tomography, or CT, scan is helpful in diagnosing hidden fractures and soft tissue damage that can't be detected with an X-ray. You lie down on a narrow table that carries you through a donut-shaped machine. The scan can last five to thirty minutes, depending on the injury and the area to be scanned.
- MRI—Magnetic resonance imaging, or MRI, uses a magnetic field instead of radiation (like a CT scan) to provide an accurate and detailed picture of an injury, particularly in soft tissues. As with a CT scan, you lie down on a narrow table. However, with MRI you are carried into the machine, not through it. If you're claustrophobic (afraid of closed spaces), let the doctor or technician know; when you go into the machine, your face and body are only a few inches from the top and sides. The technician will probably offer you a set of headphones to help block out the sound, which resembles little hammers tapping all around you.
- Ultrasound—Ultrasound uses sound waves to look for soft tissue injuries, particularly in areas such as the rotator cuff in your shoulder. The technician will put a warm jellylike substance on the area to be looked at and then roll the ultrasound "wand" back and forth across the injured area, capturing various images.
- X-ray—During an X-ray, the area with an injury is placed in between the X-ray camera and the X-ray film. The camera briefly exposes the injured area to radiation, and the image shows up on X-ray film. X-rays are primarily used to diagnose broken bones.

> ### ? Did You Know?
>
> According to the National Institute of Arthritis and Musculoskeletal and Skin Diseases, more than twenty-five thousand people sprain an ankle *every day* in the United States.[21]

of a direct blow or sudden twist, wrists as a result of falling and trying to brace the fall.

What are the best ways to prevent it?

- Engage in regular resistance training to strengthen muscles and ligaments.
- Wear athletic shoes that are appropriate for your sport and that fit you properly.
- Replace athletic shoes that have lost their tread or that are worn down on one side.
- Warm up before and cool down after each practice and game. Make stretching a big part of your warm-up/cooldown.
- To ward off fatigue, stay hydrated with water and sports drinks, and fuel your body with carbohydrates before every practice and game. Tired athletes are more likely to get injured (more on proper eating and drinking habits in chapter 4).[22]

What are the symptoms? Symptoms of a sprain include pain, swelling, bruising, an inability to move the injured joint, and an inability to put any weight on the injured joint. You might hear a pop or feel a tear, a sign that you might have a torn or ruptured ligament.

It happened; now what? When treating a sprain, the first concern is to stop or reduce swelling. Remember the acronym RICE: rest, ice, compression, elevation. If you think you sprained something, stop what you're doing and put ice on the joint as soon as possible. Wrap the injured joint in an elastic bandage; the compression will also help reduce swelling. The final step is to elevate the sprained ankle, knee, or wrist above the level of your heart. If you heard a pop and/or are unable to put any pressure on the joint, you should see a doctor right away. He or she will probably do an X-ray to rule out a break.

Strain

What is it? A strain is a twist, pull, or tear of a muscle or tendon; tendons are the cords of tissue that attach muscle to bone. A strained muscle is often called a pulled muscle.

The Dreaded ACL Tear

The most common knee injury among athletes is a torn ACL, or anterior cruciate ligament. The ACL and the PCL (posterior cruciate ligament) form an X at the center of the knee joint and stabilize the knee in front-to-back motion. An ACL injury is a type of sprain that usually occurs in one of three ways:[23]

1. During a sudden stop, pivot, or change in direction at the knee joint; common in soccer, football, field hockey, and basketball
2. When the knee is hyperextended, or straightened, beyond the normal range; can happen on bad dismounts in gymnastics and awkward landings in basketball
3. When the knee receives a direct blow, usually to the outside of the knee or lower leg; happens when a football player is tackled from the side or when a soccer player is slide-tackled

Whereas most ankle sprains heal with rest, ice, and possibly physical therapy, more than 70 percent of ACL tears must be repaired with surgery. Teenagers are more susceptible to ACL tears because their ligaments are still growing, making the knee a weak link. Though sports medicine experts aren't sure why, female athletes who participate in contact sports such as soccer are seven times more likely to injure their ACLs than men who play the same sports.[24]

Shoe On or Off?

If you sprain your ankle, should you (a) leave your shoe on to keep the swelling down or (b) take your shoe off and start icing? The answer is *b*. The longer you wait to take your shoe off, the more painful it's going to be because the swelling is going to make it harder to take off.

How does it happen? If you've watched many track meets, you've probably seen a sprinter suddenly slow up and grab the back of his or her thigh. Most likely, the runner just pulled (or strained) a hamstring muscle. In sports that involve gripping—tennis, golf, rowing—strains of the wrist or forearm are common. Strains are also common in contact sports such as football, hockey, and wrestling.

What are the best ways to prevent it? The prevention methods for a strain are basically the same as those for a sprain: stretch as part of your warm-up and cooldown at every practice and game, use resistance training to strengthen your muscles, and delay fatigue by eating right and staying hydrated. See the list under the Sprain section for more details on strain prevention.

What are the symptoms? The symptoms of a strain include pain, muscle spasms, and weakness in the affected area. You might also experience swelling and cramping.

It happened; now what? RICE therapy is important in treating strains as well as sprains. As soon as you feel the pull in your muscle, stop and get off the practice or playing field. Put ice on the strained area and elevate it as much as possible. If you have an elastic bandage, wrap the injured muscle. You should see a doctor to find out how much damage was done and what he or she suggests for rehabilitation.

❓ What Is the Most Serious Injury You Have Suffered While Playing?

"My left arm broke after a girl pushed into me during the hurdles and I hit the ground."—Anna, 19, track and field

"I pump-faked and the dude jumped right on top of me. It messed up my foot for about a week."—Joseph, 20, basketball

"I twisted my knee at softball practice. We were working on hitting and when I swung the bat, my knee twisted."—Janira, 15, softball

"A deeply bruised shoulder. I went to tackle someone and my teammate hit him at the same time. My arm got stuck between them and the ground and it pulled my arm and slung me to the ground."—Davon, 19, football

"In tennis it's very easy to throw your shoulder if you don't swing correctly and I've done it several times."—Caitlin, 16, tennis

Chronic Injuries

Unlike acute injuries, chronic injuries happen over time. Some people call them repetitive stress or overuse injuries because they result from repeating certain motions over and over—for example, throwing a baseball or swinging a golf club. Teenage athletes who play the same sport all year are more likely to develop overuse injuries because they don't give their joints and muscles a break. When they don't have time to recover, the ligaments, tendons, and muscles in the overused joints can become irritated, inflamed, and/or torn.

Bursitis

What is it? Bursitis is an inflammation, or swelling, of the bursa in a joint due to repetitive stress or overuse. (The bursa is a small fluid-filled sac that helps movement in joints.)

How does it happen? Bursitis in the shoulder is common among athletes who perform repeated overhead movements. In volleyball, for example, the bursa in the shoulder can become inflamed due to repeated serving and spiking. Tennis players and golfers often get bursitis in the elbow, which is also called tennis elbow.

What are the best ways to prevent it? For bursitis as well as most chronic injuries, the best prevention is to avoid overuse:

- Listen to your body. If your shoulder or knee or elbow starts hurting, consider cutting back your practice time for a while.
- Take breaks during practice (every thirty minutes or so) to let your muscles and joints recover.
- Warm up before and cool down after every practice and game. Make sure you carefully stretch the joints that you use the most.

What are the symptoms? Pain and swelling in the affected joint are the main symptoms, and both come on gradually. You might also experience tingling or numbness in the injured joint.

It happened; now what? If you think you have bursitis, stop the activity that's causing the pain and see your doctor as soon as possible. The best thing you can do is rest the affected joint. The doctor may give you rehab exercises to perform after the pain and swelling have disappeared.

Osgood-Schlatter Disease

What is it? Osgood-Schlatter is not actually a disease; it's an overuse injury of the knee in which the tendon that connects the kneecap to the shinbone becomes irritated and inflamed. Osgood-Schlatter is a common source of knee pain in teenagers.

How does it happen? The injury is most common among active teenagers who are going through a growth spurt. During a growth spurt (girls start around age eight to thirteen; boys around age ten to fifteen), bones, muscles, and tendons are all growing rapidly but not necessarily evenly. As a result the area between the knee and the shinbone is weak and easily aggravated by the repetitive running and jumping of sports such as soccer, football, and basketball. Osgood-Schlatter is more common in boys, probably because in general boys are more involved in sports than girls, but this is changing. The good news is that the "disease" usually goes away on its own after a year or two.[25]

What are the best ways to prevent it? Unfortunately, you really can't prevent Osgood-Schlatter disease. Some teen athletes experience it, and some don't. You can, however, reduce the severity of the symptoms by warming up and cooling down as part of any practice or game. Make sure you stretch your leg muscles—quadriceps (front of your thigh) and hamstrings (back of your thigh) in particular.

What are the symptoms?

- Osgood-Schlatter disease usually only affects one knee.
- The pain worsens when you're playing and stops when you're resting.
- The pain and swelling are located just below your knee and above your shinbone.

It happened; now what? The only way to escape the pain of Osgood-Schlatter disease is to stop playing, and this is what doctors suggest if the pain is really bad. If the pain is mild, you can keep playing, but make sure you're honest with yourself, your parents, and your coach about the pain level. After each practice or game, put ice on your knee and shin to reduce the swelling. Your doctor might also suggest an anti-inflammatory such as ibuprofen to keep inflammation down.[26]

Shin Splints

What is it? Shin splints are an overuse injury involving pain along the inside and front of the lower shinbone. Some people have pain on the outside of the shin.

How does it happen? Shin splints are most common in cross-country runners and triathletes who run long distances on hard surfaces. According to Dr. Jordan Metzl, a sports medicine physician, shin splints are especially common in runners who overpronate, or roll their foot toward the inside more than normal. This overpronation puts extra pressure on the inside of the shinbone.[27]

? Do You Overpronate?

How do you know if you overpronate when you run? Look at the bottom of your running shoes. If they are worn down on the inside part of the heel more than on the outside, then you overpronate. If the outside is more worn down, then you underpronate. To help prevent shin splints, overpronators should look for running shoes that offer motion control to compensate for the foot's tendency to roll inward. REI, an outdoor recreation store, has information on its website about choosing the right running shoe: www.rei.com/expertadvice/articles/running+shoes.html.

What are the best ways to prevent it? Stretching the upper and lower calf muscles is an important way to prevent shin splints (always warm up before you do any stretching, even if you just jog in place for a few minutes):

1. Stand facing a wall.
2. Put both hands on the wall and extend one leg straight behind you, keeping both heels on the floor. Keep your front knee behind your big toe.
3. Lightly push against the wall. You should feel a stretch in the upper calf of your back leg (the gastrocnemius muscle). Hold for thirty seconds.
4. From the same position, slightly bend your back knee, still keeping your heel on the floor. Now you should feel the stretch in your lower calf (the soleus muscle). Hold for thirty seconds.
5. Repeat both stretches on the other leg.

Dr. Metzl also suggests buying shoes and orthotics to compensate for overpronation. Look for running shoes made to control motion, that is, that prevent the foot from rolling in. A knowledgeable salesperson will be able to help you find shoes in this category. Also, get over-the-counter orthotic inserts to provide arch support.[28] You can find orthotics at stores such as Walgreens or CVS.

What are the symptoms? Pain is the main symptom. It is usually localized to the inside and front of the lower shinbone. Some people experience pain on the outside of the shin.

It happened; now what? Shin splints can be very painful, but they're fairly easy to get rid of. As soon as you start feeling pain in your shins, start icing your shins after each workout. You should also examine the bottom of your shoes to see if they're excessively worn out on the inside half. You might consider replacing your

What Is the Most Serious Injury You Have Suffered While Playing?

"I tore my ACL. It happened when I was running to block on punt and I turned in the opposite direction and my leg planted and twisted."—Requan, 16, football

"I broke my ankle. It happened in practice. I was jumping and I just landed on my ankle wrong."—Jacque, 22, volleyball

"During a match I over-extended my shoulder, which created a knot behind my shoulder."—Corey, 20, wrestling

"A broken finger. A girl basically grabbed my finger and twisted it until it broke."—Samantha, 17, water polo

"I was hit in the head with a concussion and got a helmet straight into my back on my spine, which jacked my back permanently."—David, 23, football

shoes or adding orthotics. If your shin splints are really bad, you might need to take some time off running to let your legs heal. To keep up your cardio fitness, you could take up cycling or rowing. When you start running again, make sure you stretch your calves so the shin splints don't return.

Stress Fracture

What is it? A stress fracture is a tiny crack in a bone that results from repetitive use. Muscles are supposed to lessen the shock of repeated impacts, but when the muscles are tired from overuse, they don't do their job correctly. As a result, bones absorb more of the stress and develop tiny cracks.[29]

How does it happen? Because the feet and legs absorb most of the weight-bearing impact, stress fractures are most common in the feet, ankles, and lower shins. Athletes who do a lot of running and jumping are most at risk; for example, gymnasts (floor exercise), runners, jumpers (long jump, triple jump), tennis players, and basketball players. Some athletes develop stress fractures because they try to do too much at the beginning of the season, or because they're training in old shoes that have lost their cushion and support. Other athletes develop stress fractures because their sport forces them to switch playing surfaces. For example, some high schools have dirt tracks, some have synthetic, and some have asphalt or cinder. Competing on different surfaces every week can put extra stress on your feet and ankles.[30]

What are the best ways to prevent it?

- Don't try to do too much too soon at the beginning of a new season.
- Give your legs a break by alternating running with other forms of cardio, such as cycling or swimming.
- Eat enough calcium and vitamin D to keep your bones strong.
- Strengthen your muscles through resistance training.
- Replace your athletic shoes if they are old and worn down on the soles.[31]

What are the symptoms? As with all chronic/overuse injuries, the pain of a stress fracture comes on gradually and is usually connected with exercise; once you stop the running, jumping, and so on, the pain subsides. You might also experience swelling in your foot or ankle, depending on where you have the stress fracture.

It happened; now what? Treatment for a stress fracture depends on where it is and how bad it is. The first step is to ice the injured area after every practice and competition. If the pain persists, you'll probably need to take time off your sport to let the bones heal, which can take six to eight weeks. If the stress fracture is in your foot, your doctor might put your foot and lower leg in a cast to ensure that the bones heal correctly.[32]

Tendinitis

What is it? Tendinitis is the inflammation of a tendon due to the repeated use of a certain muscle group. Tendons are the cords of tissue that connect muscle to bone. When muscles are overused in repetitive sports motions, the related tendons become frayed, torn, and irritated.

How does it happen? As with all overuse injuries, tendinitis results from repetitive stress to a certain muscle group. The most commonly affected areas include the following:

- Shoulder, due to the overhead motion involved in throwing (baseball, softball, water polo)
- Knee, due to repetitive jumping; sometimes called jumper's knee (long jump, basketball, volleyball)
- Elbow, due to the motion involved in swinging a racquet or club (tennis, golf)

Shoulder Injuries

The shoulder is the most movable joint in your body, but it's also the most unstable. Muscles, tendons, and ligaments all keep upper arm bone anchored to the shoulder socket, and it's easy to damage these soft tissues through both repetitive stress and sudden events.

Sports that involve an overhead throwing motion put the most strain on the shoulder joint—for example, baseball, softball, and water polo. Most often, sports injuries to the shoulder are chronic, that is, they happen gradually as a result of this repetitive overhead motion. Bursitis and tendinitis are two examples that have already been mentioned, and they often happen in conjunction with each other and with another repetitive stress shoulder injury called impingement syndrome. Repeated overhead throwing can irritate the rotator cuff (the group of four muscles that stabilizes the shoulder) and its tendons. When this happens, the tendons become inflamed (tendinitis) and can become pinched against bone. This pinching of the rotator cuff and its tendons is called impingement syndrome.[33]

Another result of repeated overhead throwing is a fraying of the rotator cuff muscles. At some point, the weakened fibers may tear. Rotator cuff tears often require surgery and months of physical therapy.

Though not as common, athletes do suffer acute, or sudden, injuries to the soft tissues of the shoulder. Acute shoulder injuries result from a direct blow to the shoulder—for example, slamming into the ice rink wall or falling directly on the shoulder—or from a sudden and/or violent pull on the shoulder joint, such as swinging the bat or throwing a long ball from the outfield (this last example usually only happens if you haven't warmed up properly).

The best defense against chronic and acute shoulder injuries is a resistance-training program designed to strengthen the rotator cuff muscles and back muscles, particularly between the shoulder blades. The later section on water polo injuries provides some shoulder-strengthening exercises.

What are the best ways to prevent it? Prevention of tendinitis is basically the same as for bursitis: strengthen the muscles around the overused joint through resistance training, stretch before and after every workout, take breaks in longer practices to let muscles rest, and know when your body needs a longer break from your sport. You can also get into the habit of icing the joint after every practice or game, whether or not you feel pain. This will help keep the inflammation and irritation down.

What are the symptoms? As with other chronic injuries, tendinitis pain increases gradually and is mainly connected with performing the repetitive motion. With tendinitis of the shoulder, you might also experience pain whenever you lift your arm over your head or when you sleep on that shoulder. With tendinitis of the knee, pain is usually localized to the front of the knee, just below the kneecap. With tendinitis of the elbow, pain is usually on the inside of the elbow joint.

It happened; now what? If you develop tendinitis, the first step is to reduce pain and swelling with rest, ice, and anti-inflammatory medication such as ibuprofen. If your tendinitis is mild, you might try wearing a Velcro strap during practice and competition. It's like a brace for your tendon. You've probably seen players

Which Sport Is the Most Dangerous?

In terms of catastrophic injuries, or injuries that potentially result in long-term disabilities (e.g., paralysis) or even death, football is by far the most dangerous high school sport. Between the 1982–1983 and 2009–2010 school years, 747 high school football players were seriously injured, and 113 of those players died of their injuries. The next closest sport is competitive cheer with 78 severe injuries and 2 deaths.[34] (See table 6.1 for the numbers of catastrophic injuries by sport.)

In terms of frequency of sports injuries, however, football is not the highest. Even though football has the most participants nationwide, two other sports have a higher rate of injuries per one hundred thousand athletes: ice hockey and gymnastics. In terms of frequency of injury, ice hockey is probably the most dangerous high school sport for both boys and girls.[35]

wearing the thin strap just below the knee or elbow joint. A sports strap like this is a good idea if you've taken time off and you're just returning to your sport.

Sport-Specific Injuries

Following is a sport-specific discussion of common injuries, usual causes, and the best prevention techniques. For more specific information on the types of injuries themselves (e.g., sprain, stress fracture), see the previous sections on injuries. Prevention techniques mentioned here are specific to each sport. For general sports safety ideas, see the first section (The Best Defense Is a Good Offense) or the prevention tips in the Acute and Chronic sections.

Table 6.1 Direct Catastrophic High School Sports Injuries, 1982–1983 to 2009–2010

Sport	Catastrophic Injuries*
Football	747
Competitive cheer	78
Track and field	65
Wrestling	60
Baseball	58
Ice hockey	25
Basketball	21
Soccer	20
Lacrosse	14
Gymnastics	13
Swimming	13

Sport	Catastrophic Injuries*
Softball	6
Field hockey	3
Cross-country	1
Volleyball	1
Golf	0
Tennis	0
Water polo	0

Source: Most of these statistics are taken from "Table I: High School Fall Sports Direct Catastrophic Injuries," "Table IX: High School Winter Sports Direct Catastrophic Injuries," and "Table XVII: High School Spring Sports Direct Catastrophic Injuries" by the National Center for Catastrophic Sports Injury Research, available at www.unc.edu/depts/nccsi/2010AllSportTables.pdf along with several other tables. The data on competitive cheer are taken from "Table I: High School Female Direct Catastrophic Injuries" by Frederick O. Mueller and Robert C. Cantu, available at www.unc.edu/depts/nccsi/2010Allsport.pdf, p. 28.

*The total number of catastrophic injuries is based on fatal injuries (those that resulted in death), nonfatal injuries (those that resulted in permanent severe disability), and serious injuries (those that were severe but did not result in permanent disability) that directly resulted from participation in the sport; Frederick O. Mueller and Robert C. Cantu, "Catastrophic Sports Injury Research: Twenty-Eighth Annual Report, Fall 1982–Spring 2010," p. 2, www.unc.edu/depts/nccsi/2010Allsport.pdf (accessed January 27, 2012).

Alpine Skiing

Because of the repetitive twisting, high-speed changes in direction, and the dynamics of falling (i.e., the foot stays stationary in boot, while the knee twists and the skis potentially catch on the ground), alpine skiers experience knee and ankle sprains more often than any other injury. The most commonly sprained ligament is the one on the outside of the knee—the medial cruciate ligament. Other common skiing injuries include fractures (collarbone), dislocations (shoulder), and cuts and bruises.[36]

Though not as common, head injuries such as concussions do happen and can be life threatening. Because they're traveling downhill, alpine skiers build up a lot of speed—often over forty miles per hour. If you fall and hit your head after traveling at that speed, the consequences can be serious. Get any head injury checked out even if it seems minor.

To prevent sprains of knees and ankles, make sure you maintain a strength and conditioning program during the off-season. When there's no snow, you can run or cycle for cardio, and you can strengthen your knees and ankles with exercises like the ones mentioned on pages 199 and 209–210, respectively. You can also prevent these injuries by warming up before you ski, including stretching of your legs: hamstrings, quadriceps, calves, and ankles.

Baseball

During his years as a high school baseball coach, Jose Morales has seen mostly minor injuries: sore shoulder, tender elbow, strained hamstring, and strained gastrocnemius (calf muscle). The sad thing is that most of these injuries could be avoided altogether. Coach Morales says that the tender elbows, for example, result from improper throwing mechanics; strained hamstring and calf muscles result from lack of stretching and warm-ups.[37]

A sore shoulder could have several causes (e.g., bursitis, tendinitis, impingement syndrome, torn rotator cuff), all related to the repetitive overhead throwing and pitching motion. Though any fielder can be affected, pitchers suffer most often from overuse injuries to the shoulder and elbow. As a result, there are now guidelines regarding number of pitches allowed per game and the number of days' rest required between games pitched. If you're a pitcher, you should know and follow these guidelines!

Here are a few tips to help you stay off the injured list:[38]

1. Warming up and stretching is not a race.
2. Don't cut corners or you will pay the consequence of sitting on the bench dealing with an injury.
3. If your shoulder or elbow starts bugging you, it might be time to stop playing year-round.
4. Pitchers: Learn pitches in the proper progression, easiest to hardest, and don't try the harder pitches before talking to your coach. The STOP Sports Injuries website suggests learning various pitches at the following ages (give or take a couple years):

Fastball	age eight
Changeup	age ten
Curveball	age fourteen
Knuckleball	age fifteen
Slider	age sixteen
Forkball	age sixteen
Screwball	age seventeen

Ankle Exercises

Try performing the following exercises three times a week to strengthen your ankles. There's no right or wrong number that you should perform, but you could start with three sets of fifteen repetitions unless stated otherwise:[39]

Range of motion exercise. Sit on the edge of a bench, bed, or couch with one foot hanging off the end about two inches. With your shoe off, "draw" small circles in the air using your toe as a "pencil"—first clockwise for fifteen seconds, then counterclockwise for fifteen seconds. Make sure you keep your toe pointed. The movement should occur at your ankle joint. After you do small circles, repeat the exercise by drawing bigger circles in each direction.

Resistance band exercises. These exercises work on range of motion against resistance. (A resistance band is a thin, flat elastic band used in physical therapy and resistance training. The bands come in different strengths and can be found at medical supply stores. Chapter 7 has more information on resistance training with resistance bands and tubes.) Sit on the edge of a bench, bed, or couch with one foot hanging off the end. Wrap the resistance band around your toe (shoes off again) and hold the ends in your hand. You're going to be moving your foot against the resistance band in four different directions: toward the inside, toward the outside, toward you, and away from you (figure 6.1). Do one direction at a time, concentrating on keeping your leg above the ankle as still as possible. You want to make sure you are working your ankle.

Toe raises. Put your shoes on. Stand behind a chair and rest your hands on the chair back. Raise up onto your toes, hold for two seconds, and then take two seconds to lower your heels back to the ground. A variation is to do one leg at a time.

Toe taps. Sit in the chair. Do this exercise one foot at a time. Keeping your heel on the ground, raise the toes of your right foot toward your body and then slowly lower them so they touch the ground.

For more ankle exercises, go to the websites cited in note 39.

Basketball

According to the STOP Sports Injuries website, the most common basketball injuries are

> sprained ankles,
> jammed (sprained) fingers,
> knee injuries,
> deep thigh bruises,
> facial cuts, and
> stress fractures of the foot.[40]

Knowing that knee and ankle injuries are common, make sure you focus on stretching and strengthening of these muscle groups. Taping your ankles might provide stability and pain relief, but don't let your ankles become dependent on the tape. Instead, do exercises to strengthen your ankles. It's also a good idea to take time off from basketball each year to give your knees, ankles, and feet a break from the constant pounding.

To prevent eye injuries, you might consider wearing protective eye goggles, especially if you wear contact lenses. It's not uncommon to get an accidental

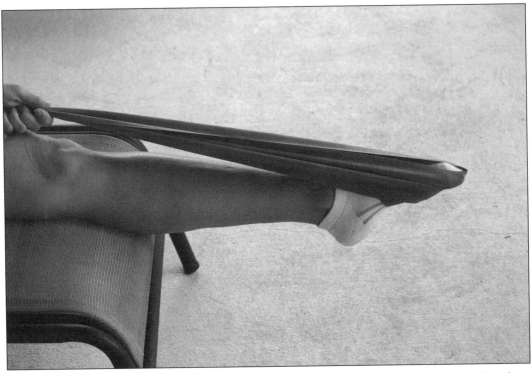

Figure 6.1 Ankle strengthening exercise with a resistance band. *Photo courtesy of Robert Fay.*

Athlete Bio: Eric Katenda, Basketball

When he graduated from high school, six-foot-nine Eric Katenda was ESPNU's number-twenty-seven-ranked power forward in the class of 2011. In May 2011, he signed to play college ball with Notre Dame, but his academic admittance was on hold until he finished a couple classes over the summer at Montgomery College in Maryland. During the summer, Eric was playing a pickup game when he went up for a rebound and got poked in the eye.

"I knew it was bad when it happened," Eric later told the newspaper, describing his injury as a "freak accident."

It turns out that the buildup of blood behind Eric's eye was so bad that it severed the optic nerve, leaving him blind in one eye. Eric says, "Right now I have no vision in my eye. . . . The doctors have told me that they can't do anything to fix that."

In August 2011, Eric started working out again, wearing specially fitted goggles for basketball. Though his future on the Notre Dame team is questionable, Eric is confident that he'll play again: "I'm going to play again. I have no doubts. I'm not worrying about anything."[41]

elbow or finger in the eye, and as Eric Katenda found out, the results can be life changing.

One sports injury not usually associated with basketball is a concussion. However, according to a story by *ABC News*, the number of basketball-related concussions rose 70 percent between 1997 and 2007, and most of the athletes injured were girls. In fact, in high school basketball, girls suffer concussions *three times as often* as guys (see Why Do Girls Suffer More Concussions? on page 219).[42] Concussions in basketball result from collisions—head to floor, head to head, or head to ball. As mentioned earlier, it's very important to recover completely before you start practicing so you don't put yourself at risk of second-impact syndrome.

Competitive Cheer

According to a report by the National Center for Catastrophic Sports Injury Research, competitive cheerleading has the highest number of catastrophic injuries

Athlete Bio: Niki Popyer, Basketball

Niki Popyer used to think about playing basketball in college. She was talented, aggressive, and hardworking, leaving it all on the court every time she played. Unfortunately, her all-out style of play resulted in multiple concussions over the years—eleven total, and seven of them basketball related. The first one happened when she was in seventh grade and Niki hit her head on the gym floor. Concussion number five happened when she was a freshman, and that one left her temporarily blind. With each concussion, the postconcussion symptoms got worse.

In 2010, when Niki was a seventeen-year-old senior, she told a reporter, "I can't concentrate in school, I have a headache 24/7 and I can't do the things I want to do because even a slight hit to the head makes me pass out. I can't play basketball, obviously, which is something I always loved to do."[43]

among female athletes. Among all sports—boys and girls—competitive cheer is second only to football. The neck/spinal cord injuries and severe concussions seen in cheerleading usually result from falls during stunts.[44]

Cheerleaders more commonly experience acute injuries such as broken fingers and ankles, sprained backs, and torn ACLs. Less common injuries include broken noses and knocked-out teeth. If any of these injuries occurs during a cheer competition, the athlete must keep going for the sake of the team, even if that means performing the rest of the routine on one leg because of a broken ankle.[45]

If you try out for a competitive cheer team, take the following steps to prevent injuries:[46]

- Make sure the coach is certified by a cheerleading safety body (such as the American Association of Cheerleading Coaches and Administrators) and is not just a gym teacher.
- Don't practice stunts or gymnastic moves such as handsprings on the bare gym floor. You should always have a mat.
- Always practice with a spotter.
- Gymnastic moves play a big part in competitive cheer routines. If you're new at gymnastics, take a class at a certified gymnastics gym.
- Strengthen your muscles with weights and other resistance training to guard against overuse injuries such as tendinitis of the wrist (from handsprings).

Athlete Bio: Jessica Urquiza, Competitive Cheer

"I would say about 75 percent of my schoolmates do NOT think cheerleading is a sport," says Jessica, age sixteen. "A lot of them think it's all just 'rah, rah, rah,' and you wave some pom-poms in the air, and that's all there is to it. But that's not all; being in shape is a HUGE part of being in cheer." When people tell her that cheerleading isn't a sport, Jessica reminds them that cheerleading involves gymnastics, which is part of the Olympics and is recognized as a sport.

Jessica tried out for a competitive cheer team as a freshman, the same year she joined her high school's cheerleading squad. Just like other sports, competitive cheer involves skills practice, strength training, and endurance (cardio) training. Though high school cheer involves some of the same skills and strength work, Jessica says competitive cheer is much more strenuous: "You have to be able to run a lot, and be tired but be able to keep going. Cardio for competitive cheer is more important than for high school cheer. You have to be able to go for two and a half minutes without stopping." And that two and a half minutes is full of back handsprings, front handsprings, cartwheels, jumping, throwing the flyer, catching the flyer—all while smiling like you're putting in no effort at all.

Jessica practices year-round with her competitive cheer team, both in private one-on-one sessions and with the whole team. It was during one of her private tumbling lessons that Jessica injured her back: "I did a back handspring and my back got a little tweaked. I

Because they perform lots of handstands, back handsprings, and other tumbling stunts, cheerleaders like Jessica are at risk for developing overuse injuries of the wrist and knee. *Photo courtesy of Alycia Collins.*

decided to just shake it off and continue with practice after [the private lesson]. However, the more and more I practiced, the worse and worse it got." It took an X-ray and a few MRIs to determine that Jessica had badly sprained her back. She was out for a few weeks and needed months of physical therapy. In addition, Jessica has tendinitis in her left wrist and permanent knee problems—both over-use injuries due to the pressure applied during back handsprings, back tucks, handstands, and so on.

Jessica and her team travel to about eight competitions a year. As of 2012, she had competed in her home state of California as well as Nevada, Hawaii, and Florida. Jessica hopes to compete as a cheerleader at the college level: "Colleges do offer full-ride scholarships for cheer just like they do for football or for any other sport."[47]

- Strengthen your abs and lower back in particular, since these are the stabilizing muscles needed for most stunts (for suggestions, see pages 205–206 in the Crew section).
- Try yoga or Pilates to increase your flexibility.
- If you do get injured, don't try to play through it. Get it checked out as soon as possible so you don't make it worse.

Crew

Most crew injuries result from overuse. The repetitive rowing motion can cause tenosynovitis (swelling of the sheath around the tendons) in the wrists and forearms, stress fractures in the rib cage, lower back pain, and patellofemoral (knee-cap) pain that gets worse when rowing, going up or down stairs, or doing squats.

Here are a few hints to prevent these overuse injuries:[48]

- If you row in cold weather, wear something to keep your wrists warm (a long-sleeved shirt, sweatshirt, etc.).
- To prevent rib stress fractures, focus on strengthening your upper back and core (made up of your abdominal, lower-back, hip, and butt muscles).
- To prevent lower back pain, your training should include core strengthening and flexibility exercises (see the core exercises for suggestions). Also take breaks to stretch between rowing intervals.

Core Exercises

No matter what your sport, a strong core can provide stability and power. The following exercises focus on your abdominals, lower back, and glutes (butt muscles); there's no right or wrong number that you should perform, but you could start with three sets of fifteen repetitions. To have a balanced core and to avoid muscle strains, it's important to work your front and back; in other words, if you do crunches for your abs, make sure you do something to work your lower back.

Crunches. This is a common exercise, but many people do it incorrectly. Lie on your back with your knees bent, hands behind your head, and elbows wide. Concentrate on using your abdominal muscles to lift your head, neck, and upper back off the floor. Don't sit all the way up; it's actually a fairly small upward movement. Think about pulling your navel toward your spine. Keep your neck straight so that you're almost looking at the ceiling as you crunch up. Don't pull on your head with your hands; your hands are there to support your neck. And lastly, don't forget to breathe: exhale as you crunch up, inhale as you lower back down. Once you have the basic move you can add variations:

Crunch up quickly (one count), then lower yourself slowly (count to three)

Count to three on the way up, then lower yourself quickly

Count to two on the way up and on the way down

Hold a dumbbell (five or ten pounds) in front of your chest as you do crunches

You can also perform the crunches and variations on a stability ball (the large inflatable exercise ball; there's one in figure 6.2) instead of the floor. To stabilize on the ball, start with your feet fairly wide apart. The closer your feet are to each other, the harder it is.

Oblique crunches. Obliques are the muscles on the sides of your abdomen. Instead of doing the basic up-and-down crunch, twist your midsection as you come off the floor. Keep your elbows wide and think about connecting your shoulder—not your elbow—toward the opposite knee as you twist. You won't actually touch shoulder to knee, but it will help you remember to keep your elbows open. Remember to pull your navel toward your spine and to breathe. For a variation lift your feet off the floor and hold your legs up so your calves are parallel to the floor. Push one foot away from you as you pull the other one toward you, and twist your upper body at the same time—shoulder toward the knee that you're pulling in. Some people call this exercise bicycle crunches. You can also do stationary oblique crunches on a stability ball. Brace your feet against a wall, lean over the ball sideways, and crunch up sideways away from the ball; then switch sides.

Back extension. You need a stability ball for this one. Lie over the ball so that your stomach is about in the middle of the ball. Place your hands near your ears. Pull your navel toward your spine, contract your glutes, and slowly lift your upper body off the ball using your back muscles (see figure 6.2). Stop when your shoulders, hips, and knees are in a fairly straight line, then slowly lower yourself back down. The person in figure 6.2 could make this exercise more difficult by moving his feet closer together. For a variation, hold your arms out in front of you in a Superman pose.[49]

Prone lat pull. The "lat" (short for latissimus dorsi) is the big, flat muscle on each side of your middle and lower back. Roll onto a stability ball so that you are in a plank push-up position, arms straight and shoulders directly over your wrists. Your hips should be on the ball; your torso should be off the front of the ball and your legs should be off the back. Keeping your hands on the floor, push back so that your arms are stretched out in front of you. Then, keeping your arms straight, pull your body back across the ball so that you end up in plank push-up position. You'll need to contract your core (pull navel toward spine) and tighten your glutes to remain stable.[50]

For more core exercises see chapter 8 in *Strength Ball Training* and chapter 5 in *Strength Band Training*; both books are listed in the Find Out More section at the end of this chapter.

Figure 6.2 Back extension exercise. *Photo courtesy of Polka Dot Images/Thinkstock.*

- Knee pain can be prevented with leg strengthening exercises and stretching. However, once you develop knee pain, you'll probably have to limit or cut out squats and stair work since this will aggravate the condition.

As with most overuse injuries, it's sometimes necessary to take time off from rowing to heal. Icing your injury and taking anti-inflammatory drugs such as ibuprofen can help decrease swelling and pain.

Cross-Country

The most common injury among cross-country runners is shin splints, an overuse injury that results from running long miles on hard surfaces. The best prevention is to find grass or dirt trails to run on instead of concrete. When that's not possible, it might help to ice your shins after a long run in order to reduce the swelling and pain. If your running shoes are old or worn down on one side, ask your parents about replacing them since worn-out shoes can contribute to shin splints. Former cross-country coach Saralyn Hannon says that in really bad cases, athletes have to supplement their cardio workouts with running in the pool or riding a stationary bike and lay off running indefinitely.[51]

Diving

Swimmers and divers are both susceptible to overuse injuries of the shoulders, but for different reasons. For swimmers, it's the repetitive overhead strokes such as freestyle; for divers, it's the repetitive flips and twists that can cause problems. These acrobatic moves can also lead to back injuries. The most important prevention step for divers involves core-strengthening and core-stabilization exercises. According to Jim Clover, coordinator at the S.P.O.R.T. Clinic in Riverside, California, divers have to make sure to work on their back muscles as well as their abs; as he says, "Whatever you do in the front, do to the back."[52] For core exercises, see pages 205–206 in the Crew section as well as the resources at the end of this chapter.

Field Hockey

According to the STOP Sports Injuries website, these are the most common field hockey injuries and their causes:[53]

Hand and wrist (fractures)—contact with ball or opponent's stick
Face (cuts, bruises, fractures, broken teeth, eye injuries)—contact with ball or opponent's stick
Ankle (sprain)—rolled ankle
Knee (ACL tear)—sudden stop or pivot
Concussion—player-to-player, player-to-ground, or player-to-goalpost contact
Overuse injuries—low back pain from bending at the waist while running; tendinitis of the hip, knee, or ankle

To prevent knee sprains, use the strengthening exercises suggested on pages 209–210; to prevent ankle sprains, try the exercises on page 199. Also make sure you warm up before every practice and game, devoting plenty of time to stretching your ankles, hips, hamstrings, and quadriceps. These tips will also help you avoid overuse injuries.

Football

As already mentioned, football has the highest incidence of catastrophic injuries in high school sports, mostly involving concussions and traumatic brain injury. As a football player, what can you do to protect your head and still play the game you love?

Knee Exercises

According to physical therapists Phil Page and Todd Ellenbecker, knee pain and injury have been linked to an imbalance of strength and flexibility between the quadriceps (front of the thigh) and the hamstrings (back of the thigh).[54] The following exercises can help strengthen both muscle groups and provide stability to the knee joint as a whole. There's no right or wrong number that you should perform, but you could start with three sets of fifteen repetitions.

Knee flexion. This exercise works your hamstrings. Tie both ends of a resistance band to a stationary object (no higher than knee level when you're seated). Sit on a bench or chair facing the place where the band is attached. Extend one leg straight out and loop the middle of the band around that ankle. Slowly flex (bend) your knee toward you, so your foot moves toward the floor. Then slowly straighten your knee back to the starting point. Make sure you sit up tall and contract your core. Repeat on the other leg.[55] (This exercise follows the same movement as the knee flexion machine at the gym, where the back of your heels rest on a padded bar.)

Knee extension. This exercise works your quadriceps. Tie both ends of a resistance band to a stationary object (no higher than knee level when you're seated). Sit facing away from the place where the band is attached. Loop the band around your ankle and foot (the band should be under the bottom of your foot and cross in front of your ankle). Start with your knee bent and your foot on the ground. Slowly extend your knee away from you until your leg is straight, then slowly return to the starting place. Make sure you sit up straight and contract your abs. Repeat on the other leg.[56] (This exercise follows the same movement as the knee extension machine, where you slip the front of your ankles behind a padded bar and press up.)

Stability ball knee flexion. This exercise works your hamstrings and your hips. Lie on your back with your heels on top of the stability ball. Put your arms out to the sides to help you balance. Squeeze your glutes and lift your hips off the ground until your ankles, knees, and hips are in a straight line. Slowly pull the ball toward you by flexing (bending) your knees. Once your feet are flat on the ball, stop and reverse the motion: extend your knees until your legs are straight and then lower your hips. When you first try this exercise, the ball will probably wobble around. Contracting your core and glutes and pressing your heels into the ball will help you stabilize.[57]

Wall squat. This exercise works your quadriceps. Stand facing away from a wall. Put the stability ball between the middle of your back and the wall. Lean against the ball and move your feet away from you slightly, keeping them shoulder width apart. Press your heels into the ground, contract your core, and slowly lower your hips toward the floor. Stop when your thighs are parallel with the floor. Your knees should stay behind your toes; if they are past your toes, readjust your position by moving your feet farther away from your body. After a slight pause at the "sitting" position, slowly extend your legs until you return to a standing position.[58]

For more knee-strengthening exercises, see the books listed in the Find Out More section.

1. Learn proper blocking and tackling techniques, no matter what position you play. The bottom line is, *don't hit with your head.*
2. Don't be afraid to admit you're hurt, especially if the injury involves your head. At a minimum, multiple concussions can leave you with constant headaches and serious concentration problems. At the other extreme, multiple concussions can lead to chronic traumatic encephalopathy (degenerative brain disease) or death (see the second-impact syndrome information on pages 181–182).
3. Find out how old your football helmet is and when it was last reconditioned. In 2011, the National Athletic Equipment Reconditioners Association (NAERA) decided that its members will no longer recondition or recertify helmets that are more than ten years old.[59] If the NAERA drew the line at ten years for the sake of safety, your school should do the same. As the player wearing the helmet, you have a right to know how old it is.
4. Find out if your school has a certified athletic trainer. If not, find out who to petition so the school can hire one. If you're told the school can't afford a certified trainer, consider contacting Advocates for Injured Athletes (A4IA). The stated goal of this nonprofit organization is "to bring a certified athletic trainer to every high school campus in America."[60] A4IA was

started by Tommy Mallon and his mom in 2009, about six months after Tommy's life was saved by a certified athletic trainer. (You can read more about Tommy, his injury, and his organization on pages 215–216 in the Lacrosse section.)

5. If you get a concussion, don't practice or play a game until you are cleared by a doctor. This might be the hardest advice to follow, especially once you start recovering from all symptoms. Be patient. It's better to miss a few games than the rest of the season or your career.

Besides concussions, football players are likely to suffer sprains and fractures of various body parts—ankles, knees, shoulders, and hands in particular. Weight

Rule Changes in Pop Warner

Concussion safety is a hot topic in professional, collegiate, and high school football. But what about the youth leagues such as Pop Warner? How do we know conditions such as chronic traumatic encephalopathy don't start with hits to the head when players are as young as five or six? It's exactly this concern that led Pop Warner—the nation's biggest youth football league—to institute some new rules in August 2012:

1. Contact will only be allowed for one-third of each practice. The term *contact* "means any drill or scrimmage in which players go all out with contact, such as one-on-one blocking or tackling drills."[61] Evidence shows that in youth football, the hardest hits often occur in practice and not games.
2. Coaches can no longer use drills that "involve full-speed, head-on blocking and tackling that begins with players lined up more than three yards apart, as well as head-to-head contact."[62]

By starting with these two rule changes, Dr. Julian Bailes, chairman of the Pop Warner medical advisory board, thinks they can eliminate at least 60 percent of the brain impacts and concussions sustained among the 285,000 five- to fifteen-year-olds who play Pop Warner nationwide.[63]

training can strengthen muscles and ligaments, which can help prevent sprains and strains. Strengthening your neck muscles can also help you keep your head up and straight when tackling, decreasing the chance of neck injuries. Eating enough calcium and vitamin D can help strengthen bones, as can year-round weight-bearing exercise.

One last injury football players are at risk for is heat exhaustion and heatstroke. These are considered indirect injuries since they aren't directly linked to the contact action involved in the sport. See chapter 4 for more details on avoiding heat exhaustion. The key is to stay hydrated, especially during pre-season two-a-days when temperatures and humidity are still high.

Golf

All in all, golf is one of the most injury-free sports. The most common injuries involve the back, shoulder, and elbow—all related to the repetitive motion involved in the golf swing. Other causes of golf-related injuries include poor conditioning, bad swinging technique, and/or lack of flexibility (range of motion)—all of which are fairly easy to correct. Here are a few prevention suggestions:[64]

- Make sure you warm up and stretch thoroughly. Golf doesn't involve the intense physical exertion of, say, basketball or soccer, but you still need to warm up and stretch. Stretching in particular will help with your range of motion. Poor flexibility is one of the biggest risk factors for injury in golf.
- Talk to your coach and make sure your swing technique is correct. If not, find out what you're doing wrong and practice until you get it right. Incorrect form can put a lot of stress on your back and shoulders.
- Stay in good cardiovascular shape so you're not tired halfway through a round. Fatigue can affect your form and lead to injury.

Gymnastics

Gymnasts are injured more frequently than just about any other athlete. Knees and ankles suffer the most trauma, though gymnasts frequently experience sprains and strains in their backs, hands, wrists, and shoulders. Many of these injuries can be avoided:[65]

1. Gymnasts who compete only on high school teams are out of shape compared to gymnasts who train year-round at gymnastics clubs, and out-of-shape athletes tend to get injured more easily. According to one statistic, club gymnasts are injured less than half as often as high school gymnasts.

If you only participate at the high school level, make sure you do all that you can to get into excellent gymnastics shape, which means consistent cardio, strength, and flexibility training.

2. High school gymnastics coaches are less likely to be trained specifically in gymnastics; untrained coaches who don't understand the proper skills progression and safety can contribute to the higher number of athlete injuries. If you only train and compete at your high school, you owe it to yourself to find out what kind of training your coach has.

3. By learning how to stick your dismounts properly, you can save your knees. Specifically, learn to bend your knees when landing in order to absorb the shock.

4. If you are nervous about a new stunt, tell your coach. Make sure you feel ready to try a more difficult move.

5. When you do feel ready to move on to something more difficult, always practice with spotters and your coach present.

6. Always warm up with light cardio and stretching.

Ice Hockey

High school ice hockey players are injured more often than athletes in any other sport, and girls get hurt three times more often than guys. One reason for the higher rate of hockey-related injuries is the playing environment. Both football and ice hockey involve high-speed collisions, but grass is not nearly as hard as ice. Also, many hockey-related injuries result from players being checked from behind and/or slammed into the glass or boards. In 2012 alone, two high school players were paralyzed after being checked from behind, one boy and one girl, both from Minnesota.[66]

According to the STOP Sports Injuries website, these are the other common ice hockey injuries, all of which result from player-to-player, player-to-ice, or player-to-boards/glass collisions:

- Shoulder injury (broken collarbone, separated shoulder)
- Knee injury (torn ligaments)

Did You Know?

Neurologists say that once you've had a concussion, you're up to four times more likely to suffer another one. Also, if you've had several concussions, it takes less of a blow to cause the injury and it takes more time to recover.[67]

- Hand/wrist injury (breaks or sprains)
- Neck/spine injury (break)

Hockey players are also at risk for overuse injuries such as chronic pain in the lower back (due to the forward skating position) and bursitis of the elbow (due to repeated collisions).[68]

To prevent acute, collision-related injuries, always wear the appropriate safety equipment: pads, helmet, mouth guard, and so on. Also, learn to skate with your head up, both so you can see what's going on and so you don't go headfirst into the boards or glass if you do get checked from behind. Preventing overuse injuries involves the same steps as in any other sport: warm up, cool down, stretch, strengthen your muscles, and don't play year-round. Important areas to empha-

Good Read: Open Ice by Pat Hughes

Sport: Ice hockey

Life apps: Career-ending injury, postconcussion syndrome, friendship, family dynamics

Summary: Sixteen-year-old Nick Taglio loves hockey. He's been playing since he was five years old, and now he's a star on his high school team. Then Nick suffers his third concussion, a grade three that knocks him out cold. After the second concussion the doctor had told Nick that one more might end his hockey career. And now Nick hears Dr. Blakeman saying, "I cannot in good conscience clear you to play hockey again."

Open Ice is the story of how Nick deals with the fact that his playing days are probably over. He's angry, frustrated, and depressed, lashing out at his parents, brother, and girlfriend. Nick is also dealing with serious postconcussion symptoms—headaches, feeling tired and "foggy," inability to concentrate—that are making it impossible to keep up in school. The dialogue is sometimes crude and explicit—exactly what you might expect from a sophomore guy who's just lost the only thing he thought he was good at.

Wendy Lamb Books, 2005

271 pages

size when stretching are your hips, hamstrings, quadriceps, and lower back (see chapter 7 for specific stretches).

Lacrosse

According to the STOP Sports Injuries website, the most common lacrosse injuries result from noncontact situations—pivoting, changing direction, and so on. These acute injuries include a

> sprain of the ankle or knee;
> torn ACL; and
> strained (pulled) quadriceps, groin, or hamstring muscle.

Though not as often, players do suffer concussions and other head injuries in lacrosse, particularly in the boys' game, which involves more player-to-player contact. Players can also develop overuse injuries such as shin splints and blisters on their feet.

Athlete Bio: Tommy Mallon, Lacrosse

Having someone on the sidelines who is trained to recognize the symptoms of concussions and other life-threatening injuries could save someone's life—just ask Tommy Mallon, a twenty-year-old former lacrosse player from California. In May 2009, just two minutes before the end of his high school lacrosse career, Tommy collided head-on with an opponent. The hit didn't look serious, but Tommy went down and didn't get up. The certified athletic trainer, Riki Kirchhoff, asked Tommy questions and looked for signs of a concussion. When Tommy told Riki that the back of his head was a little numb, she knew something was seriously wrong. Tommy wanted to get up and play; Riki made him stay on the ground and had someone call an ambulance.

At the hospital Tommy learned that he had burst his C1 vertebrae (the top vertebrae on the spinal column) and a fragment of bone had bisected his spinal cord. "If I had gotten up, I probably would have died or been a quadriplegic," Tommy said later, adding that Riki "basically saved my life." Tommy spent months in a neck brace and halo brace, in addition to months of therapy and treatment.

As of 2012, Tommy was a junior at the University of San Diego. He wasn't able to play lacrosse or other contact sports, but he could hang out with friends and play a little pickup basketball. As he put it, "I'm limited. . . . But I'm alive."[69]

In October 2009, Tommy and his mom started Advocates for Injured Athletes (A4IA), an organization that provides grants that help high schools hire certified athletic trainers like the one who saved Tommy's life. As part of A4IA, in 2011 they started Athletes Saving Athletes, a program in which certified trainers teach "student athletes to recognize the signs and symptoms of serious injury and to help serve as first responders in emergency situations."[70] For more information on either of these programs, go to the A4IA website at www.injuredathletes.com. Click on the "Watch Our Story" link to watch a video of Tommy's injury and hear from the trainer who helped him.

History of Lacrosse

When French missionaries arrived in North America in the 1600s, Native Americans were already playing a form of lacrosse; they called it the Creator's Game. The sport played a part in their religion and was used to resolve conflicts and heal the sick. Around forty-eight different tribes played the game, and the rules varied by tribe. For example, some used one rock or stick as a goal; others used two goalposts.

The French missionaries were intrigued by the Native Americans' sport, and they started playing on their own. By 1800s, the French were avid players, calling the game lacrosse, or literally, the crooked stick. They drew up the first set of rules in the 1860s; the women's game today still follows these basic rules with limited stick contact and no body contact. The men did as well until the 1930s, when the men's version of lacrosse became more physical. Today, guys wear helmets and pads, whereas the women only wear protective eyewear.

Today, lacrosse is one of the fastest growing sports in the United States at all levels—youth, high school, and college.[71]

To prevent sprains, strains, and tears, lacrosse players should stay in shape all year—cardio, weight training, and stretching. In the off-season, try cycling or swimming as a form of cardio so you give your legs a rest and avoid shin splints. Always wear properly fitting protective equipment, and always report an injury, especially if it involves your head.

Nordic Skiing

Nordic, or cross-country, skiers are injured far less frequently than alpine skiers, probably because they don't build up the same speed or make the same quick changes in direction. Still, the most common injuries are the same for both sports: sprains of the ankles and knees. With Nordic skiers, the injuries have more to do with the type of free-heel binding on the skis. Injuries to the knees and ankles often occur in situations where the ski edge "catches" or where the ski stops and the skier keeps going.[72]

Injury prevention is the same as it is for alpine skiing: stay in shape all year long. During the off-season, use running or cycling to keep up your endurance and use weights and stretching to keep your muscles and ligaments strong and flexible. Nordic skiing is all about aerobic endurance or lung capacity. If you don't keep up your endurance training in the off-season, you're more likely to suffer a fatigue-related injury once the season starts.

Soccer

Most soccer injuries involve the legs: kicks to the shin, sprained ankles and knees, strained hamstrings or quadriceps. The most serious of these injuries is a torn ACL, which seems to happen more often as athletes move into high school and the level of play becomes more competitive. Injuries to the legs usually result from illegal plays (e.g., slide-tackling from behind) or poor field conditions.

Head injuries in soccer are not as common but tend to be more serious. They usually result from player-to-player collisions, incorrect heading technique, or collisions with the goalpost. According to one study, goalposts were responsible

Did You Know?

In sports played by girls and guys, girls suffer more concussions. In high school soccer, for example, the number of concussions among female players is 68 percent higher than the number among male players.[73]

Use Your Head . . . Correctly

- Make contact with the ball on your upper forehead, approximately where your hairline starts. Don't use the side or top of your head.
- Tuck your chin in toward your chest.
- Use your arms and upper body to "pull" your head into the ball. You should hit the ball actively; don't let the ball hit you.

for twenty-two soccer player deaths between 1982 and 2002; players either hit their head on the goalpost or the goalpost fell on them.[74]

There are several things you can do to prevent soccer injuries:

1. Make sure you warm up thoroughly before every practice or game. Jog around the field, stretch (focus on your leg muscles in particular—hamstrings, quadriceps, calves), and then pass the ball with a teammate, starting off a short distance apart and slowly increasing the distance. Then move into other warm-up drills, including shots on goal. Never take full-power shots on goal before warming up! That's a sure way to pull a muscle.

2. Learn how to head the ball correctly. If you're embarrassed about not knowing, ask your coach in private (see Use Your Head . . . Correctly above for a few key tips).

3. Check out the goalposts at your school. Are they anchored down all the time? Is there padding on the posts? If the answer to either of these questions is no, talk to your coach and/or the athletic director at your school. With so many injuries caused by goalposts, it only makes sense to make them as safe as possible. One study showed that padding reduces the force of impact by 31 to 63 percent.[75]

4. Don't slide-tackle someone from behind. For one thing, it's illegal and unsportsmanlike; for another, it's one of the main causes of knee and ankle injuries in soccer.

5. Make resistance training a regular part of your fitness program. Your goal isn't to bulk up, so focus on lighter weights and more repetitions. Stronger athletes are less prone to injury.

Softball

Softball pitchers don't have the same injury problems as baseball pitchers because the underhand throw is a more natural motion. Softball fielders, however, are at

Why Do Girls Suffer More Concussions?

The short answer is, no one really knows. It's possible that hormones have something to do with it, since guys and girls have different hormones protecting their brains. It also could be related to the fact that guys generally have stronger necks than girls or the fact that guys and girls have different styles of play.

It's interesting to note that although girls suffer more concussions, they also receive less information about concussions, the symptoms, and the long-term effects seen in postconcussion syndrome. It's almost like female athletes, and their coaches, think of concussions as being a guys' injury. The truth is that studies show girls suffer more symptoms and take longer to recover than guys.

Girls, if you hit your head and experience *any* of the concussion symptoms discussed in this chapter (dizziness, headaches, foggy feeling, double vision, and so on), tell your coach and/or your parents. If you keep playing with a concussion, no matter how "mild," you risk adding to your brain injury. Here's how one writer described the repeated head injuries suffered by a female soccer player: "Melissa's head was like an egg that scrambled without ever cracking."[76]

risk of developing overuse injuries in their throwing shoulder—everything from tendinitis to a torn rotator cuff. Mark Margo, a softball coach in Illinois, says he worries more about his pitcher's arm when she's playing outfield. To prevent overuse injuries, Margo has his fielders "drill at shorter distances at the start of the season to build arm strength."[77] In addition, softball players can strengthen their shoulder muscles off the field using the rotator cuff exercises suggested in the Water Polo section (pages 226–227).

Coach Margo says the most dangerous injury in softball is pitchers getting hit by line drives. He thinks the distance from the mound to home plate should be lengthened to help prevent these injuries. That may or may not happen, so you softball pitchers should consider wearing a face mask, mouth guard, and even shin guards. Kirsten, a twenty-year-old pitcher, knows what it's like to have the ball come straight back at you: "During the first round of regionals, a lefty hitter slapped the ball, and it came back quick down the middle and hit me dead on the

Good Read: Under the Baseball Moon by John H. Ritter

Sport: Softball

Life apps: Friendship, dreams, the mystical, sports injury

Summary: Glory Martinez and Andy Ramos live in a laid-back California beach town where the locals all know each other and people skateboard or walk barefoot from place to place. Glory dreams of playing on the U.S. national softball team; Andy wants to be a big-time musician playing a unique fusion of Latin, jazz, rock, and hip-hop on his trumpet. They have a mystical, inexplicable link—Glory pitches like a rock star whenever Andy plays his trumpet in time with her actions on the mound; Andy plays like someone much older than fifteen whenever Glory is in the audience supporting him. Then some mysterious man makes promises to Andy, and weird "voodoo" starts happening for both characters, including an injury that almost ends Glory's dream.

Told from Andy's point of view, the story includes realistic descriptions of competitive fast-pitch softball. The author has a unique, flowing writing style that matches the laid-back, beach-town setting.

Philomel Books, 2006

283 pages

shinbone, which caused my shin to split open, and the swelling went all the way down to my foot. . . . I had to sit out for a few weeks from travel ball."[78]

Swimming

According to high school swimming coach John Gottschalk, the most common swimming injuries involve the shoulders. Both rotator cuff injuries (such as impingement syndrome) and sub-scapula (under the shoulder blade) muscle pulls result from the repeated overhead motion of the swimming stroke. Swimmers who compete in the breaststroke often experience a different set of injuries related to the kicking motion. The breaststroke kick is not the up-

> ### Did You Know?
>
> Swimming events in the first three Summer Olympics took place in open water—in 1896, swimmers competed in the cold Bay of Zea near Pireas, Greece; in 1900, they swam in the river Seine; and in 1904, swimmers competed in a man-made lake in St. Louis, Missouri. It wasn't until the 1908 games in London that swimming events moved to the pool.

and-down motion of the freestyle or backstroke; it involves a bend-open-snap motion, often called the frog kick. As a result of the repeated stress on the knees and hips, breaststroke swimmers sometimes develop tendinitis in their knees and hips.[79]

Preventing shoulder injuries involves two steps: (1) warming up/stretching before every practice and meet and (2) strengthening the shoulder muscles. There are several ways to stretch your shoulders and upper back; you can ask your coach for swimming-specific suggestions or check out the tips in chapter 7. To strengthen your rotator cuff muscles, Coach Gottschalk recommends exercises from the Water Polo Planet website (www.waterpoloplanet.com), some of which are described on pages 226–227 in the Water Polo section.

Here are a few other injury-prevention suggestions:[80]

- Make sure your stroke technique is correct for your arms and legs. Talk to your coach if you're not sure.
- Strengthen your core—abdominals, hips, butt, and lower back. Don't forget the lower back. To avoid strained muscles, you need to strengthen your front (abs) and back.
- To avoid overusing your arms, try cross-training, especially during the off-season. For example, work on endurance through cycling or running. Work on strength using weights or resistance bands.

Tennis

Most tennis injuries happen gradually, not as the result of one traumatic event. Overuse injuries include

tennis elbow (bursitis due to repeated swinging motion),
tennis toe (pain under toenail from repeated contact with the shoe during sudden stops),

stress fractures of the foot (due to inadequate cushion in shoes and doing too much too soon), and

shoulder tendinitis or bursitis (due to bad mechanics and repeated overhead motion).[81]

One acute injury tennis players experience more often is a strain, especially of the calf muscle. It usually results from a quick, sudden movement to return a ball.

The good news about tennis injuries is that they are fairly easy to prevent.

- Following the suggestions in Picking the Right Shoe will help you avoid painful tennis toe and stress fractures.
- Maintaining a year-round cardio and strength program will help you avoid stress fractures when the season starts. Working on specific muscle groups such as the rotator cuff can help you prevent tendinitis and bursitis.
- Warming up before every practice or match will help you avoid muscle strains. Make sure you jog for a few minutes before you stretch, and make sure you stretch your calf muscles, as well as your hip flexors, hamstrings, quadriceps, wrists, and shoulders.

Picking the Right Shoe

To avoid common overuse injuries such as tennis toe and stress fractures, it's important to have the right kind of shoe. Here are a few tips from Dr. Lloyd Nesbitt, a podiatrist (foot doctor) from Toronto:[82]

1. Buy shoes that are made for the side-to-side movement involved in racquet sports.
2. Don't wear running shoes, which are made for forward motion and don't have enough ankle support.
3. Make sure you have enough room to move your toes. You should have about a finger's width of room between your toe and the shoe.
4. Look for shoes with a well-padded sole, especially under the balls of your feet and your heel.

Athlete Bio: Nathan Wolitarsky, Track and Field

Sometimes you can be taken out of action by injuries that occur off the playing field. That's what happened to Nathan Wolitarsky, an eighteen-year-old shot-putter from California.

Nathan started shot putting in seventh grade and continued into high school, where he added the discus to his events. After a successful four years, Nathan finished third on his school's all-time shot put list and eighth on the all-time discus list. Four colleges recruited Nathan for their track and field teams. He says he decided on UCLA "because of the great history of their throwers, as well as the school's academic excellence."

In September 2011, Nathan was about a month away from moving in the dorms when he got into a serious car accident. He was driving down a street near his house and hit a tree at one hundred miles an hour. It's a miracle that he survived. Nathan broke five ribs as well as bones in his face; he suffered a compound fracture and dislocation of his right knee; he tore the ACL, PCL, and patella tendon in his right knee; and he shattered his right kneecap. As of January 2012, Nathan had undergone six surgeries on his right knee and had begun physical therapy, which will continue until full range of motion in his knee returns. How long will that take? Nathan says, "The doctors do not really have a set time. It all depends on my recovery. . . . It's going to take a tremendous amount of work to get to where I want to be, but staying focused and dedicated will get me there."

Though Nathan had to withdraw from his first year of college, he says he still has a good chance of competing at UCLA: "The coach has left the door open for me. I hope to begin school in September 2012."[83]

Nathan says, "As much as one would think I am disappointed, I am not. The reality is that I am a walking miracle who was given a second chance at life, and that along with the love and support of my family and friends keeps me going." *Photo courtesy of Pogos Kuregyan.*

Track and Field

Field events (especially pole vault and discus) account for most of the acute injuries in track and field. The number of pole vaulting injuries has decreased as more high school vaulters have started wearing protective headgear. Discus injuries often involve someone not paying attention and getting hit with the discus.

The main acute injury in running events is a strained muscle, usually the hamstring, quadriceps, or groin. Overuse injuries in running events are more common. The repetitive pounding on the track can result in shin splints, stress fractures, and tendinitis of the knee and hip.

The key to preventing most track injuries is stretching. Shin splints, pulled muscles, and tendinitis can all be avoided if you diligently stretch your muscles before *every* workout and meet. Here are a few stretching dos and don'ts for track; see chapter 7 for more on flexibility training in general:

- *Do warm up before you stretch.* Jog around the track for five to ten minutes and then start stretching.
- *Do take your time.* It's not a race.
- *Do focus on the muscles in your lower body*—calves, hamstrings, quadriceps, groin, hip flexor, and lower back.
- *Don't bounce.* Slowly sink into each stretch and hold it for around thirty seconds.
- *Don't stretch cold muscles.* This can cause injuries before you even hit the track.
- *Don't hold your breath.* On each exhaled breath, try to sink into the stretch a little deeper.

My, How Times Have Changed

When American Thomas Burke won the 100-meter dash at the first modern Olympics in 1896, he did it without the help of starting blocks or super-light shoes. His time: 12.0 seconds. Changes in training methods and equipment have resulted in faster times, so much so that high school guys *and girls* have beat Burke's gold medal time. As of 2012, Jeff Demps held the boys' U.S. high school record of 10.1 seconds; Angela Williams held the girls' record of 11.11 seconds.[84]

Volleyball

In general, volleyball players suffer fewer injuries than athletes in other major sports. However, they are susceptible to various chronic injuries because the game involves repeated hitting and jumping. If you're playing both high school and club volleyball, you're even more likely to experience one of these three overuse injuries:[85]

1. Rotator cuff tendinitis (due to repetitive overhead motion of serving and spiking)
2. Patellar tendinitis, or inflammation of the kneecap tendon (due to repetitive jumping)
3. Lower back pain (muscle strain due to exaggerated movements—reaching to dig the ball, overreaching on spike, etc.)

The most common acute injuries among volleyball players include

sprained ankles (the most common volleyball injury);
broken, dislocated, or sprained fingers; and
torn ACLs.[86]

To prevent both overuse and acute volleyball-related injuries, incorporate the knee, shoulder, and ankle exercises discussed in this chapter. Also make sure to stretch and strengthen your lower back using exercises from Core Exercises on pages 205–206. Weight training should be part of your year-round fitness program, not just during the season.

Water Polo

According to Paul Rave, who has coached at the club and college level, water polo injuries are nearly always caused by overuse. The sport-specific motions are not natural, so the repetitive stress is especially hard on the joints. The treading water motion (egg beater kick), for example, can cause tendinitis in the knees. The constant throwing and shooting can cause tendinitis in the shoulder. Coach Rave says that "in the beginning of the season, a lot of these injuries happen because they [the players] haven't been training on the break and they go too hard too fast. . . . The kids really need to be in shape and have the strength to support hard training."[87]

As suggested by Coach Rave's comment, the best way to prevent water polo–related injuries is to be in shape before the season begins, which means year-round strength and endurance training.

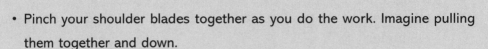

Shoulder Exercises

The following exercises work on your rotator cuff—the group of muscles and tendons that stabilizes your shoulder. In order to truly work your rotator cuff, concentrate on the following as you perform each exercise:

- Pinch your shoulder blades together as you do the work. Imagine pulling them together and down.
- Don't lift/shrug your shoulders toward your ears.
- Keep your wrist straight.
- Keep your back straight and your abs contracted.

There's no right or wrong number that you should perform, but you could start with three sets of fifteen repetitions unless stated otherwise.[88]

Internal rotation. Tie one end of a resistance band or tube to a stationary object; the band should be about waist high. Stand next to the object (*not* facing it) and take the other end of the band in the hand nearest the object. Keep your elbow next to your side and bend it to 90 degrees with your hand in front of you and your forearm parallel to the ground (see figure 6.3). Pull the band away from the attachment point and across your body, keeping your elbow next to your side. Slowly return. Turn around so your other arm is next to the attachment point. Repeat.

External rotation. Tie one end of a resistance band or tube to a stationary object; the band should be about waist high. Stand next to the object (*not* facing it) and take the other end of the band in the hand farthest from the attachment point. Keep your elbow next to your side and bend it to 90 degrees with your hand in front of you and your forearm parallel to the ground (figure 6.4). Pull the band away from the attachment point until your rotation motion stops. The tendency is to twist your body as you pull the band out and across, but don't do it. Keep your elbow next to your side and your body still. Slowly return. Turn around and take the band in the other hand. Repeat.

Scaption. Stand with one foot in front of the other. Place the middle of a resistance band or tube under your front foot and hold the ends in your hands, arms at your sides (the tubes might be easier to use since they have handles). Keeping your arms straight, raise your hands in front of you and slightly to the sides. Keep your thumbs pointing up and stop when your hands reach shoulder height. Remember to keep your shoulders down; don't shrug up toward your ears.

For more exercises, go to the Water Polo Planet website (www.waterpolo planet.com/HTML_Mike_pages/mr31_Strength_Training.html), which has video demonstrations of seven different exercises for your rotator cuff.

- To prevent tendinitis in your knees, focus on strengthening and stretching your hamstrings, quadriceps, and hips. To give your knees a break from the egg beater motion, do at least some of your off-season cardio out of the pool—running or cycling, for example.
- To prevent tendinitis in your shoulder, focus on strengthening your rotator cuff and your core. In water polo, you're throwing without help from your legs, which can put extra strain on your shoulder and upper back.

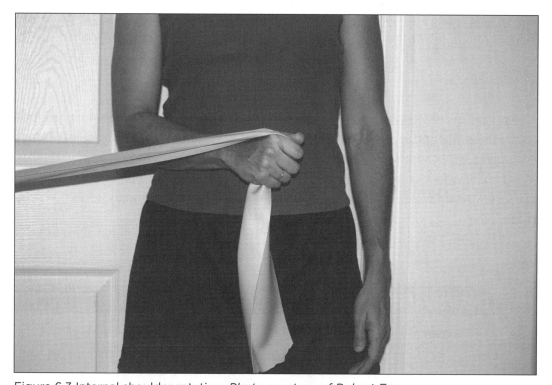

Figure 6.3 Internal shoulder rotation. *Photo courtesy of Robert Fay.*

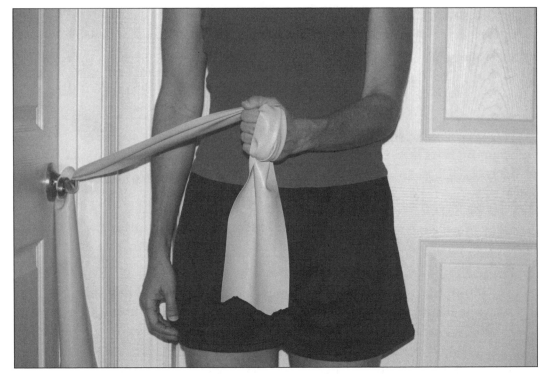

Figure 6.4 External shoulder rotation. *Photo courtesy of Robert Fay.*

Strengthening your abs, lower back, and hips can help stabilize your body when you throw and take some of the strain off your shoulder.[89]

Wrestling

According to former high school coach Aaron Cantrell, "most wrestling injuries result from putting joints in unnatural positions. The best way to prevent injury is to make sure these joints are strong through off-season weight training."[90] The joints most affected are the shoulders, knees, and ankles; ligament sprains and tears can occur when an arm or leg is bent too far or is suddenly jerked out of place.

Did You Know?

Men's water polo is the longest-standing Olympic team sport. It has been included in every Olympics since 1900. Women's water polo didn't become an Olympic sport until one hundred years later, at the 2000 Olympics in Sydney.[91]

Other common wrestling injuries include

concussions;

prepatella bursitis (bursitis of the kneecap due to repetitive slamming into the mat);

cauliflower ear (severe bruising of the ear due to being repeatedly hit); and

MRSA (deadly skin infection caught from body-to-body contact).[92]

One of the best ways to prevent injuries in contact sports such as wrestling is having a coach who knows and teaches correct form and technique. Does your coach attend clinics to learn the latest research on safety, conditioning methods, and skills instruction? Does your coach (or athletic trainer) monitor weight loss, making sure it is done safely in accordance with the NFHS rule (see chapter 4)?

Here are a few tips on preventing injuries in wrestling:

1. Strengthen your neck muscles to guard against concussions and neck injuries.
2. Always wear properly fitting headgear to guard against cauliflower ear.
3. Use the exercises presented in this chapter to strengthen your ankle, knee, and shoulder joints. Also strengthen the muscle groups surrounding these

Athlete Bio: Luke Hampton, Wrestling

Freak accidents happen in wrestling, just as they do in many other sports.

On December 3, 2011, seventeen-year-old Luke Hampton was competing in a wrestling tournament. He charged his opponent in an attempt to pin him, but Luke lost his grip and went headfirst into a padded wall. The impact broke two vertebrae, leaving Luke paralyzed from the neck down. The athletic director, and former wrestling coach, at Luke's high school said he had never heard of such an injury in wrestling.

Prior to his injury, Luke was North Carolina's top-ranked Class 1A wrestler at 182 pounds. He was also the leading rusher on the football team, and he helped coach little kids on a club wrestling team.

Luke has been told that he'll never walk again, but Luke's coach doesn't believe it. "We all know he's going to walk again," Coach Derrick Calloway said. "Just because they told him he can't do it, he'll do it."[93]

joints; for example, strengthen your quadriceps and hamstrings to help prevent knee injuries.

4. To minimize the risk of catching MRSA, shower before and after wrestling practices and matches, wear clean clothing at each practice, and sanitize the wrestling mats with antiseptic solution after each practice. You might get teased for being a clean freak, but that's better than catching MRSA any day.[94]

Rehabilitation and Recovery

If you do suffer an injury, you'll have to undergo a recovery period before you resume play. This is possibly the hardest part of being injured, especially when you're nearly back to full strength and all you want to do is get off that bench and play. As mentioned earlier, it's extremely important to stay out of the game until you're completely healed, whether you suffered a concussion, a sprained ankle, a torn rotator cuff, or one of the many overuse injuries. Going back too soon can result in reinjury, prolonged rehabilitation, and even life-threatening consequences.

> "For my back, I took the entire summer off from volleyball. I worked forty hours a week and lifted three to four times a week to get my body strength back up."—Noah, 20, volleyball

Your specific recovery process will depend on the type, extent, location, and initial treatment of the injury. Here are some general pieces of the rehab pie:

1. Doctor—Don't try to self-diagnose using the Internet. Go to the doctor and get a professional diagnosis and road map for recovery.
2. Surgery—It's not required for everyone, but if you tore your ACL or rotator cuff or suffered a compound fracture, surgery might be the only way to get back in the game.
3. Physical therapy—Whether or not your injury requires surgery, you will probably need some kind of physical therapy (PT) to strengthen the injured area. PT involves stretching and strengthening exercises, both under the supervision of the physical therapist and at home. Don't neglect the home portion of your PT! If you want to start playing again, you need to regain strength, mobility, coordination, endurance, and flexibility; the only way to do that is by doing your exercises. The knee, ankle, and shoulder exercises provided in this chapter are often used as part of PT. See the Find Out More section for a helpful article on PT.

4. Exercise—This step needs to be taken slowly and under the direction of a physical therapist or doctor, especially if you had surgery. You don't want to undo the surgeon's repair job by doing too much too soon.

5. Return—As much as you're looking forward to playing again, you're probably going to be a little nervous too. Will you be able to hit the ball as hard? Will you be able to make the same sharp cuts? Will you be able to throw or serve like you used to? If you're wearing a knee or ankle brace, it might take a little getting used to. Sometimes the mental side of recovery is as hard as the physical side. See the Find Out More section for an article by sports psychologist Alan Goldberg on the mental side of injuries and recovery.

Find Out More

Books

Furgang, Kathy. *Frequently Asked Questions about Sports Injuries.* New York: Rosen, 2008.

Goldenberg, Lorne, and Peter Twist. *Strength Ball Training.* 2nd ed. Champaign, IL: Human Kinetics, 2007.

Page, Phil, and Todd Ellenbecker. *Strength Band Training.* 2nd ed. Champaign, IL: Human Kinetics, 2011.

Shannon, Joyce Brennfleck, ed. *Sports Injuries Information for Teens.* Detroit, MI: Omnigraphics, 2004.

Online Articles

Chan, Jenny, and Joseph Brownstein. "11 Injury-Prone High School Sports." *ABC News,* November 13, 2008. abcnews.go.com/Health/PainManagement/story?id=6198970&page=1#.TyF1hYF5f_R.

Claussen, Drew. "Concussions End Jake Deitchler's Career." *Minnesota Daily,* January 17, 2012. www.mndaily.com/2012/01/17/concussions-end-jake-deitchler%E2%80%99s-career. Jake Deitchler is a former Olympian, a three-time Minnesota State High School champion wrestler, and now, a former collegiate wrestler. After talking with a concussion specialist about his repeated head injuries, Jake retired though he still had eligibility left at the University of Minnesota.

Goldberg, Alan. "Rebounding from Injuries: The Mental Side of Athletic Injuries." Competitive Advantage. www.competitivedge.com/resources_rebounding_from_injury.htm (accessed April 6, 2012).

Keating, Peter. "Heading for Trouble." *ESPN: The Magazine*, 2009. sports.espn
.go.com/espnmag/story?id=3958650. This article tells the story of Melissa
Inzitari, a college soccer player who suffered a severe concussion and tried to
keep playing. Two years later, she was still suffering from postconcussion syndrome—depression, personality changes, and blindness in her left eye. When
she finally saw a neuropsychologist, Melissa discovered she had brain damage
and her soccer career was over. She went on to coach soccer and teach girls
about the seriousness of concussions.

KG Investments. "Q&A Articles: Injuries." TeenGrowth.com, last updated February 14, 2012. www.teengrowth.com/index.cfm?action=info_
sub&SubCategory=sports_Injuries&CatDesc=Sports&SubDesc=Injuries&
Category=sports. This web page contains a list of questions from teens aged
thirteen to eighteen related to sports injuries. Click on the question for the
answer.

National Institute of Arthritis and Musculoskeletal and Skin Diseases. "Handout
on Health: Sports Injuries," April 2009. www.niams.nih.gov/Health_Info/
Sports_Injuries.

———. "Questions and Answers about Sprains and Strains," April 2009. www
.niams.nih.gov/Health_Info/Sprains_Strains.

The Nemours Foundation/KidsHealth. "Concussions." TeensHealth, reviewed
January 2011. kidshealth.org/teen/safety/first_aid/concussions.html.

———. "Osgood-Schlatter Disease." TeensHealth, reviewed November 2010.
kidshealth.org/parent/general/aches/osgood.html.

———. "Physical Therapy." TeensHealth, reviewed May 2011. kidshealth.org/
teen/your_body/medical_care/pt.html (accessed April 6, 2012).

Schwarz, Alan. "Girls Are Often Neglected Victims of Concussion." *New
York Times*, October 2, 2007. www.nytimes.com/2007/10/02/sports/other
sports/02concussions.html?scp=6&sq=concussions&st=cse. This article highlights the experiences of Hannah, Kate, and Sarah, three high school athletes
who sustained multiple concussions and suffered debilitating and sometimes
scary symptoms for months afterward. All three were faced with the reality
that if they didn't stop playing (or at least take a season off), they could cause
permanent damage to their ability to concentrate, read, remember, and more.
The article also emphasizes the importance of being honest about any head
injury you receive, whether you're a guy or girl.

Websites and Organizations

Advocates for Injured Athletes (www.injuredathletes.org). This is the organization started by former lacrosse player Tommy Mallon and his mother. For a

summary of Tommy's injury experience and his reason for starting this organization, click on the "Watch Our Story" link.

American Orthopedic Society for Sports Medicine (www.sportsmed.org/Patient/). The "Patient Education" page of the American Orthopaedic Society for Sports Medicine (AOSSM) website has a ton of info regarding sports injuries and their prevention. The "Sports Tips" link offers two different lists that provide tip sheets for a wide variety of sports and injuries.

Centers for Disease Control and Prevention (www.cdc.gov/concussion/HeadsUp/high_school.html). There are several places on the CDC's website where you can find information on traumatic brain injuries and concussions in sports. Through the link given here you can access the CDC's Heads Up materials on high school sports in particular. At the bottom of the page there is a link to the Heads Up fact sheet, which has information on concussion symptoms and prevention, as well as what to do if you think you (or a teammate) has a concussion.

National Institute of Arthritis and Musculoskeletal and Skin Diseases (www.niams.nih.gov). This website has information on sports injuries in general as well as specific types such as sprains, strains, tendinitis, and more. Search for a topic using the letters at the top of the home page.

Sports Legacy Institute (www.sportslegacy.org). According to the organization's website, "The mission of the Sports Legacy Institute is to advance the study, treatment and prevention of the effects of brain trauma in athletes and other at-risk groups." You can read about the serious risk that multiple concussions pose to teen athletes. Under the "Education Programs" tab, click on "For Athletes." At the bottom of the page, there's a link to the CDC's fact sheet mentioned earlier.

STOP Sports Injuries (www.stopsportsinjuries.org). Because of the rising number of acute and chronic injuries among young athletes, the AOSSM started a campaign called STOP Sport Injuries. The website has links to sports-injury-related videos, the free monthly newsletter, and sport-specific resources, all with the goal of stopping injuries and keeping players like you in the game. The "Sports Injury Prevention" link takes you to a list of injury prevention tips for twenty-five different sports.

Notes

1. Laura Atkinson, e-mail to author, January 23, 2011.
2. Atkinson, e-mail.
3. Scripps Howard News Service, "Most Common High School Sports Injuries," *ABC2News .com*, October 25, 2010, www.abc2news.com/dpp/news/health/concussions/most-common -school-sport-injuries (accessed February 14, 2012).

4. Dave Bryan, "Ben Roethlisberger since the Injury," *Steelers Depot* (blog), January 6, 2012, www.steelersdepot.com/2012/01/ben-roethlisberger-since-the-ankle-injury/ (accessed January 30, 2012).

5. Gerry Dulac, "Pittsburgh Steelers Playoff Report: Ben Roethlisberger Says Ankle Feels Worse," SportingNews, January 4, 2012, aol.sportingnews.com/nfl/story/2012-01-04/pittsburgh-steelers-playoff-report-ben-roethlisberger-says-ankle-feels-worse#ixzz1kxLSMyFq (accessed January 30, 2012).

6. Andrew E. Lincoln et al., "Trends in Concussion Incidence in High School Sports: A Prospective 11-Year Study," *American Journal of Sports Medicine*, January 29, 2011, ajs.sagepub.com/content/early/2011/01/29/0363546510392326.abstract (accessed January 30, 2012); Centers for Disease Control and Prevention, "Concussion in Sports," www.cdc.gov/concussion/sports/ (accessed January 30, 2012).

7. Mayo Clinic staff, "Postconcussion Syndrome," Mayo Clinic, September 29, 2011, www.mayoclinic.com/health/postconcussion-syndrome/DS01020 (accessed February 7, 2012).

8. Alan Schwarz, "Girls Are Often Neglected Victims of Concussion," *New York Times*, October 2, 2007, p. 1, www.nytimes.com/2007/10/02/sports/othersports/02concussions.html?scp=6&sq=concussions&st=cse (accessed February 13, 2012).

9. Centers for Disease Control and Prevention, "Heads Up: Concussion in High School Sports: Fact Sheet for Athletes," June 2010, available at www.cdc.gov/concussion/HeadsUp/high_school.html#2.

10. Donald C. Collins, "NFHS Tightens Concussion Rules," Moms Team, www.momsteam.com/team-experts/nfhs-concussion-rule-requires-immediate-removal-after-suspected-concussion (accessed January 27, 2012).

11. Sean Gregory, "Hard Knocks: How to Keep High School Kids with Concussions on the Bench," *Time*, February 2, 2009, pp. 63–64.

12. Jorge Castillo, "Seemingly Ordinary Game, Then a Player Dies," *New York Times*, October 20, 2011.

13. Gregory, "Hard Knocks," 64.

14. Gregory, "Hard Knocks," 64; Castillo, "Seemingly Ordinary Game."

15. Gregory, "Hard Knocks," 63–64.

16. Mayo Clinic staff, "Dislocation: First Aid," Mayo Clinic, www.mayoclinic.com/health/first-aid-dislocation/FA00009 (accessed January 31, 2012).

17. The Nemours Foundation/KidsHealth, "Broken Bones," TeensHealth, reviewed August 2009, p. 2, kidshealth.org/teen/diseases_conditions/bones/broken_bones.html# (accessed January 31, 2012).

18. Quoted in George White, "Know Your Health Pro . . . Dr. Michael Magee," *Florida Today*, July 31, 2011.

19. The Nemours Foundation/KidsHealth, "The Facts about Fractures and Broken Bones," in *Sports Injury Information for Teens*, ed. Joyce Brennfleck Shannon (Detroit, MI: Omnigraphics, 2004), 94.

20. American Orthopaedic Society for Sports Medicine (AOSSM), "Media Room: Common Diagnostic Procedures and Medical Treatments," in Shannon, *Sports Injury Information*, 59–60.

21. National Institute of Arthritis and Musculoskeletal and Skin Diseases (NIAMS), "Questions and Answers about Sprains and Strains," April 2009, www.niams.nih.gov/Health_Info/Sprains_Strains/ (accessed January 28, 2012).

22. NIAMS, "Questions and Answers about Sprains and Strains," in Shannon, *Sports Injury Information*, 90.

23. Aetna, "ACL (Anterior Cruciate Ligament) Injuries," InteliHealth, updated February 17, 2011, www.intelihealth.com/IH/ihtIH/WSIHW000/9339/25425.html (accessed February 1, 2012).
24. Aetna, "ACL Injuries."
25. The Nemours Foundation/KidsHealth, "Osgood-Schlatter Disease," TeensHealth, reviewed November 2010, p. 1, kidshealth.org/parent/general/aches/osgood.html (accessed February 2, 2012).
26. The Nemours Foundation/KidsHealth, "Osgood-Schlatter Disease," 2.
27. Jordan Metzl, *Shin Splints* (video), www.drjordanmetzl.com/ (accessed February 2, 2012).
28. Metzl, *Shin Splints.*
29. American Academy of Orthopaedic Surgeons (AAOS), "Stress Fractures of the Foot and Ankle," reviewed July 2009, orthoinfo.aaos.org/topic.cfm?topic=a00379 (accessed February 3, 2012).
30. AAOS, "Stress Fractures."
31. AAOS, "Stress Fractures."
32. AAOS, "Stress Fractures."
33. NIAMS, "Questions and Answers about Shoulder Problems," in Shannon, *Sports Injury Information*, 123, 133.
34. National Center for Catastrophic Sports Injury Research, "Table I: High School Fall Sports Direct Catastrophic Injuries," p. 2, www.unc.edu/depts/nccsi/2010AllSportTables.pdf (accessed January 27, 2012); Frederick O. Mueller and Robert C. Cantu, "Catastrophic Sports Injury Research: Twenty-Eighth Annual Report, Fall 1982–Spring 2010," pp. 26, 28, www.unc.edu/depts/nccsi/2010Allsport.pdf (accessed January 27, 2012).
35. Mueller and Cantu, "Catastrophic Sports Injury Research," 13; Jenny Chan and Joseph Brownstein, "11 Injury-Prone High School Sports," *ABC News*, November 13, 2008, 5–6, abcnews.go.com/Health/PainManagement/story?id=6198970&page=1#.TyF1hYF5f_R (accessed January 26, 2012).
36. Mike Langram, "Alpine Ski Injuries," Ski-Injury.com, www.ski-injury.com/specific-sports/alpine (accessed February 9, 2012).
37. Jose Morales, e-mail to author, January 18, 2012.
38. Morales, e-mail; AOSSM, "Preventing Baseball Injuries," STOP Sports Injuries, 2010, www.stopsportsinjuries.org/baseball-injury-prevention.aspx (accessed March 21, 2012).
39. Stana Landon, "12 Ways to Build Ankle Strength for Top Performance," Active.com, www.active.com/fitness/Articles/12_Ways_to_Build_Ankle_Strength_for_Top_Performance.htm?page=2 (accessed March 22, 2012); Manuel A. Escalante, "Ankle Strengthening Program," www.csuchico.edu/~sbarker/injury/ankle/ankle_rehab.pdf (accessed March 22, 2012).
40. AOSSM, "Preventing Basketball Injuries," STOP Sports Injuries, 2010, www.stopsportsinjuries.org/basketball-injury-prevention.aspx (accessed February 5, 2012).
41. Diamond Leung, "Injury Leaves Eric Katenda Partially Blind," ESPN.com, August 6, 2011, espn.go.com/mens-college-basketball/story/_/id/6839154/notre-dame-fighting-irish-recruit-eric-katenda-blinded-eye-injury (accessed February 5, 2012).
42. *Blow to the Head* (video), *ABC News*, September 13, 2010, abcnews.go.com/Health/WellnessNews/basketball-concussions-head-injuries-rise-teen-sports/story?id=11603847#.Ty7cavkt3XN (accessed February 5, 2012); Peter Keating, "Heading for Trouble," *ESPN: The Magazine*, 2009, sports.espn.go.com/espnmag/story?id=3958650 (accessed February 9, 2012).
43. Quoted in Courtney Hutchison, "Basketball and Concussions: How to Protect Your Teen," *ABC News*, September 13, 2010, abcnews.go.com/Health/WellnessNews/basketball

-concussions-head-injuries-rise-teen-sports/story?id=11603847#.Ty7cavkt3XN (accessed February 5, 2012).

44. Maura Judkis, "Cheerleading Accounts for Most Catastrophic High School Injuries," *U.S. News.com*, August 15, 2008, health.usnews.com/health-news/blogs/on-medicine/2008/08/15/cheerleading-accounts-for-most-catastrophic-high-school-injuries (accessed February 6, 2012); also, see sources from note 30.

45. Judkis, "Cheerleading."

46. Maura Judkis, "5 Tips for Cheerleading Safety," *U.S. News.com*, August 15, 2008, health.usnews.com/health-news/family-health/articles/2008/08/15/5-tips-for-cheerleading-safety (accessed February 6, 2012); AOSSM, "Preventing Cheerleading Injuries," STOP Sports Injuries, 2010, www.stopsportsinjuries.org/cheerleading-injury-prevention.aspx (accessed February 6, 2012).

47. Jessica Urquiza, e-mails to author, January 2, January 19, and February 6, 2012.

48. AOSSM, "Rowing Injury Prevention," STOP Sports Injuries, 2010, www.stopsportsinjuries.org/rowing-injury-prevention.aspx (accessed February 8, 2012).

49. Lorne Goldenberg and Peter Twist, *Strength Ball Training*, 2nd ed. (Champaign, IL: Human Kinetics, 2007), 226.

50. Goldenberg and Twist, *Strength Ball Training*, 228.

51. Saralyn Hannon, e-mail to author, January 7, 2012.

52. Quoted in Chan and Brownstein, "11 Injury-Prone High School Sports," 7.

53. AOSSM, "Field Hockey Injury Prevention," STOP Sports Injuries, 2010, www.stopsportsinjuries.org/field-hockey-injury-prevention.aspx (accessed February 6, 2012).

54. Phil Page and Todd Ellenbecker, *Strength Band Training*, 2nd ed. (Champaign, IL: Human Kinetics, 2011), 97.

55. Page and Ellenbecker, *Strength Band Training*, 52.

56. Page and Ellenbecker, *Strength Band Training*, 53.

57. Goldenberg and Twist, *Strength Ball Training*, 110.

58. Goldenberg and Twist, *Strength Ball Training*, 118.

59. NAERA, home page, www.naera.net (accessed February 8, 2012).

60. Advocates for Injured Athletes, "About Us," www.injuredathletes.org/about/about.html (accessed May 26, 2012).

61. Tom Farrey, "Pop Warner to Limit Practice Contact," ESPN, June 15, 2012, espn.go.com/espn/story/_/id/8046203/pop-warner-toughens-safety-measures-limiting-contact-practice (accessed June 29, 2012).

62. Anahad O'Connor, "Trying to Reduce Head Injuries, Youth Football Limits Practice," *New York Times*, June 13, 2012, www.nytimes.com/2012/06/14/sports/pop-warner-football-limits-contact-in-practices.html (accessed June 29, 2012).

63. O'Connor, "Trying to Reduce Head Injuries."

64. AOSSM, "Golf Injury Prevention," STOP Sports Injuries, 2010, www.stopsportsinjuries.org/golf-injury-prevention.aspx (accessed February 8, 2012).

65. Chan and Brownstein, "11 Injury-Prone High School Sports," 4; SafeUSA, "Gymnastics Safety," in Shannon, *Sports Injury Information*, 330.

66. Chan and Brownstein, "11 Injury-Prone High School Sports," 6; Cameron Smith, "High School Hockey Player Paralyzed after Hit into Boards," *Pep Rally: A Y! Sports Blog*, January 2, 2012, rivals.yahoo.com/highschool/blog/prep_rally/post/High-school-hockey-player-paralyzed-after-hit-in?urn=highschool-wp10640 (accessed April 6, 2012); Cameron Smith, "Minnesota Mother: 'You Don't Get Paralyzed from Falling,'" *Pep Rally: A Y! Sports Blog*,

January 16, 2012, sports.yahoo.com/blogs/highschool-prep-rally/minnesota-mother-don-t-paralyzed-falling-164124017.html (accessed April 6, 2012).

67. "Head Injuries in Football," *New York Times*, October 21, 2010, topics.nytimes.com/top/reference/timestopics/subjects/f/football/head_injuries/index.html (accessed February 7, 2012).

68. AOSSM, "Hockey Injury Prevention," STOP Sports Injuries, 2010, www.stopsportsinjuries.org/hockey-injury-prevention.aspx (accessed February 7, 2012).

69. Lylah M. Alphonse, "Advocates for Injured Athletes Aims to Arm Student Athletes with Life-Saving Knowledge," Shine, April 20, 2012, shine.yahoo.com/team-mom/advocates-injured-athletes-aims-arm-student-athletes-life-031200089.html (accessed May 26, 2012).

70. Advocates for Injured Athletes, "Programs: Athletes Saving Athletes," www.injuredathletes.org/programs/programs.html (accessed May 26, 2012).

71. US Lacrosse, "About the Sport: Overview," www.uslacrosse.org/UtilityNav/AboutTheSport/Overview.aspx (accessed October 30, 2011); Human Kinetics, with Thomas Hanlon, *The Sports Rules Book: Essential Rules, Terms, and Procedures for 54 Sports*, 3rd ed. (Champaign, IL: Human Kinetics, 2009), 164.

72. Mike Langram, "Nordic/Telemark Ski Injuries," Ski-Injury.com, www.ski-injury.com/specific-sports/Nordic (accessed February 9, 2012).

73. Keating, "Heading for Trouble."

74. SafeUSA, "Soccer Safety," in Shannon, *Sports Injury Information*, 340–41.

75. SafeUSA, "Soccer Safety," 341.

76. Keating, "Heading for Trouble."

77. Chan and Brownstein, "11 Injury-Prone High School Sports," 2.

78. Chan and Brownstein, "11 Injury-Prone High School Sports," 3; Kirsten Frame, author's sports survey, November 30, 2011.

79. John Gottschalk, e-mail to author, January 19, 2012; AOSSM, "Preventing Swimming Injuries," STOP Sports Injuries, 2010, www.stopsportsinjuries.org/swimming-injury-prevention.aspx (accessed February 10, 2012).

80. AOSSM, "Preventing Swimming Injuries."

81. Lloyd Nesbitt, "Timely Tips for Tennis Types," in Shannon, *Sports Injury Information*, 348; AOSSM, "Tennis Injury Prevention," STOP Sports Injuries, 2010, www.stopsportsinjuries.org/tennis-injury-prevention.aspx (accessed February 10, 2012).

82. Nesbitt, "Timely Tips," 346–48.

83. Nathan Wolitarsky, author's survey, February 21, 2012.

84. "The Evolution of the 100 Meter Race," 100 Zone, www.100zone.8m.com/Evolution.htm (accessed November 12, 2011); "High School Records—Boys," *Track and Field News.com*, www.trackandfieldnews.com/tfn/records/records.jsp?listId=15 (accessed November 12, 2011); "High School Records—Girls," *Track and Field News.com*, www.trackandfieldnews.com/tfn/records/records.jsp?listId=16 (accessed November 12, 2011).

85. AOSSM, "Preventing Volleyball Injuries," STOP Sports Injuries, 2010, www.stopsportsinjuries.org/volleyball-injury-prevention.aspx (accessed March 24, 2012).

86. AOSSM, "Preventing Volleyball Injuries."

87. Paul Rave, e-mail to author, January 29, 2012.

88. The following three exercises are taken from Page and Ellenbecker, *Strength Band Training*, 35, 36, and 34, respectively.

89. AOSSM, "Water Polo," STOP Sports Injuries, 2010, www.stopsportsinjuries.org/water-polo.aspx (accessed February 10, 2012).

90. Aaron Cantrell, e-mail to author, January 2, 2012.

91. Francois Fortin, ed., *Sports: The Complete Visual Reference* (Willowdale, ON: Firefly Books, 2000), 84.

92. AOSSM, "Wrestling Injury Prevention," STOP Sports Injuries, 2010, www.stopsports injuries.org/wrestling-injury-prevention.aspx (accessed February 13, 2012).

93. Mason Linker, "Allegheny Star Wrestler Suffers Sever Spinal Cord Injury," *Winston-Salem Journal*, December 7, 2001, www2.journalnow.com/news/2011/dec/06/1/alleghany-star -wrestler-suffers-severe-neck-injury-ar-1684885/ (accessed February 13, 2012).

94. AOSSM, "Wrestling Injury Prevention."

TRAINING ON
YOUR OWN

....

"I'm usually up at 5:30, 6 o'clock working out. My whole mind-set is always, someone else is sleeping, so I want to be working while they're sleeping."
—Chris Paul, Los Angeles Clippers point guard[1]

"Being an athlete requires sacrifice, discipline & heart. There is no winning without hard work."—Serena Williams, U.S. tennis player[2]

The goal of this chapter is to help you become a better athlete, not just a better player in your particular sport. Recall from chapter 1 that sports require different skills and abilities; this chapter focuses on the physical fitness skills (speed, strength, agility, etc.) as opposed to technical and mental skills such as dribbling, serving, or blocking out the crowd. The better athlete (i.e., the one who is more physically fit) is often the better player.

Before you start trying any of the tips and workouts listed here, talk to your coach or athletic trainer. They know your strengths and weaknesses and can help you prioritize workouts (e.g., work on speed or agility first? Strength or endurance?) They can also evaluate whether you're doing the exercises correctly. Form is extremely important. It's not really practice that makes perfect; it's practicing the skill correctly.

Before starting a training program on your own, consider the following tips so you stay safe and make the most of your training efforts:

1. Talk to your coach before you start. Find out what physical fitness area he or she thinks you need to work on.
2. Set SMART goals for the fitness area(s) you're trying to improve. Make your goals specific, measurable, achievable, recorded, and time-framed.[3]
3. Listen to your body and take days off when needed. If you're really sore from a hard workout, take an easy jog or swim or just warm up and stretch.

Why Warm Up?

Before you start the real work of any training session, slowly jog (or skip or swim or cycle) for five to ten minutes. Then take five to ten minutes to stretch (suggested stretches can be found later in this chapter). Do not skip the stretching stage, especially if you're working out in cold weather. It's important to do both parts of this warm-up in this order because

- the slow exercise warms up your muscles, ligaments, and tendons and prepares your body for hard work;
- stretching is more safe and effective when your muscles are warm; and
- you reduce the risk of injury when your body is warmed up.

The warm-up routine also signals to your mind that it's time to go to work (remember the importance of routines for mental toughness from chapter 3).[4]

It's better to undertrain than overtrain; you don't want to end up injured because you tried to do too much (see chapter 6 for more on overuse injuries).
4. Always warm up before you start the intense part of your workout, and then cool down afterward.
5. Stay hydrated. Drink lots of water or sports drink before, during, and after a training session, especially when it's hot and when you're working out for more than thirty minutes at a time.
6. Find a workout partner, both for motivation and for safety (especially in the weight room). Even if you're not doing same weights or reps or exercises (you might be working on speed; he might be working on strength), you can still go to the gym or track together.

Why Cool Down?

After you finish a strenuous workout, your body needs time to cool down. Jog (or swim or cycle) slowly for five to ten minutes to let your body cool off and get rid of some lactic acid, which is what causes muscle soreness. Then stretch for another five to ten minutes. Stretching after your workout also reduces muscle soreness and improves flexibility.[5]

Have You Ever Heard of Shinty?

- Shinty is played almost entirely in Scotland. There are a few clubs in the United States, but in Scotland it's a national sport.
- It's a fast-paced game that's similar to lacrosse and field hockey.
- Players use curved sticks called camans to try to put the ball in their opponent's goal.
- Unlike lacrosse and field hockey, in shinty players can stop the ball with their feet.[6]

Each section in this chapter provides tips on improving one of the following physical fitness skills: speed, strength, power, endurance, agility, and flexibility. Though I've narrowed my discussion to six fitness skills, there are others—balance and quickness, for example—and you'll find sidebars with keys points on each of these.

Speed

Many sports involve the need for speed, or the ability to move very fast in one direction for a short period of time; for example, track and field (sprints, long

Speed Training Tips

- Before starting a speed workout, make sure your body has fully recovered (that is, no lingering tiredness or soreness) from any previous training.
- Always use proper sprinting technique. Ask your coach for feedback on your technique to make sure you are practicing correct form during your workouts.
- Always give yourself enough rest after each set during a speed workout.
- Vary your speed training so that you have light, medium, and hard days. It's not a good idea to have back-to-back hard days.[7]

jump), football, baseball, softball, field hockey, lacrosse, soccer, gymnastics, ice hockey, and swimming. Developing speed for your sport involves a combination of interval training and speed drills. Ask your coach to help you come up with a balanced workout plan with the right combination of activities.

Here are a few workouts that can help you develop running speed,[8] which involves increasing explosive strength and foot speed, among other things. Remember to ask your coach for help in deciding which drills to combine on the same day.

1. *Sprints*—Run six 20-yard sprints at full speed, walking back to the starting point after each sprint. After you finish all six, take a short jog—maybe three minutes. Then repeat the exercise with fifteen-yard sprints and ten-yard sprints. (This drill works on speed endurance.)
2. *Hill sprints*—Find an area with a slight to moderate hill. Run approximately thirty yards up hill at 75 percent effort with one minute rest after. Repeat three times. Then run approximately twenty yards all out with one minute rest. Repeat four times. (This drill improves running strength and power.)

Quickness

One aspect of speed is quickness, or the ability to react or accelerate quickly.[9] Being quick is important in sprint events. Speed on the track or in the pool is important, but the winner is often the one who reacts first at the sound of the gun. In other sports, athletes need to react quickly to moving objects. A hockey goalie needs quickness to stop a screaming puck. A third baseman needs quickness to catch a line drive.

As with straight speed, quickness can be developed through drills. Quickness is best drilled by the specific needs of your sport. In some sports, it helps to have quick feet and legs; running, hopping, and jumping through "agility ladders" can improve this skill. In other sports, it helps to have quick hands and arms; try quick catch-and-release drills and activities that involve reacting to fast-moving and/or bouncing balls. For specific drill ideas, check out the books and websites in the Find Out More section at the end of this chapter.

3. *Butt kicks*—While jogging, lift your legs back so you kick your butt with your heels. Pump your arms as you would while sprinting. (This drill works on foot speed.)
4. *Stairs*—Run up stairs in a football stadium for four to eight seconds, then walk back down and repeat. (This drill works on starting power and acceleration.)
5. *Bounding*—Bounding, hopping, and jumping are all plyometric exercises designed to increase explosive power and speed. In bounding, you run, drive your free knee up so your upper leg is parallel to the ground, and jump a little on each step. (This drill works on power and stride length.)

For more suggestions, see chapter 3 in *Training for Speed, Agility, and Quickness* and other resources listed in the Find Out More section at the end of this chapter.

Strength

Athletes who want to be fast also need to be strong. Leg strength in particular powers an athlete down the track or field. Swimming speed comes from strong leg and shoulder muscles. Strength is also important in sports that don't involve speed: wrestling and water polo, for example. Actually, every athlete should work on muscular strength; it's the force behind longer hits, higher jumps, and harder kicks. As mentioned in chapter 6, strength training also prevents injury, since strong muscles, tendons, and ligaments can stand more stress and strain.

> "My junior year in high school I began to take a weight lifting class and my game really started to improve because I started to hit the ball much longer and was able to control my shots a lot better."
> —Jessica H., 20, golf

Resistance Training

When most people hear the words *strength training*, they think of the weight room. It's true that free weights and weight machines are important for building muscle and overall strength, but they're not the only way. The key to strength training is performing exercise against resistance, and that resistance can come from weights, bands/tubes, and even your own body weight.

To start with, here's a quick review of some basic resistance exercises mentioned throughout this chapter. (Some other basic exercises—toe raises and

Resistance Equipment

The resistance exercises suggested here involve minimal equipment. You can probably find all of it at the gym or in the school weight room. If you want to be able to work out at home, here are a few things to buy:

- Dumbbells: You probably want three different sizes to start with, something that feels light, medium, and heavy. In general, the lighter weights are for shoulder exercises (overhead shoulder presses, front shoulder raises); the medium are for arms (biceps, triceps); and the heavier weights are for back, chest, and leg exercises (rowing, chest press, squats, lunges). Remember: You're going to be doing multiple sets and repetitions (reps), so your heaviest weights shouldn't be something you can barely lift once.
- Resistance tubes or bands: These elastic tubes/bands come in a range of strengths indicated by different colors. The color–resistance strength combos vary by the manufacturer, so you'll have to test them to see what feels light, medium, and heavy. The tubes are, well, tubes and usually have handles. The bands don't have handles, but you can easily wrap them around your hands; the bands are two to three inches wide and lie flat. You should try both types to see which you like better. There's no difference in terms of their effectiveness in resistance training, though tubing is often preferred for upper body exercises and bands for lower body.[10]
- Stability ball: This is the bigger exercise ball that people often use for abdominal crunches. The size you should get depends on your height:[11]

  Five foot nine and shorter—45 cm or 55 cm
  Five foot ten to six foot three—55 cm or 65 cm
  Six foot four and taller—65 cm or 75 cm

- Medicine ball: This is a weighted ball a little smaller than a basketball that's used for a variety of core, arm, and chest exercises. Before buying a medicine ball, talk to a coach or trainer and try using one so you know what weight to get.

abdominal crunches, for example—are discussed in chapter 6 in the sidebars on ankle and core exercises, respectively. Chapter 6 also has a review of the location of the major muscle groups.) Each of these exercises can be performed alone or with hand weights or resistance bands/tubes. There are many variations to these basic moves, so make sure you learn these first. Please consult your coach or a reliable website or book to make sure your form is correct. With each exercise, the general guideline is three to five sets of eight to twelve reps, with about a minute of rest between sets.

1. *Bicep curls* (biceps)—Hold the weights in your hands, palms facing front, arms at your sides. Lift your hands toward your shoulders focusing on using your bicep muscle. Keep your elbows close to your body. Lower the weight to the starting position and pause before starting the next rep. Don't jerk your body to help you lift the weight.
2. *Chest flies* (pectorals)—Lie on your back with your arms straight out to the sides (perpendicular to your body), elbows slightly bent, palms facing up. Keeping your elbows slightly bent, raise both arms until the dumbbells meet; it should look like you're hugging a big tree. Exhale while you lift your arms. Lower both arms to the starting position and inhale. Don't let your arms go lower than your shoulders.
3. *Chest press* (pectorals; also called bench press)—Lie on your back with elbows bent at a 90 degree angle, hands in the air. Hold the weight with your palms facing front. Press up until your arms are extended, exhaling as you do so. Pause briefly and then lower the weight slowly to the starting position. If you perform this exercise on a bench, don't let your elbows drop lower than your shoulders.
4. *Lunges* (quadriceps, hamstrings)—Stand with one leg in front of the other, front foot flat on the floor. Lift the heel of your back foot so you are balancing your back toes. Lower your body straight down so your back knee comes close to the ground. Keep your back straight. Keep the knee of your front foot in line with your front ankle and behind your big toe. Keep the hip of your back leg over your back knee.
5. *Rowing* (back)—Put one foot on a step. Hold a dumbbell in the hand opposite the foot on the step (if your left foot is on the step, hold the dumbbell in your right hand). Put your non-dumbbell hand on the bent knee. Bend over slightly at the waist; place the dumbbell hand approximately level with the opposite knee, arm straight, palm facing your knee. Pull the dumbbell hand straight up. Your elbow should go past your back and your hand should stop right next to your rib cage. Focus on squeezing your shoulder blades together as you lift. Switch to the other hand, with the other foot on the step.

6. *Shoulder press* (shoulders)—Lift your arms so your upper arms are parallel to the floor at shoulder height, elbows pointed away from your body and hands in the air toward the ceiling (think "muscle man" flexing his biceps). Hold one weight in each hand, palms facing front. Lift both arms straight up until the weights meet, then lower to the starting position. Exhale on the way up, inhale on the way down.

Strength-Training Tips

- Check with your coach or team trainer before you start a resistance-training program to make sure you have the proper form for each exercise. If your form is wrong, you won't be working the muscle you think you're working no matter how many reps you do. You're also more likely to injure yourself if your form is incorrect. The Find Out More section also has websites that show proper form.
- Alternate days to give your muscles a rest. Work upper body (chest, back, arms) one day and lower body (legs, hips, abs) the next.
- Spend more time on the muscles you need for your sport, but don't neglect the other muscles—especially abs and lower back. A strong core provides stability and balance.
- Know what muscle you're working on with any given exercise. Focus on using that muscle as you lift, pull, or push.
- Don't hold your breath. Exhale when you're doing the work; for example, exhale when you lift during a bicep curl, inhale when you lower.
- Use slow and controlled movements. If you find yourself swinging or bouncing the weight into position, you should use a lower weight. It's better to go lighter and use correct form.
- Pause briefly in between reps to make sure your muscle is doing the work and that you are not bouncing or using momentum.
- Contract your core during every exercise, not just when you're working on abs. Concentrate on pulling navel toward spine, and remember—don't hold your breath.

7. *Squats* (quadriceps)—Stand with your feet about shoulder width apart. Stick your butt out and sit back into the squat position, exhaling as you sit. Focus on putting your weight on your heels. Keep your knees behind your toes. Use your arms for balance or hold a weight in each hand by your sides. Contract your core as you squat.

8. *Triceps dips* (triceps)—Sit on the edge of a bench (or on the floor with your back to a low step). Put your hands on the edge of the bench/step so that your fingers curl down and under. Extend your legs in front of you (the straighter they are, the harder this exercise is). Keeping your butt close to the bench, slowly lower your body by bending your elbows. Your elbows should point straight back. Don't raise your shoulders toward your ears. Straighten your elbows and return to the starting position.

There are four main ways to get resistance training. Here are a few suggestions for each; there are many more resistance exercises to choose from, depending on your sport and your strength needs:

1. Using your *body weight*—push-ups, abdominal crunches, pull-ups, triceps dips, squats, stationary lunges, calf raises (also called toe raises)
2. Using *resistance bands or tubes*—bicep curls, triceps kickbacks, shoulder press, rowing, knee extension (see chapter 6), knee flexion (see chapter 6)
3. Using *dumbbells*—bicep curls, triceps kickbacks, chest flies, shoulder press, squats, lunges, calf raises
4. Using *weight machines*—whatever your gym has available

Dumbbells and resistance bands/tubes are a good choice for a few reasons. First, you can work muscles in different ways not possible with a weight machine. For example, with dumbbells you can work your biceps in two different ways just by changing the way you hold the weight: horizontally (the usual bicep curl) or vertically (also called hammer curls). Second, with a few sets of dumbbells and/ or a few resistance bands, you can easily have a friend come over and work out at home instead of having to go to the gym. Third, resistance bands/tubes are easy to pack so you can take them with you when you go on vacation.

Circuit Training

To add variety and challenge to your strength workout, try circuit training. Choose eight to fifteen exercises using a variety of resistance methods. If you're at the gym you can include the weight machines, but you can also create a circuit at home using body weight, resistance band/tube, and free weight exercises. Each

What Is Cross-Training?

Authors Gary Morgan and George McGlynn define cross-training as "using another sport, activity, or training technique to help improve performance in the primary sport or activity."[12]

If you're a skier who cycles in the off-season to maintain aerobic endurance and strong quadriceps, a golfer who uses resistance training to increase core strength for more powerful drives, a football player who runs track to work on speed, or a wrestler who takes a Pilates class to work on flexibility, then you're using cross-training. Chances are that every one of you engages in some kind of cross-training. Keep it up! Cross-training is a great way to improve your performance while avoiding overuse injuries and burnout (boredom with the same old workout).

Here are a few more benefits of cross-training:[13]

- For truly seasonal sports (skiing, snowboarding), cross-training provides a way to maintain endurance and muscle strength when you can't participate in your primary sport.
- Cross-training works different muscles than your primary sport—and/or the same muscles in different ways—which strengthens your body overall and helps prevent injuries.
- Cross-training allows you to keep working out while you're recovering from an injury. For example, if you injured your shoulder playing water polo, you can still ride a stationary bike or run in the pool to work out your lower body.
- Cross-training can give you a much-needed mental break without compromising your need to keep training. See Try Something New on page 250 for more cross-training suggestions to reboot your motivation.
- Cross-training can allow you to work longer and harder without injuring yourself. If you're a cross-country runner, you might be susceptible to shin splints. Rather than log more miles on the pavement and risk getting shin splints, you could get more cardio endurance training through a less jarring activity such as cycling or swimming.

exercise equals one "station" in the circuit. Organize the stations so that you don't work the same muscle two times in a row. Move through the circuit, performing one set at each station. When you get to the end of the circuit, rest for a few minutes and then start over. Complete the circuit two to three times. The beauty of circuit training is that you can include different exercises or the same exercises in a different order so it's always a new workout.

Here's an example of an eight-station strength circuit you could try at home:

1. Push-ups
2. Lunges (with or without weights)
3. Biceps curls with resistance bands/tubes (see figure 7.1) or weights
4. Squats (with or without weights)
5. Rowing with a resistance band tied to a doorknob
6. Triceps dips
7. Calf raises (with or without weights)
8. Crunches (alone or while holding light weight)

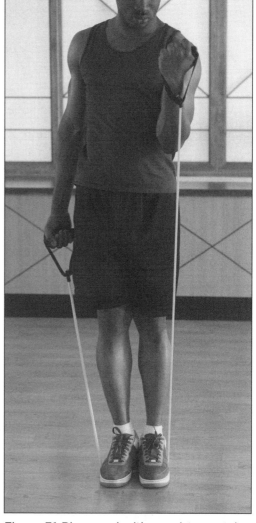

Figure 7.1 Bicep curl with a resistance tube. To make the exercise harder, step "higher" on the band so the amount of band between your foot and the handle is shorter. You can also curl both arms at the same time. *Photo courtesy of Jupiterimages/Thinkstock.*

You can vary the circuit to meet your individual sport needs. For example, if you need to work on leg strength, pick four or five that focus on legs (e.g., squats, lunges, calf raises, knee flexion, leg press) and then put other body parts in between.

Power

Power is a combination of speed and strength needed for fast, explosive movements—a hockey shot, golf swing, tennis serve, soccer kick, and so on. Increase

Try Something New

Variety is the spice of life, even when it comes to training. If you find yourself increasingly unmotivated to work out, it might be because you're tired of doing the same thing day after day, week after week. Lack of motivation can lead to skipped workouts and unaccomplished goals. There are so many ways to work on speed, strength, and the other fitness aspects; why not try something completely different? (Fact: Variety is actually better for your muscles anyway; see the information on muscle confusion on page 251.)

Here are a few suggestions:

- Try a different way of getting in your cardio endurance training. If you usually run, try cycling or swimming. If you usually swim, try running or rowing. You'll be increasing your lung capacity and working different muscle groups at the same time.
- As another cardio alternative, take a Spinning class at the gym. In most classes, you do different kinds of "rides" during the course of the class. You might do a three-minute heavy-gear hill ride followed by thirty-second sprints on a light gear followed by four-, eight-, and sixteen-count "jumps" on a medium gear. You can make the class as easy or hard as you want since you set the gear level.
- Try a different kind of resistance training. If you usually use weights, try using resistance bands or tubes instead. To do bicep curls, for example, step on the band, wrap the band around your hand (or hold the handle on a tube), and curl (see figure 7.1). For more resistance band/tube exercises, see *Strength Band Training*, which is listed in the Find Out More section.
- Another way to vary resistance training is to take a Strong class at the gym. Each teacher uses different resistance equipment, everything from bands to a stability ball to a barbell with weights. You might even try Pilates or yoga to work on flexibility in addition to core strength.

- For an all-around conditioning workout, try a home program such as P90X or Insanity, both available at Beachbody.com. These workouts involve speed, strength, power, and endurance training. Warning: You're going to sweat *a lot*, so have a towel and water or sports drink handy. Both workouts involve intense, nonstop activity (running, jumping, boxing, squats, push-ups, and things you've never even heard of!), so make sure you're up for it.

your power, and you will increase the height you can jump, distance you can shot put, and the force with which you hit a baseball or softball. According to strength and conditioning specialists Lorne Goldenberg and Peter Twist, athletic power comes from the body's "speed center," which is made up of the muscles in the abdomen, lower back, hips, and glutes (butt). Goldenberg and Twist say that "in sport, those muscle groups initiate, assist, and stabilize all movement."[14]

Unfortunately, athletes who need a strong speed center don't always know how important it is. Instead of working on this core area, athletes often focus on "power" muscles such as quads and chest. Goldenberg and Twist report they've known guys who can bench press three hundred pounds, and yet once they're standing, they're easily knocked off balance because their core is weak.[15] The key is to strengthen your core along with your legs, chest, and so on.

There are many ways to increase your power. The following exercises involve quick, explosive (power) movements; for example, quick release of a medicine

Muscle Confusion

According to fitness instructor Robyn Kaczynski, "muscle confusion is a training method used to stimulate muscles in different ways to continue growth." Practically, muscle confusion involves changing your workout often—at least every six to eight weeks, but even as often as every week or every workout—so your muscles are constantly being worked in different ways. For example, you could change the weight, number of repetitions, number of sets, and/or rest time between sets. Kaczynski says, "I personally never do the same workout two times in a row. Some days I will use heavy weights and fewer repetitions, others I will use lighter weights and more repetitions. . . . It's all about mixing it up so the body can't get used to a particular workout."[16]

ball, lifting a dumbbell quickly and lowering it slowly. If you were working on pure strength, you might pick your heaviest weight and lift and lower at the same speed; for example, two counts up, two counts down. To work on power, however, use your medium weight and focus on quick, explosive lifts and slow, controlled returns; for example, count to one going up and count to three while lowering. Don't forget to exhale when you're doing the work. For more power exercises, see chapters 6 and 7 in *Sports Power* as well as other resources in the Find Out More section.

1. Using a *medicine ball*, you can work on just about any muscle group. A few sample exercises are the chest pass (works chest, shoulders, and back; mimics basketball chest pass), overhead throw (works back and core; mimics basketball pass and soccer throw-in), and axe chop (works core; good for any power sport).
2. Using a *stability ball*, you can work on your speed center (abs, lower back, hips, glutes), as well as legs, arms, shoulders, upper back, and chest. There are literally hundreds of exercises you can do with a stability ball—crunches, hamstring curls, push-ups, balancing, bridging, and more. By incorporating the ball into various exercises, you work on core stability as well as the other muscle groups. In figure 7.2, for example, the person

Figure 7.2 Chest flies on a stability ball. In the bridge position, keep your head and neck supported by the ball, abs contracted, glutes squeezed, and hips up so your body is in one straight line or "bridge." *Photo courtesy of Chris Clinton/Thinkstock.*

is doing chest flies while "bridging" on the ball, thus working glutes and abs as well as chest. Goldenberg and Twist's book *Strength Ball Training* categorizes the ball exercises by muscle group and has a handy chart at the beginning listing all the exercises by muscle group, equipment needed (stability ball, medicine ball, or both), and page where the description is found.

3. *Plyometrics* is specifically designed to develop explosive power. The exercises include rapid, repeated stretching and contracting of muscles: jumping, bounding, and hopping, for example. Before you try any plyo exercises, talk to your coach or trainer. Plyometrics involves high-impact activity and can result in injury if not performed correctly. For examples of plyometric workouts, see *Training for Speed, Agility, and Quickness* listed in the Find Out More section at the end of this chapter.

4. *Circuit training* can be used to develop power as well as strength. You can basically use the same circuit stations as in your strength circuit, just change the weights and the way you perform the exercises. Use medium weights and perform a medium number of reps. Lift quickly and lower slowly, even if doing push-ups, triceps dips, or another exercise using just your body weight. Every exercise should involve bursts of power.

Endurance

There are really two kinds of endurance: aerobic and anaerobic. During *aerobic* exercise (think cardio—running, rowing, cycling, swimming), the body uses oxygen to break down food to fuel activity; during *anaerobic* exercise (short bursts of activity—sprinting, jumping), the energy comes from what is stored in the muscles and no oxygen is required. In sports requiring aerobic endurance, the key is good lung capacity, so you can take in and use as much oxygen as possible; athletes who compete in cross-country, Nordic skiing, and distance swimming events, for example, need excellent cardiovascular stamina. Athletes who compete in stop-and-start sports—volleyball, football, and gymnastics, for example—need muscular endurance so they can go all out for a couple minutes (or less) at a time.

> "I see races as a great way to push myself to the absolute physical edge and although I'm not very competitive, I like to push myself as far as I can go."
> —Annalise, 18, Nordic skiing

Aerobic

No matter what your sport, you can improve your overall performance by increasing your aerobic endurance. This kind of lung capacity/stamina is the foundation

History of Nordic Skiing

Nordic skiing is named after the Norse people who settled the northern European region in the ninth century. Today that area is more commonly called Scandinavia and includes the countries of Norway, Denmark, and Sweden.

Over four thousand years ago, people in this area started using skis as a way to travel and hunt in the snow. In the 1700s, army units in Norway started skiing for fun, and cross-country (or Nordic) skiing became a competitive sport in the late 1800s. Cross-country skiing has been part of the Winter Olympics since 1924 (for men; women's events started in 1952). For the most part, Nordic countries—for example, Norway and Sweden—dominate Olympic cross-country events.[17]

for all other fitness training. Aerobic stamina enables you to keep going at higher intensity longer than your competitor. A wrestler or golfer or tennis player who doesn't tire easily can focus on skill and technique instead of catching his or her breath. So, even if your sport isn't Nordic skiing or cross-country, try adding some endurance training to your workout routine.

Here are some ideas. Your endurance training should contain a mix of the following:[18]

1. *Steady pace cardio*—Run (or swim or cycle or row) for about thirty minutes at 70 to 80 percent effort. It should be a pace that is challenging but not so hard that it prevents you from carrying on a conversation with someone.
2. *Interval training*—Intervals involve alternating hard work and rest. For example, you might run one lap around the track (four hundred meters) at a fast (not all-out) pace, then rest for two minutes and run another lap. Do a total of six fast laps. The same interval idea can be applied to swimming, rowing, or cycling for a little variety in your cardio.
3. *Fartlek training*—*Fartlek* means "speed play" in Swedish. This workout is basically the same as interval training, but fartlek sessions are less structured.

For example, start the workout as a steady pace jog. After five minutes or so, run hard to a certain destination—a tree or stop sign, for example—then start jogging again. After a few minutes, pick another destination and run hard until you reach it. The key is to vary the length of the hard runs, making some only ten yards and some one hundred yards or more. You can add variation by finding an area with hills so that some of your jogging and sprinting is done both up- and down-hill. Another variation involves changing the mode of exercise to cycling, rowing, or Nordic skiing.

Anaerobic

Many team sports involve repeated periods of all-out effort followed by short periods of rest: competitive cheer, football, and volleyballare just a few examples. To develop the needed anaerobic endurance, muscles must be trained to go all out over and over with short breaks in between. Here are a couple ideas:[19]

1. *Interval training*—This workout is similar to interval training for aerobic endurance, with two basic differences: the work periods involve shorter distance and faster speed. So, instead of running one lap (four hundred meters) at 70 to 80 percent, you run one hundred or two hundred meters at closer to 90 percent. Do five sprints, resting in between for about ninety seconds.
2. *Circuit training*—Circuit training for endurance is a little different than for strength or power. You still want to set up around eight to twelve stations, but this time a few of the stations should include sprint variations along with the resistance exercises. Your goal is to work for thirty seconds at each station, then rest for sixty seconds, and repeat the circuit three times. Here's a sample endurance circuit:

   - Calf raises
   - Triceps dips
   - Straight sprint
   - Crunches
   - Lunges
   - Football stance fast feet (change direction every five seconds)
   - Push-ups
   - Squats
   - Suicides (back-and-forth sprints, touching the floor before you run back)

Athlete Bio: Derek Ort, Wrestling

Officially, Derek Ort started wrestling in the eighth grade. Unofficially, he started at age five. "My brother wrestled before me, so he would come home and practice his moves on me," says Derek, age eighteen. Joining a wrestling team in high school was a no-brainer. "It's a family tradition," Derek says, and thanks to his brother, Derek had already learned how to defend himself.

Derek also played two years of football, but he says the training for wrestling was much harder: "Our warm-ups were harder than the entire football practice. . . . There were a couple football players that came in [to wrestling practice]; they quit the next day because it was too hard for them. And some schools that are bigger into wrestling . . . their warm-ups are harder than our entire [wrestling] practice."

According to Derek, wrestling training is so demanding because it involves strengthening the whole body. "We use a lot more of our bodies and all that. We use our neck muscles. We roll around on our heads. They use weights a lot . . . , but we never did. We would do cross-fit training: a minute of push-ups, then you go run, then a minute of sit-ups. We would sprint back and forth. We had a 'fun run' . . . two to three miles."

As a senior in 2011, Derek wrestled his way through districts and regionals to make it to the state meet—and he did so with a broken pinky finger and pneumonia. He finished just one match shy of placing. Derek was recruited by Edinboro University in Pennsylvania, but the wrestling program didn't have any scholarships available. "There are very few wrestling scholarships," he says. "You have to be *really* good. You would have to win state to get a college scholarship." But all is not lost. "I want to finish my two years of college [in Florida]; that way I can go up to Edinboro and wrestle. I had a meeting with the assistant coach. They didn't have any scholarships available, but if I were to go that school I would be automatically put on the roster."

As of 2012, Derek wasn't wrestling, but he was still using sports to stay in shape. His sport of choice now is ultimate Frisbee; as he says, "that's just nonstop cardio."[20]

If you're completing your circuit in a gym, you can hop on the treadmill, stationary bike, or elliptical machine for the sprints, or just run in place. To add some difficulty to the circuit workout, you can

increase the work time to forty-five seconds,
decrease the rest time to thirty seconds, or
increase the number of times around the circuit to four.[21]

Agility

John Graham, a certified fitness instructor and strength coach, defines agility as "the ability to decelerate, accelerate, and change direction quickly while maintaining good body control without decreasing speed."[22] Many sports involve short bursts of energy in all different directions—left, right, vertical, backward, forward, and diagonal—and sometimes in combination. Think of the following sports scenarios, all of which happen on a regular basis and all of which require agility and balance:

- A basketball player dribbles the ball downcourt, cuts right around the screen, drives left and diagonally toward the basket, and jumps to make the shot.
- A tennis player sprints sideways to return a serve, then stops her momentum and reverses direction to return the volley, and then sprints diagonally backward to return the next volley.
- A running back cuts right, then left, then spins off a tackle and sprints toward the end zone.

According to Graham, "agility is a critical and often overlooked component of athletic performance. . . . Athletes that can develop their quickness in different directions will be better athletes," no matter what their sport.[23] They will have better control over their bodies due to increased "kinesthetic awareness," or knowing where one's body is in space. Gymnasts and divers have this trait in abundance; they can flip and twist through the air and still stick the dismount or find the water for a smooth entry. Kinesthetic awareness can help in any sport that involves multidirectional movement at speed.

So, how do you improve agility? Some fitness experts suggest that agility training should mimic the movements you perform in your sport—for example, sprinting left, stopping, then sprinting right; diagonal sprint then vertical jump; backward run, then turn and sprint. Agility also involves flexibility, especially in

> ## Balance
>
> Agility is closely connected with balance or stability. A strong core (abs, lower back, hips, glutes) is essential for remaining balanced while cutting, juking, changing direction, and so on. Here are a few ways to strengthen your core and improve your balance:
>
> 1. Perform resistance exercises while bridging on the stability ball (as in figure 7.2). From the bridging position you can do chest press, chest flies, and skull crushers (another triceps exercise). Make sure you focus on contracting your core, squeezing your glutes, and keeping your hips up.
> 2. Perform resistance exercises while standing on one leg or while standing on a half stability ball (one side is flat and rubberized, and the other side looks like a regular stability ball; you can stand on either the ball side or the flat side to work on balance). You can do bicep curls, squats, triceps kickbacks, and shoulder press on one leg or on the half ball. Make sure you contract your core to keep yourself stable. According to fitness instructor Robyn Kaczynski, standing on one leg helps increase core strength and balance "because the less contact you have with the floor the more you force the core to engage."[24]
> 3. Take Pilates or yoga classes. Almost all of the poses and exercises involve balance and focus on strengthening the core.

the hip area, so take a look at the next section for stretches to increase flexibility. Chapter 4 in *Training for Speed, Agility, and Quickness* has over fifty different exercises; here are just a few examples:[25]

1. *Carioca*—Start with legs about shoulder width apart. Step sideways so right foot goes in front of left leg. Then step and cross your left foot behind your right leg. Repeat right foot in front of left leg, then left foot behind right leg. (This exercise works on balance, sideways speed, footwork, and hip flexibility.)
2. *Shuttle*—There are numerous variations on this drill. Start with your legs about shoulder width apart, one foot on either side of the middle line. Turn to the right, sprint to a line about five yards away, and touch the line

History of Cheerleading

The history of cheerleading in the United States is closely linked to the history of college football. In 1869, Princeton and Rutgers played in the first intercollegiate football game. Within ten years, Princeton had a pep club leading cheers from the stands. Like the football team, the pep club was all guys.

One of the Princeton yell leaders was Thomas Peebles. After he graduated in 1884, Peebles moved to Minnesota and introduced the pep club idea at the University of Minnesota. Soon, guys from other colleges and universities started leading cheers from the stands in order to encourage the team and create a high-energy environment.

In 1898, a University of Minnesota student named Johnny Campbell took the pep club idea to a new level. With his team struggling to rebound from a three-game losing streak, Campbell grabbed a megaphone, jumped onto the field, and led the crowd in coordinated cheering. Many people consider this to be the invention of modern cheerleading.

In 1923, girls were finally allowed to join cheer squads, again at University of Minnesota, but cheerleading still didn't become a female-dominated sport until the 1940s, when many young men left to fight in World War II. It was also during the 1920s that pep squads started using more tumbling and gymnastics moves in their cheers.

Here are a few more highlights in cheerleading history:

- 1960s: Most high schools and grade schools have cheerleading programs.
- 1970s: Cheer routines are introduced, often to music. The first clinics are started to teach skills, stunts, pyramids, and so on.
- 1982: The first National Cheerleading Competition airs on ESPN.
- 2004: The first World Cheerleading Championships take place and includes the top fourteen teams.
- 2010: The seventh World Cheerleading Championships takes place and includes sixty countries.[26]

with your right hand. Stand up, turn to the left, sprint past the middle line to the far line (ten yards away), and touch it with your left hand. Stand up, turn to your right, sprint back to the center line. (This drill works on ability to change direction, footwork, and reaction time.)

3. *Stand up*—Sit on the ground, knees bent, feet flat on the ground, palms on the ground at your sides. Get up to a standing position as quickly as possible. The action should be explosive. Practice rolling to one side or the other to get up. Repeat. (This drill works on total body agility and kinesthetic awareness.)

Flexibility

Flexibility is especially important in sports like competitive cheer, wrestling, diving, and gymnastics, which involve a wide range of lunging, twisting, and flipping motions. However, every athlete should make flexibility training a top priority since flexible muscles, ligaments, and tendons are able to withstand more strain and stretching, thus reducing the likelihood of injury. Unfortunately, flexibility is probably the most neglected aspect of physical fitness.

The single best way to increase your flexibility is to make stretching part of *every* workout. Here's a list of basic stretches for the major muscle groups used in sports. They are arranged in order from larger to smaller muscle groups. For more stretches, along with photographs and/or drawings, go to the Mayo Clinic website (www.mayoclinic.com/health/stretching/SM00043) or consult two of the books listed in the Find Out More section: *Cross-Training for Sports* (chapter 4) and *Fitness Training for Girls* (chapter 5).

1. *Hips and glutes stretch*—Lie on your back with your feet flat on the floor and your knees bent. Place your right ankle on your left knee so you form the shape of the number four (this stretch is sometimes called the figure 4 stretch because of this pose). Grab your left leg with hands and slowly lift your left leg toward you. You should feel a stretch in your right hip and glute. Add to the stretch by gently pushing against the inside of your right knee with your right elbow. This pushing away will stretch more of the outside of your right hip. Switch legs to get your left hip and glute.

2. *Hamstring stretch*—Lie on your back with both knees bent. Put your right leg straight in the air with the sole of your foot facing the ceiling. Grab your right leg near your knee and lightly pull toward you until you feel a stretch in the back of your right thigh and calf. Switch legs and repeat.

3. *Lower back, glutes, and hip stretch*—Sit up straight with both legs flat on the floor. Bend your left leg and cross it over the right so that your left foot is flat on the floor on the outside of your right leg. Keeping your back straight, twist your

Figure 7.3 Stretch for your lower back, hips, and glutes. Some people call this the pretzel stretch. *Photo courtesy of Ryan McVay/Thinkstock.*

upper body to the left; place your left hand behind you and your right elbow on the outside of your bent left knee (see figure 7.3). Keep twisting slowly until you feel a stretch in your back, as well as your hips and glutes. Switch legs and twist in the opposite direction.

4. *Groin stretch*—Sit up straight on the floor with your knees bent and soles of your feet touching in front of you. Slowly pull your feet toward you and push down gently on your knees using your elbows. You should feel the stretch in your inner thighs, hips, and lower back. This stretch is also called the butterfly stretch.

5. *Hip flexor stretch*—Kneel on your right knee. If you're on a hard surface, fold a towel and put it under your knee. Put your left foot in front of you, bending

Stretching Tips

- Always warm up before you stretch. As mentioned earlier, warm muscles can be stretched more thoroughly and safely. Ideally, you should jog, walk, cycle, or swim for five to ten minutes before stretching.
- Never bounce. Stretching should be a slow, smooth motion to the point where you feel tension, not pain. Then stop and hold the stretch.
- Hold each stretch for about thirty seconds. According to *Fitness* magazine, "Anything less than twenty seconds won't make a significant difference in lengthening muscle fibers and tissue."[27]
- Take slow, deep breaths as you stretch. As you exhale, try to sink deeper into the stretch—slowly.
- When you stretch, start with the larger muscle groups (e.g., quadriceps, lower back) and finish with the smaller muscle groups (e.g., shoulders, triceps). The exercises in this section follow this progression.
- As mentioned earlier, it's a good idea to incorporate stretching into your cooldown after a hard workout. Your muscles are really warm at that point, so it's a great opportunity to improve your flexibility. Stretching after a workout also reduces muscle soreness.

your knee at a 90 degree angle. Slowly let your hips sink toward the floor and lean forward a little (figure 7.4). You should feel stretch in your right hip flexor—the front hip area of your back leg. If your front knee goes past your toes when you lean forward, move your front foot a little farther away from you. Switch legs and repeat.

6. *Quadriceps stretch*—Stand up straight, bend your right leg behind you, and grab your right foot. Pull your right heel slowly toward your butt. Make sure your right knee is pointed straight down and your legs are close together (see figure 7.5). You may need to steady yourself by holding on to a chair or wall. You should feel the stretch in the front part of your bent leg. Switch legs and repeat.

7. *Calf stretch*—Stand facing a wall. Put both hands on the wall, extend your right leg straight behind you, and push against the wall. Make sure both feet are completely on the floor, facing forward. You should feel a stretch in the calf of the back leg. Switch legs and repeat.

Figure 7.4 Hip flexor stretch. To feel a deeper stretch in your back hip flexor, lean forward slightly, but don't let your front knee go past your toes. *Photo courtesy of Robert Fay.*

8. *Chest stretch*—Grab hands behind your back, around butt level. Squeeze your shoulder blades together so your shoulders go back and you feel a stretch in your pectoral muscles (chest) and the front part of your shoulders. Don't hunch your shoulders; pull down with your hands.

9. *Shoulder stretch*—Bring your right arm across your body just below shoulder level. Keep that arm straight and hold it with your left hand above or below the elbow, pulling slightly with your left hand. Switch arms and repeat.

10. *Triceps stretch*—Take your right arm and hold it straight up. Bend at the elbow and place your hand in the center of your upper back. Using your left hand, lightly press down on your right elbow. Switch arms and repeat.

You might find it helpful to perform each triceps stretch in conjunction with the shoulder stretch; that is, move directly into the right triceps stretch after stretching the right shoulder. Then do the left side.

Find Out More

Books

The following books contain specific exercises and drills for improving different areas of physical fitness. Most drills and exercises are accompanied by an illustration as well as an explanation of the goal (that is, the body part to be strengthened

Figure 7.5 Quadriceps stretch. Keep your knee pointed straight down and gently pull your heel toward your butt. *Photo courtesy of Jupiterimages/ Thinkstock.*

or the specific skill to be improved), the setup, and the step-by-step directions. *Training for Speed*, *Cross-Training for Sports*, and *Strength Band Training* also provide sport-specific workout suggestions. You can probably find all of these books at your local library.

Brown, Lee E., Vance A. Ferrigno, and Juan Carlos Santana, eds. *Training for Speed, Agility, and Quickness*. Champaign, IL: Human Kinetics, 2000.

Gaede, Katrina, Alan Lachica, and Doug Werner. *Fitness Training for Girls*. San Diego, CA: Tracks Publishing, 2001.

Goldenberg, Lorne, and Peter Twist. *Strength Ball Training*. 2nd ed. Champaign, IL: Human Kinetics, 2007.

Morgan, Gary T., and George H. McGlynn. *Cross-Training for Sports*. Champaign, IL: Human Kinetics, 1997.

Page, Phil, and Todd Ellenbecker. *Strength Band Training*. 2nd ed. Champaign, IL: Human Kinetics, 2011.

Sandler, David. *Sports Power*. Champaign, IL: Human Kinetics, 2005.

Online Articles

KG Investments. "Q&A Articles: Fitness." TeenGrowth.com, updated February 14, 2012. www.teengrowth.com/index.cfm?action=info_sub&Sub Category=sports_Fitness&CatDesc=Sports&SubDesc=Fitness&Category= sports. This web page contains a list of questions from teens aged thirteen to eighteen related to various aspects of fitness. You might find that you've had some of the same questions but were too embarrassed to ask someone. Click on the question for the answer.

Mayo Clinic Staff. "Slide Show: A Guide to 10 Basic Stretches." Mayo Clinic, February 23, 2011. www.mayoclinic.com/health/stretching/SM00043.

Walters, Lexi. "Our Top 8 Stability Ball Exercises." *Fitness*. www.fitness magazine.com/workout/gear/equipment/best-stability-ball-exercises/.

Websites

Dumbbell-Exercises.com (www.dumbbell-exercises.com). Click on the "Dumbbell Exercises" link for information on more than seventy-five dumbbell exercises.

Resistance Band Workouts (resistancebandworkouts.com). Click on the links at the top for resistance band exercises for your back, chest, abs, and more. Some exercise explanations include video.

Notes

1. Quoted in *Chris Paul's Conditioning Workout* (video), Yahoo! Sports, sports.yahoo.com/elite -athlete-workouts/chris-paul (accessed January 9, 2012).

2. Quoted in "Tweet This," *Florida Today*, January 8, 2012.

3. Youth Sport Trust (Great Britain), *The Young Athlete's Handbook* (Champaign, IL: Human Kinetics, 2001), 84.

4. Youth Sport Trust, *Young Athlete's Handbook*, 27.

5. Youth Sport Trust, *Young Athlete's Handbook*, 28.

6. *The Sports Book: The Games, the Rules, the Tactics, the Techniques* (London: Dorling Kindersley, 2007), 171.

7. Doug Lenz and Andrew Hardyk, "Speed Training," in *Training for Speed, Agility, and Quickness*, ed. Lee E. Brown, Vance A. Ferrigno, and Juan Carlos Santana (Champaign, IL: Human Kinetics, 2000), 18–19.

8. Youth Sport Trust, *Young Athlete's Handbook*, 46–47; Lenz and Hardyk, "Speed Training," 66, 76.

9. Ian Pyka and Diane Vives, "Quickness Training," in Brown, Ferrigno, and Santana, *Training for Speed*, 147.

10. Phil Page and Todd Ellenbecker, *Strength Band Training*, 2nd ed. (Champaign, IL: Human Kinetics, 2011), 8.

11. Lorne Goldenberg and Peter Twist, *Strength Ball Training*, 2nd ed. (Champaign, IL: Human Kinetics, 2007), 18.

12. Gary T. Morgan and George H. McGlynn, *Cross-Training for Sports* (Champaign, IL: Human Kinetics, 1997), 3–4.

13. Morgan and McGlynn, *Cross-Training for Sports*, 4–5.

14. Goldenberg and Twist, *Strength Ball Training*, 5.

15. Goldenberg and Twist, *Strength Ball Training*, 5.

16. Robyn Kaczynski, e-mail to author, February 29, 2012.

17. "Cross Country Skiing Equipment and History," Olympic.org, www.olympic.org/cross-country-skiing-equipment-and-history?tab=history (accessed October 24, 2011).

18. Youth Sport Trust, *Young Athlete's Handbook*, 34–35.

19. Youth Sport Trust, *Young Athlete's Handbook*, 37.

20. Derek Ort, interview with author, December 3, 2011.

21. Youth Sport Trust, *Young Athlete's Handbook*, 37.

22. John F. Graham, "Agility Training," in Brown, Ferrigno, and Santana, *Training for Speed*, 80.

23. Graham, "Agility Training," 80.

24. Kaczynski, e-mail.

25. Graham, "Agility Training," 84, 86.

26. "History of Cheerleading," The International Cheer Union, cheerunion.org/Content.aspx/History (accessed October 30, 2011); Varsity, "Being a Cheerleader—History of Cheerleading," www.varsity.com/event/1261/being-a-cheerleader-history.aspx (accessed October 30, 2011).

27. "How Long Should I Hold a Stretch?" *Fitness*, www.fitnessmagazine.com/workout/tips/expert-advice/how-long-should-i-hold-a-stretch/ (accessed March 28, 2012).

8

PLAYING IN COLLEGE

··

"If you want to play college sports, there's a college that wants you. . . .
You have to find it."—Lenny Paoletti, athletic director at
Holy Trinity Episcopal Academy, Florida[1]

Some of you might already have college coaches recruiting you. Maybe they saw you play at a club tournament or they read your combine scores online, and they took the initiative to contact you. Congratulations! This chapter provides you with some things to keep in mind as you make a final decision about your college career.

For the rest of you: Don't wait to be noticed! Whether you're a freshman or a senior, there are steps you can take now to market yourself to college coaches. It takes a lot of work and a good dose of realism about your athletic potential, but you can put yourself in a place to be recruited. If you really want to play your sport in college, read on to find out what you can do to make it happen.

What Are Your Options?

When it comes to college sports, most people think of the schools they see on television—Ohio State, LSU, Notre Dame, and so on. These schools all belong

> "The best part of my college career no doubt was the relationships I was able to form with not only my teammates but my coaches and the athletic department staff. . . . Unless you go through something like a collegiate sport with someone, it is difficult to truly understand the extreme hardships and extreme triumphs that make college sports what they are. Putting that much work into something with other people creates bonds that are very unique and special."—Lauren, 22, track and field (NCAA Division I)

"It's really important to keep an open mind. . . . When I first started my heart was set on going to California to play. I was getting recruited by a lot of top-25 schools at the time like LSU and Wichita [State], but I was like, 'No way am I going to Kansas, no way am I going to Louisiana.' . . . Really look at every school, not just the state that it's in, but everything they have to offer."—Emily, 23, volleyball (NCAA Division I)

to Division I of the NCAA (National Collegiate Athletic Association). But did you know that there are two other divisions in the NCAA, as well as two other completely separate college athletic associations? And all have opportunities for you to play sports at the college level. According to the College Sports Scholarships website, of the available athletic scholarships, less than 15 percent are given to Division I student-athletes. The other 85 percent are awarded to players in NCAA Division II, the NAIA (National Athletic Intercollegiate Association), and the NJCAA (National Junior College Athletic Association).[2]

Although you might have your heart set on a certain Division I college, you would be smart to explore all your options. There are so many factors involved in college sports placement:

- How many other players does that school already have at your position?
- How many scholarships does the coach have to offer? Are they full scholarships? If not, how much would you have to pay for tuition, books, room and board, and so on?
- Are you academically eligible for a Division I school?
- Does the school have the academic major you want to pursue?
- Do you like the snow or the desert or humidity?
- Do you like being in an area with beautiful scenery and little nightlife, or do you want to be in a major city where there's a lot to do?

In order to fully enjoy your college playing experience, you need to find the best fit *for you* on every level—athletically, academically, and socially. You are more likely to

"I feel super blessed to have had the experience that I've had [at Colorado State University] but I know kids that didn't like it. We had the same exact experience, and it was perfect for me and it wasn't what they wanted."
—Jacque, 22, volleyball (NCAA Division I)

History of Football

In the 1860s, male college students at several East Coast universities started playing a wild new game. It was a rugby-soccer variation that was extremely rough—so much so that several college campuses banned it. Athletes at one of these universities—Princeton—started playing a modified game, one that had more rules and was not quite so violent. Many people consider this to be the start of modern American football, though the game still resembled rugby more than the game we know today.

At first, football was strictly a college sport played at the prestigious universities; Rutgers and Princeton played the first official collegiate game in 1869. This early game was played with twenty-five players to a side and different rules about kicking and carrying the ball. Around 1877 a Yale player named Walter Camp started making changes to distinguish the new game from rugby. Rule changes credited to Camp include the following:

- Teams limited to eleven per side
- Creation of quarterback and center positions
- Creation of a line of scrimmage
- Teams switch possession after a set number of downs (at first it was three downs to move five yards; it later switched to the current system of four downs to get ten yards)

Even with some rule changes, this new game was very rough. In 1905 alone, 18 players were killed and 159 were seriously injured. President Teddy Roosevelt demanded that the game be made safer. This is when pads and other protective equipment were introduced, though the leather "helmets" still didn't provide much padding.

Football became a professional (paid) sport in 1892, and the American Professional Football Conference was formed in 1920. In 1921 the pro league changed its name to the National Football League as we know it today.[3]

find the perfect spot if you keep an open mind and explore all your options. There might be something out there that you've never thought of.

National Collegiate Athletic Association (NCAA)

The NCAA is a nonprofit organization that oversees the sports programs at schools that are members. According to the NCAA website, the association was started in 1906 "to protect young people from the dangerous and exploitive athletics practices of the time"—specifically in football, which was a much more violent and unregulated sport back then.[4] As of 2012, there were twenty-three NCAA sports, and more than 1,200 colleges and universities belonged to the organization. Among other things, the NCAA enforces rules on eligibility and manages the national championship in each sport. The NCAA is by far the best known of the college athletic associations.[5]

There are three NCAA divisions, each with different requirements regarding the number of sports offered, the number of scholarships offered, and the number of competitions. Schools decide which division to join by determining which set of requirements they are able to meet given their student enrollment, financial situation (how much money they can allot toward sports facilities, equipment, scholarships, etc.), and fan support (how many people will pay to watch the sport and buy the sport paraphernalia). Then each school must meet the NCAA requirements for that division each year. See table 8.1 for the basic differences between the three divisions.

Division I

NCAA Division I represents the top level of collegiate athletic competition. The schools are well known, the games are televised (in some sports, anyway), and the

"The biggest difference for me was the time commitment. Whereas in high school, meetings/film/practice would usually last from 3pm to 6pm (3 hours), college players are spending about 4 hours a day in mandatory film study, team meetings, weights, and practice. That was just mandatory time spent. If you were a hard worker and diligent student of the game you would spend hours more studying game film and researching your opponent and usually putting extra time in the weight room. It really takes over your life."
—Josh, 24, football (NCAA Division II)

Table 8.1 Differences among the NCAA Divisions

	Division I	Division II	Division III
Number of sports required	At least seven for men and seven for women *or* six for men and eight for women	At least five for men and five for women *or* four for men and six for women	At least five for men and five for women
Number of team sports required	At least two for men and two for women	At least two for men and two for women	At least two for men and two for women
Number of athletic scholarships allowed	Varies by sport	Varies by sport	None; no sports-related financial aid is allowed
Attendance requirements	Minimum average for men's football (17,000 for home games)*	None	None

Source: Data from NCAA Eligibility Center, "Divisions," pp. 2–4, web1.ncaa.org/ECWR2/NCAA_EMS/NCAA_EMS.html# (accessed May 27, 2012).

*This average only applies to Division I-A schools.

athletes are considered elite; it's the big time as far as college sports goes. Many young athletes dream of playing Division I, which is exactly why the competition to get there is so fierce.

So what does it take to play Division I? Talent, hard work, commitment, mental toughness, and desire. Training and competing at the Division I level are physically, mentally, and emotionally demanding. The pressure to win is intense, especially if you're playing on a scholarship in a highly ranked program. "There's a lot of expectation to win and to work hard. Usually they make that pretty clear when you're getting recruited," says Jacque, age twenty-two. Jacque played Division I volleyball at Colorado State University on a full-ride scholarship. "They are paying you to be there and to play, and it's an investment and it's your job. They

"College is so much more physically demanding. . . . Lifting three to four times a week and practicing five days a week . . . practicing as a freshman at the level of twenty-two-year-old men. . . . I remember the first three weeks of lifting in practice. My entire body would just be sore every day."
—Noah, 20, volleyball (NCAA Division I)

take it very seriously and they take you very seriously. It's fun and everything, but it certainly is a job. It forces you to grow up really, really quickly."[6] Before you start pursuing a Division I athletic career, ask yourself: Am I willing to work that hard? Can I handle the pressure to perform and win? To succeed at the top college level, you really have to want it.

In addition, you probably have to do more than play on your high school team if you want to have a chance of playing Division I. Coaches want players who are committed to their sport and who continually strive to get better. Depending on your sport, that might involve one or more of the following:

- Trying out for and making a club/travel team
- Attending summer camps to work on skills
- Participating in combines to test your overall athleticism
- Participating in showcase events where college coaches come check out high school talent

All of these athletic extras involve time and money, so your parents need to be on board. Also, see what you can do to help out financially. You probably won't have time for a part-time job, but you can save your allowance or do odd jobs for neighbors. Chances are that people will appreciate that you're taking responsibil-

"The biggest difference in playing a Division I sport is the commitment. In high school, most of us were 'valuable' parts to the team so practice was run how we wanted and we had much more room for having fun. In college our sport is our job and the hours we put in on the court are hard and efficient and you must go 100% at all times, no excuses. The competition is so high and nobody ever is sure who will be on the starting lineup. I just take it way more seriously now."—Dane, 21, volleyball (NCAA Division I)

Athlete Bio: Jacque Davisson, Volleyball

When Jacque, age twenty-two, started high school, she thought basketball was going to be her sport. Then she tried out for volleyball. It was the first time she had actually played real six-on-six indoor volleyball, and Jacque got hooked. She went on to play all four years, earned all-league honors several times, and led her team to the California Interscholastic Federation Southern Section championship during her senior year. Jacque also joined a club team as a sophomore, and after seeing her play at tournaments, several college coaches started recruiting Jacque.

After considering offers from different universities, Jacque accepted a full-ride scholarship from Colorado State University (CSU) and learned almost immediately that playing in college is a lot tougher than playing in high school. "In college the sport you play is your main job. . . . We get in the weight room at 6:15 a.m. We're working hard, and we're going hard every single time. We don't mess around. When you go to practice, you work hard. Leave all your crap at the door, you play volleyball for two and a half hours, and then you can pick up your life later."

Academics are also tougher at the college level, and Jacque says she was lucky to have a coach who understood that school stress sometimes affects athletic performance. However, she also learned that coaches expect players to take advantage of the tutoring and other help that's available to them as student-athletes.

Jacque says, "I love playing volleyball because of the way I approach the game. I am a very loud and energetic player, and I love that I am that way because it draws people to the game. The best feeling is hearing someone say after a match that watching you play has made them fall in love with the game." *Photo courtesy of Nick Lyon.*

One of the best parts of Jacque's college experience was the community support for women's volleyball. She says, "We were the big sport on campus. . . . It's a cool experience to be a big deal for a little while."

Besides athletics, Jacque chose CSU for academic reasons: "I narrowed it down based on what I thought I wanted to major in—which was veterinary medicine, which turned out to be not something I wanted to major in—so I went to the school with the best vet school in the nation." Jacque ended up changing her major to health and exercise science, and she's hoping to start a career in sports medicine.

But not yet. After graduating from CSU in 2011, Jacque accepted an offer to play volleyball professionally in Finland. As of 2012, she had just finished her first season as a pro. Not bad for someone who didn't think of playing volleyball until she was a high school freshman.[7]

ity for your athletic future and will gladly pay you for washing/waxing cars, mowing lawns, shoveling snow, and so on.

For many student-athletes, part of the Division I dream is receiving a full-ride athletic scholarship, and rightly so. If you score a full ride, *everything* is paid for—tuition, books, room and board—and you don't have to pay it back. You can't beat that! But full rides are hard to come by since the NCAA has regulations about the number of scholarships that each head coach can offer to incoming athletes.

In some Division I sports (called *head-count sports*), the NCAA limits the number of athletes that can be recruited each year by each school. Coaches have a set number of athletic scholarships, and each one is a full ride. In Division I women's basketball, for example, each school has fifteen full-ride scholarships available, so each school can recruit up to fifteen female basketball players each year. There are very few head-count sports; in fact, there are only two for men and four for women (the number in parentheses refers to the number of athletes each school fielding a team in one of these sports can recruit each year):[8]

Men
Basketball (13)
Football (85)[9]

Women
Basketball (15)
Gymnastics (12)
Tennis (8)
Volleyball (12)

In other Division I sports (called *equivalency sports*), the NCAA limits the number of scholarships but not the number of athletes. In other words, coaches can divide one scholarship among several athletes so that each player gets a partial ride. For example, each Division I men's cross-country team gets five scholarships. Because the coach is limited on the number of scholarships and not on the number of "heads" he can recruit, he might decide to give out two full-ride scholarships and divide the other three scholarships among six athletes, for a total of eight new recruits. The NCAA rules regarding scholarships in equivalency sports allow for more athletes to be recruited, but few actually receive a full ride. Here are some of the Division I equivalency sports (the number in parentheses refers to the number of scholarships available to each school; a coach is free to divide these scholarships and recruit more than this number of athletes each year):[10]

Men	*Women*
Baseball (11.7)	Softball (12)
Golf (4.5)	Golf (6)
Gymnastics (6.3)	
	Field hockey (12)
Ice hockey (18)	Ice hockey (18)
Lacrosse (12.6)	Lacrosse (12)
	Rowing (20)
Soccer (9.9)	Soccer (12)
Swimming (9.9)	Swimming (14)
Tennis (4.5)	
Track and field (12.6)	Track and field (18)
Volleyball (4.5)	
Water polo (4.5)	Water polo (8)

"The best part about my college athletic experience is by far being able to play the sport that I love, regardless of the pain and regardless of the injuries, at such a high level. The fact that I was able to contribute to such a high level program, day in and day out, is inspiring and has definitely left a positive mark. Nothing can replace the competitive spirit and passion with which we practiced and lifted as a team."
—Noah, 20, volleyball (NCAA Division I)

Title IX and the NCAA

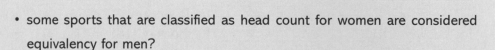

Look back at the lists of scholarships available for various Division I sports. Did you notice that

- some sports that are classified as head count for women are considered equivalency for men?
- in almost every case where there is a men's and women's team, women have more scholarships available?

What's up with that? It all goes back to Title IX. Because NCAA schools have to offer women the same opportunities as men and because football takes up such a big portion of the men's available resources, schools often have to cut their offerings for men in other sports. Even Division I schools that don't have football programs are limited to the same number of scholarships in other men's sports. Long Beach State (in California), for example, doesn't have a football program, but it still only has 4.5 scholarships available for men's volleyball. The "quotas" are applied across the NCAA, not on a school-by-school basis.

It's a Fact

Crazy as it sounds, you might be better off turning down a partial athletic scholarship. Noah, age twenty, did just that. He was offered a partial scholarship to play volleyball at UCLA, a Division I school. Because men's volleyball is an equivalency sport, the coach only had 4.5 scholarships to divide among all the potential recruits. As a result, Noah was not offered very much money. NCAA rules prohibit athletes from taking both athletic scholarship money and nonathletic financial aid, so Noah chose to accept the latter. Though he signed to play volleyball at UCLA, he turned down the athletic scholarship because he got more money from other financial aid.[11] (If you find yourself in a similar situation, just be open with the college coach, as Noah was. The coach should understand your desire to get the best financial package possible. Plus, the coach will have more money left to offer other potential recruits.)

Even if you impress a Division I coach with your athletic talent, you still have to meet the academic qualifications, which includes a 2.0 GPA in your sixteen core classes (math, science, English, and social science; see table 8.2 for the exact breakdown) and a good score on the SAT or ACT. The lower your GPA, the better you need to do on your SAT or ACT (see the NCAA Eligibility Center website for the "sliding scale"). According to Alison Bell, director of college counseling at Holy Trinity Episcopal Academy in Florida, you can really help your recruiting prospects by excelling in the classroom: "The word *student-athlete* is crucial. Your academic profile is as important if not more so in your athletic placement because you have more leverage the better your academic profile is."[12] If a coach has to decide between equally talented athletes—or even between a number-one recruit and a number-ten recruit—he or she will most likely choose the better student. Division I coaches are under pressure to keep the academic performance of their players up. They're not going to risk signing you if there's an equally talented second baseman (or striker or running back) with a stronger academic profile.

Did You Know?

Athletic scholarships, whether partial or full ride, are only guaranteed for one year. They are reevaluated each year.

The NCAA Eligibility Center

If you want to play at an NCAA Division I or Division II school, you must register with the NCAA Eligibility Center (also known as the Clearinghouse) in order to have your academic and athletic eligibility verified. As of 2012, the cost of this certification process was sixty-five dollars for U.S. students and ninety-five dollars for international students. You are responsible for registering and for providing the Eligibility Center with the required information according to the following timeline:[13]

- Register with the Eligibility Center at the beginning of your junior year of high school.
- Send your SAT or ACT scores directly to the Eligibility Center; the code is 9999.
- Have your guidance counselor send an official transcript to the Eligibility Center after your junior year.
- Have your guidance counselor send your final official transcript to the Eligibility Center after you graduate. The transcript must be sent directly from the high school to the Eligibility Center.

You can also use the Eligibility Center to explore the sports teams at various NCAA schools. Click on the "Sports" link at the top, then click on the sport you're hoping to play. From here you can find out which divisions have teams in your sport and then you can explore the teams at different schools in each division. Make sure you take advantage of this feature of the Eligibility Center. It's a great way to research team records, coaches, rosters, and the schools themselves as you narrow your options.

See the Eligibility Center website (www.eligibilitycenter.org) to register and to get more information on the steps you need to take.

"Having the opportunity to play in front of 4–6,000 screaming fans every Friday and Saturday night was one of the most exhilarating experiences I have ever endured. It is something that I truly miss and a feeling that I will never forget!"—Emily, 23, volleyball (NCAA Division I)

Division II

Division II schools aren't as widely known as Division I schools, but they still have high-quality sports and academic programs. Some colleges and universities choose to join Division II instead of Division I because the requirements are better matched with their enrollment, athletic support base, and financial situation. Division II schools don't have to fund quite as many athletic programs and they don't have any head-count sports, which means most Division II athletes receive partial scholarships and not full rides.

The athletic competition is still tough, as is the competition for scholarships. In general, Division II schools have fewer scholarships to hand out in each sport compared with Division I. Participating in sport-specific summer camps, club/travel teams, and combines can all boost your recruiting prospects, and so can excellence in the classroom. As at Division I, coaches at Division II are looking for recruits they don't have to babysit. They want responsible, self-disciplined student-athletes. Academically, Division II schools are just as challenging as Division I schools. As of August 1, 2013, incoming Division II freshmen have a sixteen-course requirement just like incoming Division I freshmen (see table 8.2 for details).

So why do high school student-athletes play at Division II? First, if you don't get recruited to play at a Division I school, Division II is an excellent

"In high school it was very laid back, and although you wanted to do well and win it felt more like an extracurricular activity than a full sports team. . . . In college, it turns into a job. Instead of being light and fun, it is taken very seriously, and because of that the fun most times is taken out of the sport."—Kirsten, 20, softball (NCAA Division II)

Table 8.2 Academic Initial-Eligibility Requirements for NCAA, NAIA, and NJCAA Schools[a]

NCAA Division I	NCAA Division II	NAIA	NJCAA
Graduate from high school	Graduate from high school	Graduate from high school	Graduate from high school or receive a high school equivalency diploma by taking a national test such as the General Educational Development (GED) Test
Take sixteen core courses: • Four years of English • Three years of math (Algebra I or higher) • Two years of natural/physical science (one year of lab if offered by high school) • One year of additional English, math, or natural/physical science • Two years of social science	Take sixteen core courses:[b] • Three years of English • Two years of math (Algebra I or higher) • Two years of natural/physical science (one year of lab if offered by high school) • Three years of additional English, math, or natural/physical science	Satisfy *two of the following three* standards: 1. Graduate in the top half your class 2. Achieve an overall high school GPA of 2.0 3. Earn a minimum score of 860 on the SAT critical reading and math sections or a composite score of 18 on the ACT	Non–high school graduates can become eligible for athletic participation by completing one term (12 credits) of college work with a GPA of 1.75; term must be taken after your high school class has graduated

- Four years of additional courses (from any area above, foreign language, or nondoctrinal religion/philosophy)

- Two years of social science
- Four years of additional courses (from any area above, foreign language, or nondoctrinal religion/philosophy)

Earn a minimum GPA of 2.0 in your core courses

Earn a minimum GPA of 2.0 in your core courses

Earn a combined SAT or ACT score that matches your core-course GPA according to the sliding scale (you can find the scale in the "NCAA Eligibility Center Quick Reference Guide" under "Resources" on the NCAA Eligibility Center website: www.eligibilitycenter.org)

Earn a minimum SAT score of 820 or ACT sum score of 68

Source: Data from NCAA Eligibility Center, "NCAA Eligibility Center Quick Reference Guide," fs.ncaa.org/Docs/eligibility_center/Quick_Reference_Sheet.pdf, and National Interscholastic Athletic Administrators Association, *A Guide for College-Bound Student-Athletes and Their Parents*, 13th ed. (Indianapolis, IN: Author, 2008).

[a] NCAA Division III is not included in this table since each college and university has its own admissions requirements. If you're interested in a Division III school, you should talk to your high school guidance counselor.

[b] These are the Division II requirements starting August 1, 2013. Before this date, students were required to take fourteen core courses—three English; two math; two science; two additional English, math, or science; two social science; and three additional in the above, religion, or foreign language.

> "In high school people play for fun or to be able to put it on their résumé. In college there is more competition and you are surrounded by true athletes."
> —Jessica H., 20, golf
> (NCAA Division II)

alternative. You could try to walk on to a Division I school, but there's no guarantee you're going to make the team, let alone get playing time. Plus, you won't get any money unless you get an academic scholarship or other financial aid. If you instead look to Division II schools, you might get to play and receive money to do so. Second, Division II might just be a better fit for you. If you take the advice given here and explore all your options, you might find a Division II school that has everything you want—academic major, location, open spot on the team, awesome coaches, and so on. Playing at the college level is about the whole student-athlete experience; for you, a Division II team might be the perfect fit.

> "The size, speed, and strength of the athletes was obviously much different. You go from being the best player on your team in high school to being on a team of all the best players from their high schools."—Josh, 24, football (NCAA Division II)

Division III

The key difference between Divisions I and II and Division III is the third line of the table 8.1: Division III schools don't give *any* sports-related scholarships to student-athletes. That doesn't mean coaches can't recruit you; they just can't offer you money related to your athletic ability. Instead, you might be offered an academic scholarship or other nonathletic financial aid. Because you're not able to receive athletic money, you don't have to register with the NCAA Eligibility Center. Academic and athletic eligibility is determined by each college, not the NCAA.

Aside from not receiving an athletic scholarship, one of the biggest drawbacks of playing at Division III is lack of exposure. Family and friends are not going to see you on television. You're probably not going to make it in the major newspapers. Your games might have few fans in the stands. You have to ask yourself how much all that matters.

So, why play at Division III? Pat Coleman, who runs the website D3sports .com, asked this question on Twitter. Here are some of the responses he received from Division III athletes:[14]

- "d3's offer u great opportunities! I turned down many d2 offers & a couple d1 cause the d3 offered alot on & off court."
- "In my case, only place to offer a chance to play FB & BASE while gettin a solid education & not just a piece of paper!"
- "Coaches care about you AND want to win, team becomes family."
- "I love playing @d3tennis because I am surrounded by my teammates— not coworkers. It's not a job. We play because we are passionate."

Types of Financial Aid

There are three basic types of college financial aid: grant, work-study, and loan.

- *Grants* are financial gifts that don't have to be paid back. Examples include athletic scholarships and scholarships based on grades or community service.
- *Work-study* is a part-time job, usually on campus. You are basically working to earn money to pay for college expenses.
- *Loans* are financial awards that have to be paid back after you leave college. Usually, you have to pay interest on top of the original amount borrowed.[15]

Remember: Full-ride scholarships are rare. Unless you're one of the lucky few who earns one, you'll be paying for part of your college education even if you sign with a Division I school. This is another reason to focus on academics as much as athletics throughout your high school career. Good grades can potentially help you earn an academic scholarship that offers more money than any partial athletic scholarship you're offered. Together with your parents, explore all your financial aid options, and don't wait until the last minute to apply. See the Find Out More section for a list of websites with information on scholarships and financial aid.

It's a Fact

Remember: Even if you meet all the academic and athletic requirements of an NCAA school, you still have to apply for admission like everyone else.

As Coleman summarizes, "Why Division III? Because you can play your sport and still be a college student, still have a life outside of your sport. You can be in a play or write for the school newspaper, run for student government. Or take a double major."[16]

Playing Division III isn't as intense as Divisions I or II, but that doesn't mean Division III is just glorified high school, as some have suggested. One father quoted on D3football.com thought that until he saw one of his son's games: "I have to admit that before my son started playing at Wabash, I thought D-III football was just trumped-up high school football. I didn't know anyone that had played it and never saw a game. That impression lasted until he was rung onto the team and I got a look at the size of some of his teammates."[17]

History of Basketball

Around 1500 the Mayans and Aztecs played a game similar to today's basketball. Called *tlachtli*, the game was part of a religious ceremony and involved putting a small rubber ball through a ring on the wall. The winners often received gifts from the crowd; the losers, however, often lost their heads—literally.

The sport as we know it today was invented by James Naismith in 1891 at what is now Springfield College in Massachusetts. He was looking for an indoor game he could play during the winter with the young men in his YMCA training school. Naismith nailed a peach basket to each end of the gym and players tried to shoot a soccer ball into the basket. The only problem was they had to stop the game to get the ball out each time someone made a basket. Amazingly, they didn't think of cutting a hole in the bottom of the basket until 1906.[18]

Today, the men's and women's college basketball player of the year receives an award named after basketball's founder: the Naismith Trophy.

National Athletic Intercollegiate Association (NAIA)

The NAIA is completely separate from the NCAA. In 1937, Dr. James Naismith, the inventor of basketball, started an annual intercollegiate basketball tournament in Kansas City, Missouri. In 1940 the participating schools formed the National Association of Intercollegiate Basketball, which became the NAIA in 1952. Basketball is still one of the biggest sports in the NAIA, having two divisions for men and women while all the other sports have just one. As of 2012, nearly three hundred colleges and universities belonged to the NAIA.[19]

As in the NCAA, each NAIA school has an overall limit on the number of scholarships it can offer in each sport. Because all NAIA sports are equivalency sports, each scholarship can be handed out as a full ride or it can be divided among two or more student-athletes. (See table 8.3 for a comparison of the scholarships available in NAIA sports versus NCAA sports.)

Table 8.3 NCAA and NAIA Athletic Scholarships Available per School[a]

	NCAA Division I	NCAA Division II	NAIA
Archery—men	0	0	0
Archery—women	5	9	0
Badminton—men	0	0	0
Badminton—women	6	10	0
Baseball	11.7	9	12
Basketball—men	13*[b]	10	11[c]
Basketball—women	15*	10	11
Bowling—men	0	0	0
Bowling—women	5	5	0

(continued)

	NCAA Division I	NCAA Division II	NAIA
Crew—men	0	0	0
Crew—women	20	20	0
Cross-country/track and field—men	12.6	12.6	5/12[d]
Cross-country/track and field—women	18	12.6	5/12
Equestrian—men	0	0	0
Equestrian—women	15	15	0
Fencing—men	4.5	4.5	0
Fencing—women	5	4.5	0
Field hockey—men	0	0	0
Field hockey—women	6.3	6.3	0
Football	85*	36	24
Golf—men	4.5	3.6	5
Golf—women	6	5.4	5
Gymnastics—men	6.3	5.4	0
Gymnastics—women	12*	6	0
Ice hockey—men	18	0	0
Ice hockey—women	18	18	0
Lacrosse—men	12.6	10.8	0

	NCAA Division I	NCAA Division II	NAIA
Lacrosse—women	12	9.9	0
Rifle—men	3.6	3.6	0
Rifle—women	0	0	0
Skiing—men	6.3	6.3	0
Skiing—women	7	6.3	0
Soccer—men	9.9	9	12
Soccer—women	12	9.9	12
Softball	12	7.2	10
Squash—men	0	0	0
Squash—women	12	9	0
Swimming/diving—men	9.9	8.1	8
Swimming/diving—women	14	8.1	8
Synchronized swimming	5	5	0
Team handball—men	0	0	0
Team handball—women	10	12	0
Tennis—men	4.5	4.5	5
Tennis—women	8*	6	5

(continued)

	NCAA Division I	NCAA Division II	NAIA
Volleyball–men	4.5	4.5	0
Volleyball—women	12*	8	8
Water polo—men	4.5	4.5	0
Water polo—women	8	8	0
Wrestling	9.9	9	8

Source: Data from College Athletes.com, "NCAA & NAIA Athletic Scholarships Limits," www
.speeddevelopment.net/NCAA_College_Scholarship_Rules_and_Limits_-_CollegeAthletes.com.pdf
(accessed April 7, 2012), and NAIA, "NAIA Guide for the College-Bound Student-Athlete," p. 2,
www.naia.org/fls/27900/1NAIA/membership/NAIA_GuidefortheCollegeBoundStudent.pdf?DB_
OEM_ID=27900 (accessed April 7, 2012).

[a]These are yearly limits; in other words, each school that fields a team in that sport has the
indicated number of scholarships available each year.

[b]Head-count sports are marked with an asterisk (*). This means coaches cannot divide the
scholarships; each one is a full-ride scholarship. All of the other scholarships may be divided
among several athletes.

[c]The NAIA has two divisions for basketball only; the scholarship numbers in this table are for
Division I.

[d]The NAIA separates cross-country and track and field scholarships, whereas the NCAA lumps
them into one category. The NAIA allows five cross-country and twelve track and field for men
and the same for women.

Academically, the NAIA requirements are not as strict as they are for NCAA
Divisions I and II. You still have to maintain a decent GPA and earn a respectable
score on either the ACT or SAT, but you don't have to take a required number of
core courses as in the NCAA (go back to table 8.2 on pages 280–281 for details and
for a comparison to other athletic associations). In 2010 the NAIA opened its own
eligibility center for determining the eligibility of incoming freshmen. It's your
responsibility to register and get your academic and athletic eligibility verified.

Why would you choose an NAIA school over one from the NCAA?

1. You don't get recruited by an NCAA school.
2. You're looking for a small-school college experience or specifically a
   Christian or Catholic college.

It's a Fact

Some student-athletes score higher on the ACT than on the SAT; for others, the opposite is true. If you can afford it, take both tests to see which one you do better on. Don't forget to submit your scores to the NCAA Eligibility Center and/or the NAIA Eligibility Center.

The NAIA Eligibility Center

If you're hoping to play at an NAIA school, you must register with the NAIA Eligibility Center. The Eligibility Center website (www.playnaia.org) doesn't say exactly which year you should register; it just says to do so early. To be safe, you should probably register at the end of your junior year. As of 2012 the cost to have your eligibility verified was sixty-five dollars for U.S. students and ninety-five dollars for international students.

Here are some other things to keep in mind:

- When you take ACT or SAT, have your score sent to the NAIA Eligibility Center. The Eligibility Center code is 9876.
- After you graduate, have your high school send your final official transcript to the NAIA Eligibility Center. The transcript must be sent directly from the high school to the Eligibility Center.
- You have the option of setting up an NAIA Connections profile in order to connect with college coaches; this step is not required but it's probably a good idea. NAIA Connections lets you create a sports résumé by answering questions about your playing experience, extracurricular activities, and more. Then you can search colleges by location, school size, and so on, and send your sports résumé straight to the coach and admissions office of up to five colleges. Creating a profile also puts you in the system, so coaches might find your résumé and contact you directly.[20]

3. Your high school GPA/academic portfolio is not up to NCAA standards, but you still want to play sports in college.

National Junior College Athletic Association (NJCAA)

Unlike the NCAA and the NAIA, the NJCAA is made up of two-year community and city colleges. The association formed in 1938 to give junior college students an opportunity to play sports as part of their college experience. The first sponsored sport was track and field, with the first NJCAA national championship taking place in 1939. When it formed, the NJCAA had thirteen junior colleges from California; as of 2012, there were over five hundred schools from across the country.[21]

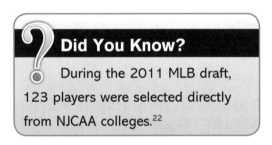

Did You Know?

During the 2011 MLB draft, 123 players were selected directly from NJCAA colleges.[22]

At the NJCAA level, athletic scholarships are called grants-in-aid. Like scholarships at the NCAA and NAIA level, they are only guaranteed for one year at a time. The NJCAA sponsors fifteen sports, the most competitive of which have up to three divisions. Grants-in-aid are only offered in division 1 and 2 sports. For men, those sports are baseball, basketball, cross-country, golf, outdoor track and field, soccer, and tennis. For women, grants-in-aid are offered in basketball, cross-country, fast-pitch softball, outdoor track and field, soccer, tennis, and volleyball.[23] The number of scholarships available varies by school.

Junior colleges are a good stepping-stone in several ways. If money is tight and you're not sure what you want to major in, start your college career at a city or community college. You can get your general education requirements out of

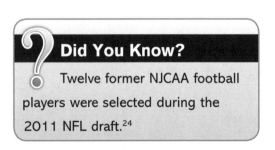

Did You Know?

Twelve former NJCAA football players were selected during the 2011 NFL draft.[24]

the way for a lot less money—possibly for free if you earn a full-ride grant-in-aid to play your sport. In addition, many junior college student-athletes are picked up by four-year NCAA and NAIA schools. This is what happened to Josh Cohen, a football player from California. After playing at the local junior college during the fall of 2008,

he put together a recruiting package and got picked up by an NCAA Division II school in the spring of 2009. Here's how Josh tells it:

After playing a year at SBCC [Santa Barbara City College] I made up a highlight tape, wrote a brief bio, and included my transcripts in a nice little package I sent out to many schools. I researched all the schools in Div. IAA that were in the top 25 in the nation and all the Div. II schools that were in the top 25 and sent my package to them. Tiffin [University] happened to be in the top 25 about 3 years ago and somehow they got on my list. I got a lot of interest from some really good Div. IAA schools but I was a mid-year transfer and they didn't have scholarship spots open yet. I would've had to come for one semester on my own dime and then my scholarship would kick in the next year. Tiffin's coach flew out to Cali to meet with me and offer me a full ride right away. I didn't want to have to pay for a semester at a four year so I went to Tiffin on a full ride right away.[25]

By playing at the NJCAA level first, you gain more skills and maturity, and NCAA and NAIA coaches know you can handle the college-level course work and athletic competition.

How to Get Recruited[26]

How do you put yourself in a place where college coaches take notice of you and want you on their team? That's the question answered in this section. If you already have several colleges calling and e-mailing you, feel free to skip to the next section on making a final decision.

There are two keys to getting recruited: First—and this is probably the most difficult part—you have to be realistic about your athletic abilities and potential. If you're five foot one and you want to play basketball at a top-ranked NCAA Division I school, you're probably going to have to rethink your options. As already mentioned, 85 percent of the available college scholarships are *outside* NCAA

> "The hardest part is managing school and golf at the same time. If I could I would be at the course all day but that is impossible with school. The worst part is when I play bad because I make golf such a big part of my life. It's not good that it happens like this, but if golf is good life is good."
> —Jessica H., 20, golf (NCAA Division II)

Good Read: Heart of a Champion *by Carl Deuker*

Sport: Baseball

Life apps: Peer pressure, underage drinking, realizing you might not play in college, father-son relationships, friendship, example of how one person's actions can affect the whole team

Summary: Seth Barham's father died when Seth was seven. Jimmy Winter's father is an alcoholic who demands perfection from his son on the baseball diamond. When they're both around twelve, Seth and Jimmy meet one Saturday on a baseball field; Jimmy is practicing with his dad and invites Seth to join them. From that moment on, Seth is a baseball fanatic. He doesn't have the natural talent that Jimmy has, but he practices hard to improve his skills.

Both boys make the JV team as high school freshmen. The next year, Jimmy makes varsity while a disappointed Seth is left on JV. Jimmy and other members of the varsity team start drinking on weekends. Eventually, the drinking leads to team suspensions and more devastating consequences.

Told from Seth's point of view, *Heart of a Champion* captures the joy of playing baseball. The game descriptions are accurate and detailed. You might find the plot is slow and even corny in parts, but if you've ever played baseball (or softball), or struggled with not making varsity, or realized that you might never play your sport in college, you will probably identify with Seth's experiences.

When it was first published in 1993, *Heart of a Champion* won several awards: ALA Best Book for Young Adults, ALA Best Book for Reluctant Readers, New York Public Library Book for the Teen Age, and Pennsylvania Young Reader's Choice Book of the Year.

Little, Brown, 2007
208 pages

Division I. You have a much better chance of getting a scholarship to play college basketball if you widen the net to include NCAA Division II, NAIA, and NJCAA schools.

Second, *you* have to take responsibility for your athletic placement. This process takes a lot of work, and you can't wait around for someone else to do it for you. You have to take the initiative to talk to your parents, coaches, and counselors; search college websites for a school that is the best fit academically, athletically, and socially; and contact college coaches with your athletic and academic profile. This section provides practical suggestions on what to do and when. The earlier you start, the better. If you're already a junior or senior, don't worry over lost time. Just get started!

1. Develop and Implement an Academic Plan.

- Start as a freshman or sophomore.
- Look at the sixteen core course requirements for NCAA Division I and II schools and sketch out a plan for taking all the necessary courses over your four years of high school. Even if you end up playing Division III, NAIA, or NJCAA, you will have taken more than enough of the necessary courses.
- Remember: The best recruit is the one the college coaches don't have to worry about, so take your schoolwork seriously. If you have the whole package—strong academics as well as athletic talent—coaches will take notice.
- Maintain a GPA of 2.0 or above in all your classes, but especially the core college-prep ones.
- As part of your plan, take the SAT or ACT in your junior year (take both if possible). Don't forget to have scores sent to the NCAA Eligibility Center and/or NAIA Eligibility Center.

> "I would have to say the best part of my college football career was the friendships I formed. Many of my former teammates are now lifelong friends. I played with and against several players who are now playing professionally and it is cool to still be in touch with them as well."
>
> —Josh, 24, football (NCAA Division II)

2. Keep Track of Your Athletic Accomplishments.

- Start as a freshman or sophomore.
- Keep a record of all the teams you play on—different sports as well as different teams for the same sport (e.g., high school soccer and club soccer).

Ways to Improve Skills and Get Noticed

There's no single right way of improving your skills and getting college coaches to notice you; it's often a combination of things. Evaluate your options and talk with your parents and coaches to find out what's best for you.

- Camps: Sport-specific skills camps usually take place during the summer, and they're often on college campuses. If possible, go to a camp at one of the colleges you're interested in attending and kill two birds with one stone.
- Club/travel ball: College coaches probably won't come to your high school games. Instead, they'll go to club/travel ball tournaments and other showcase events where they can see a lot of high school talent in one place. Club/travel ball is a big time and money commitment, so make sure you talk to your parents about it.
- Combines: Athletic combines involve a series of tests in general athleticism, for example, a forty-yard sprint, vertical jump, and three-hundred-yard shuttle. At the end of the one- or two-day event, you receive a score that college scouts look at to see how you match up to athletes across the country. Combines are most often used by football players, but there are also combines for soccer, lacrosse, basketball, and a few other sports. The Find Out More section has a list of websites you can search for info on upcoming combines in your area.
- Private coach: You and your parents could hire a coach to work on a certain skill or to improve your overall fitness. However, private coaches usually aren't cheap.

- Keep a sports journal of your personal best achievements—fastest times, highest or longest jumps, highest number of rebounds, most strikeouts in a game, most goals for the season, and so on.
- Keep articles and photos that appear in the local paper or the school newspaper. Don't forget to check online versions of the newspapers.
- Have someone take video of your games, meets, and so on. These can be used later when you put together a recruiting video.
- Add to your list of accomplishments by taking every opportunity to improve your skills; for example, work hard in practice, listen to your coaches, attend summer skills camps, participate in athletic combines, and join a club/travel team.

3. Check Out College Websites.

- Start as a freshman or sophomore.
- As you do research, create three lists: (1) colleges you're interested in whether or not you play sports there, (2) colleges that are actively recruiting you to play there (this list might not be formed until your junior year), and (3) colleges to whom you are actively marketing yourself, athletically speaking. Ideally, your final choice will be a school that appears on two or three of these lists.

> "I heard [this advice] so many times but didn't really take it to heart: pick a school where if you break your leg, you'll still be happy."—Noah, 20, volleyball (NCAA Division I)

- Look at *all* aspects of the college, not just the athletic team you're interested in: academic majors, average class size, location (both distance from home and whether it's in a small town, big city, etc.), school size, extracurricular activities, and so on. As already mentioned, you're looking for the best overall fit. You want to find a school where you'll be happy even if you get hurt and can't finish your athletic career—a school that can prepare you for life after college, which, for most of you, will not include playing on a professional sports team.
- Do a detailed search on the athletic team and coach. This step requires self-analysis and honesty; you're basically trying to determine how you match up against those who play your position/compete in your races to see if you have a chance at making the team. Most college websites allow you to look at the athletic bios of players on the roster. You can see their year in school (freshman, sophomore, etc.), height/weight, stats, and

accomplishments—club teams, fastest times, awards, and so on. By seeing who's already on the team in your position, you can tell what the coach is looking for in a keeper, outside hitter, or shortstop.

- Once you find a school that seems like a good all-around fit, fill out a prospective player questionnaire and e-mail it to the coach. A link to this form is usually located on the team web page; it might be called "Prospects" or "Recruit Questionnaire" or "Recruiting Form" or "Prospect Questionnaire." So that you have some playing time under your belt, you might wait until the end of your sophomore year/beginning of your junior year to start contacting coaches. Then you'll have more accomplishments to report. If the coach e-mails you back, respond!
- If possible, visit some of the schools on your three lists. Try to attend a summer skills camp at a college you're interested in.
- Remember to look beyond NCAA Division I. Research schools in Divisions II and III as well as in the NAIA.

4. Assemble Your Team—Parents, Coaches, and Guidance Counselor.

- Start as a freshman or sophomore.
- Talk to your parents, coaches (both high school and club), and guidance counselor about your desire to play sports in college. You need help from all of them to make this process happen. If you change your mind somewhere in the process—maybe you decide to pursue a high jump scholarship instead of one in basketball—you need to tell the various members of your team so everyone knows what's going on.
- Keep your parents in the loop since they'll probably be driving you to practices, tournaments, camps, SAT/ACT testing sites, and so on; they'll also be forking out some money for these things. Your parents can help you sort through the details of recruiting offers, think of questions to ask col-

Be Honest

As you go through the athletic placement process, be honest with yourself about the level of competition you can mentally and emotionally handle and still enjoy your sport and your college experience. After some self-evaluation, you might decide that you'd be more happy playing NCAA Division III or NAIA, where the competition is tough but not overwhelmingly intense.

lege coaches, and organize the paperwork that has to be filled out, signed, and sent by certain deadlines.

- Ask your high school coach for suggestions on skills camps, combines, and club/travel teams. Tell your coach you're thinking of playing in college, and ask for suggestions on what you need to work on. Also, maintain a good relationship with your coach; he or she will probably give feedback to college coaches who ask him or her about your skills, attitude, work ethic, and coachability.

- If you play club/travel ball, talk to your club coach about your desire to play in college. Club coaches often have more connections to colleges than high school coaches do. Emily, a former Division I volleyball player, says her club coaches had a huge part in helping her get recruited. When Emily realized the first college she chose was a bad fit, she went back to her club coaches, who put her in touch with four Division I schools and helped her through the whole transferring process.[27]

- Talk to your school counselor about the colleges on your three lists, and tell him or her you're hoping to earn an athletic scholarship. Your counselor can give you details on each college's academic requirements, application deadlines, and so on. Remember: You still have to apply to each college/university like everyone else.

- Find out if your counselor is the one who sends out transcripts; if not, find out who does. You and/or your parents will need to sign a release form so the school can send your transcript to various people who request it. College coaches might request an unofficial transcript before they get far in the recruiting process. They're probably not going to waste their time watching you play if you have a low GPA. You also might need to have an official transcript sent to the eligibility center or college at end of your junior year, definitely after you graduate.

- Talk to your counselor about nonathletic financial aid—scholarships related to academics, community service, extracurricular activities, and so on. Make sure you ask about financial aid early, probably by the end of

"I felt almost like a famous person in college. I would go to the store and people would come up to me telling me they were my biggest fans and would ask for my autograph. It was such a rewarding feeling knowing how much people enjoyed watching me play and I knew that all the hard work I was putting in was paying off in more ways than I could have ever imagined!"—Emily, 23, volleyball (NCAA Division I)

your sophomore year. You want to make sure you know all the different options and that you get your applications in on time. Full-ride athletic scholarships are hard to come by, so you want to make sure you have a backup plan.

Don't Be Shy

If you don't have college coaches recruiting you, you're going to have to market yourself. This is no time to be shy about tootin' your own horn; if you want money to play in college, you need to sell coaches on your athletic talent and accomplishments. You won't get recruited based on an athletic résumé alone, but you can pique coaches' interest to find out more about you.

---

5. Create and Send Out an Athletic Résumé.

- Start sending out your résumé early in your junior year.
- In your résumé include academic achievements (GPA, SAT/ACT scores, scholastic awards, etc.) as well as athletic. Coaches want to know right up front whether you'll be able to hack college course work.
- Include information on your athletic accomplishments in all sports played, not just the one you're hoping to play in college. Many coaches are looking for all-around athletes, not just players of a particular sport. Include number of years on each team, position(s) played, individual awards received (e.g., league MVP), team awards (e.g., state champions), and so on. Also include information on club/travel teams, tournaments, and showcases. See figure 8.1 for one example of how to organize this information in your résumé. (For more sample résumés, see Miller Place Athletic Department's "The Student-Athlete's Game Plan" or Varsityedge.com, both listed in the Find Out More section.)
- Don't overload your résumé with statistics such as batting averages, rebounds, goals scored, and so on. Dave Galehouse of Varsityedge.com says these numbers can be subjective, and they don't tell the whole story. Galehouse gives the example of a field goal kicker who made five out of fifteen attempts during the season. That looks bad on paper, unless you know that seven of the ten missed field goals were blocked because of a poor offensive line. On the other hand, personal bests in timed races and field events are objective stats; these should be included if they are noteworthy.[28]

- Make sure your athletic résumé is clear, well organized, and as brief as possible—ideally one page. College coaches are busy people; they want to be able to look over your résumé and quickly find out what they need to know.
- Carry copies of your résumé with you whenever you go to tournaments, camps, or showcases. You never know when you might find yourself talking with a college coach.
- Create a web page athletic profile as well as a paper version of your résumé. Some coaches prefer to handle everything electronically—correspondence through e-mail, viewing highlight videos on YouTube, and reading profiles on a web page.
- Talk to your high school and/or club coaches for suggestions on what to add. You can also check out the Varsityedge.com website under "Recruiting Info." Have a coach and a parent look over your résumé, both to make sure it's grammatically correct and to make sure you haven't forgotten anything that would help you market yourself.
- Create a video of athletic highlights to send with your résumé. Might need help from someone who does video editing. Make sure your name and jersey number are clearly stated/written at the beginning. Each clip should also start with an arrow pointing to you or a circle around your number. You can search YouTube for examples (as of 2012, the video created by Requan, a sixteen-year-old football player from Florida, was available at www.youtube.com/watch?v=sASR7gAfEgM).
- Send the résumé and video/DVD to coaches at colleges you're interested in playing for, either via snail mail or via e-mail. Include an intro letter (see figure 8.2 for example). The Miller Place Athletic Department suggests that you handwrite the envelope if you snail-mail your résumé and DVD. College coaches receive thousands of recruiting films from scouting agencies, and they sometimes disregard anything that looks like it's from an agency. If you handwrite the envelope, the coach will know it's not from an agency.[29]

6. Register with at Least One Eligibility Center.

- Register in your junior year.
- Decide whether you want to register with the NCAA, the NAIA, or both. If there's a chance you'll end up at a Division I or II school or in the NAIA, you must register with the appropriate eligibility center to have your eligibility verified.
- Don't forget to have SAT/ACT score sent, as well as official transcripts. See the website for each eligibility center for details on what you need to do. Both websites are listed in the Find Out More section at the end of this chapter.

Jamie Johnson
123 Victory Lane, Merryland, CA 91234
Cell: 818-555-0987 Home: 818-555-6543
johnson.jamie@mymail.com

Date of birth	10/10/1990
High school	Lincoln High School
Year of graduation	2008
GPA	3.8
SAT [or ACT] score	1480
Height	6' 1"
Block jump	9' 5"
Approach jump	9' 10"
Academic achievements	National Honor Society
	Principal's Award
	Rotary Student of the Month
	Winner of the 2008 G. H. Jones Journalism Award
Other activities	Editor of the school newspaper: Grade 12
	Co-editor of the school yearbook: Grade 12
	Reporter for the school newspaper: Grades 10, 11, 12
Volleyball	High school varsity: Grades 9, 10, 11, 12
	Position: Outside hitter
	State champions, division 6A: Grade 12
	First team all-league: Grades 10, 11, 12
	Southland Volleyball Club: Grades 10, 11, 12
	Second place at Junior National Championships: Grade 11
Basketball	High school varsity: Grades 10, 11, 12
	JV: Grade 9
	Position: Forward
Softball	High school varsity: Grade 10
	JV: Grade 9
	Position: Left field

Figure 8.1 Sample athletic résumé

"The best thing was creating friendships with the girls because they understand your day-to-day schedule and stress and what goes on, because they have to deal with it too. And also, it's just a fun time to be around people with the same interests. Also, the competitive nature is awesome."

—Kirsten, 20, softball (NCAA Division II)

March 1, 2012

Christopher Coach
USA University
123 University Avenue
College Town, PA 45678

Dear Christopher Coach,

I am writing to let you know I am interested in playing intercollegiate [insert your sport]. Sports have been a major part of my life throughout high school, and I look forward to continuing my playing career in college. I am looking for a school that offers a challenge both academically and athletically, and your university fits this description perfectly. USA University has a long tradition of excellence both in the classroom and on the playing field.

Enclosed you will find a copy of my academic and athletic résumé, as well as a DVD containing highlights from my athletic career. Please send me information on your school's academic and athletic programs as well as an application for admission.

Thank you very much for your time. I hope we have a chance to meet in the near future.

Sincerely,

Alex Athlete

Enclosure

Figure 8.2 Sample letter

Making a Final Decision

You did it. You successfully attracted the attention of two or three college coaches. They're calling or writing nearly every week, just to say hi or to tell you about their season or to try to convince you to commit to their school. Now what? Alison Bell, director of college counseling, says, "You want to stay in the driver's seat for this. You do not want to be at the whim of a college coach."[30] College coaches have a job: build the best possible team. Once they decide you have what they want to build that team, they want an answer—will you come play for us? Coaches want to know if they should move on to the next prospective student-athlete, and they will pressure you to make a decision as soon as possible.

"In college the pace of an average practice and competitions are much faster and the mood is much more serious. In high school a lot of participants are playing whatever sport they play as an extra-curricular activity. In college, especially when on a scholarship, the sport which you play becomes somewhat of your job, your means to pay for your education."
—Lauren, 22, track and field (NCAA Division I)

This is where you need your team—parents, coaches, and counselors—to help you stop and think. The college coach knows his or her offer is in the team's best interest, but is it the best fit for you? Have you looked at all aspects of that college—academic, athletic, and social? Are you still waiting to hear back from a couple schools you really want to go to for academic and athletic reasons? This is *your* college experience and it's much bigger than just your athletic placement, so make sure you really think about what *you* want out of that experience.

Athlete Bio: Roger Bush, Football

If you're really good, college coaches will find you. You'll be getting e-mails, letters, and phone calls from the day coaches can legally contact you in your junior year. Roger Bush, a sixteen-year-old running back, is one such talented athlete. In December 2011, he showed me a six-inch-high stack of mail from Division I colleges across the country that wanted him to join their football program—UCLA, Stanford University, Kansas University, Georgia Tech, Florida State, and the University of Wisconsin, among others—and that stack just kept growing.

College coaches started watching Roger as a freshman in 2009. A standout on the freshman team, Roger moved up to varsity before the year was over. But Roger didn't take his talent for granted. As he says, "You can always get better. Either you get better or you get worse, and I like to get better." In an effort to get better, Roger participated in two combines and trained at a facility for athletes who want to play at the college level. At the suggestion of his football coach, he also took up track during his junior year, specifically the 400 meters and the pole vault. Roger says, "In football I break out a lot but then I don't have the endurance to keep going, so that's why track, I think, is going to help me . . . to keep the endurance, to keep my legs moving; that way they don't get tired."

The first day college coaches can directly contact a high school athlete is September 1 of the player's junior year. On September 1, 2011, Roger started getting e-mails and letters from coaches across the country. At least fifteen different schools contacted him, and as of May 2012, Roger and his parents were still discussing his options. He was looking at the depth chart for each team, and he also wanted to make sure the school was a good fit academi-cally. Roger liked Georgia Tech's

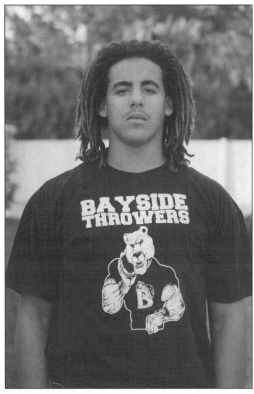

Roger says, "Football is not a game where you think you want to play it. This is, you do or you don't. . . . I want to play it. I love it. I'd do anything to play football." *Photo courtesy of the author.*

strong program in computer-aided design, and the school is fairly close to his home in Florida so his parents could even come to home games. But Georgia Tech had a lot of running backs coming in, so there would be a lot of competi-tion for playing time. Roger was also considering the University of Wisconsin because he felt like he fit into their program; "they run the ball a lot, they're a pro-style offense and that's what I like to do." But Wisconsin is very different weather-wise and it's a long way from Florida.

Though Roger was looking toward his future, he was also concentrating on his upcoming senior year: "I'm really trying to focus on my team. We're a big unit and we're trying to move forward to a state championship this year, but it all takes the seniors making progress and being leaders and all that, so I just want to be a leader on the team and hopefully we can move to a state championship this year."[31]

No Talking!

The NCAA has very specific guidelines regarding contact between you and the college coaches recruiting you. Though it's technically the coach's responsibility to follow the rules, you should know what they are so you don't lose eligibility because of someone else's mistake.

According to NCAA rules, up until September 1 of your junior year, coaches

- *can* send you information about sports camps happening on campus.
- *cannot* call or e-mail you. You can call the coach before that time, but if you have to leave a message, the coach cannot (and should not) call you back.
- *cannot* send you recruiting information.

After September 1 of your junior year, coaches

- *can* e-mail you or send you letters via snail mail.
- *can* send you information about the athletic program and the school itself.
- *cannot* call you.

Starting July 1 after your junior year, coaches

- *can* call you once a week.
- *can* contact you in person, as long as you don't meet on the campus itself. A coach cannot initiate a meeting on campus until after September 1 of your senior year.

The NAIA and NJCAA don't have the same guidelines. According to the National Collegiate Scouting Association, "NAIA and NJCAA coaches have no restrictions on contacting potential recruits. They can call, email, text, send direct messages on Facebook, post to a recruit's wall, and chat online—anything at any time."[32]

Official Visits

Part of the decision-making process will involve visiting the schools. If a college is really interested, the coach might offer to have you come on an official visit, which means the college pays for the whole trip—plane, food, hotel if necessary. However, the NCAA and NAIA have specific rules regarding official visits:[33]

1. You get a total of five official visits to college campuses. That's not five to each campus, but five total; you actually only get one official visit per school.
2. You can't take an official visit until after the first day of classes during your senior year of high school.
3. You have to give the college coach an official copy of your transcript and ACT or SAT score before you can make an official visit.
4. An official visit cannot last longer than forty-eight hours (two days).

You and your family can take as many unofficial visits as you want; it just means your parents are paying for those trips.

Before you visit each college, sit down with your parents and think of questions to ask the coach. Jacque, who played volleyball at Colorado State University, says her mom wrote down every single question she could think of, and she got Jacque to do the same. Then when the coach would ask if they had any questions, her mom would take out her list and say, "As a matter of fact . . ." When I asked Jacque if she had any advice for high school athletes hoping to play in college, she brought up this topic of asking questions: "Make sure you ask all the questions that you want the real answers to. Sometimes coaches will try to sugarcoat things to make things seem better than they might actually be." She also said it really helped having someone outside the situation (her mom) think of questions that didn't occur to her as a sixteen- or seventeen-year-old.[34]

Did You Know?

Some student-athletes have gone into their senior year trying to be recruited for one sport, and by the end of the year they get recruited to play another sport. If you're a multiple-sport athlete, that's another reason to keep your options open.[35]

Questions to Ask

The following questions are taken from *Guide for College-Bound Students Athletes and Their Parents*. This is only a partial list; see the guide for more ideas:[36]

1. What is the attitude of the professors in my prospective department toward athletes?

2. Does your school have an athletic study table or tutors available? What other kinds of academic support are available?

3. Will I live with regular students or athletes? Can I live off campus if I so desire?

4. How many hours a day are involved with the athletic program? During the off-season, will I be expected to work out daily, participate in off-season practice and conditioning, and so on?

5. How many classes am I likely to miss each semester/quarter due to travel and so on? Do professors allow athletes to make up assignments or tests?

6. If I am eligible for an athletic scholarship, are there any circumstances under which I could lose it? (e.g., injury, academics, disciplinary procedures, playing performance)

7. How much of the total cost does my scholarship cover? What is the difference between the financial assistance offered and the total cost of attending the college each year?

8. What GPA must be maintained to keep my scholarship?

9. Is there an athletic trainer available for the athletic teams? Can I see the training room?

10. How does the team travel? (e.g., by private car, school vehicle, bus, or plane)

Here's a checklist of things to keep in mind for each visit, official or unofficial:[37]

- Bring copies of your athletic résumé, unofficial transcript, and any other paperwork the coach asked you to bring.
- Ask the coach about seeing the training room, campus, and classrooms used by professors in your department. You might even ask about meeting with a professor in your desired major.
- If possible, schedule your visit for a school day and try to sit in on an actual class.
- Attend a team practice. Talk with the players about their experiences as athletes and as students. Ask the freshmen and sophomores about their first-year experiences.
- Be observant. Make mental notes about the condition of the athletic facilities and the campus itself, as well as names of people you met and conversations you had.
- When you get home, write the coach a thank-you note, no matter who actually paid for the trip.

After each visit, you should sit down with your parents and evaluate your experience. Here are a few things to consider:[38]

1. Did the coaches seem knowledgeable and competent?
2. Did the coaches' answers to your questions seem honest and sincere?
3. Did the coaches and trainers seem like people you could trust?
4. Did the coaches seem concerned about your academic experience as well as your athletic one?

> "Enjoy playing your sport now and know that once you get to Division I at a major university, it becomes your job and sometimes it's hard to keep the love for sport when coaches are in your face and your mistakes are amplified. . . . It is a huge sacrifice on many levels to play Division I sports in college, and you had better be ready to give up a lot in order to compete at that level. Also, there's no guarantee that you will be a starter once you get to college. But the experience prepares athletes for their future in terms of hard work, dedication, team spirit and determination."
> —Dane, 21, volleyball (NCAA Division I)

5. Did you like the feel of the team as a whole—players and coaches?
6. Given your current training and abilities, does it seem like you would see significant playing time?
7. Did you like the size, location, and general atmosphere of the school?
8. If you got hurt and could not continue your athletic career at this college, would you still be happy as a student?

Transferring

Even if you do all your homework and think you've found the perfect fit on every level, things happen: the coach who was awesome off the court turns out to be a nightmare on the court; the coach you really liked leaves, and the new one doesn't run the program the same way; the competition for playing time is way tougher than you imagined; the small town is actually a little too small; and so on. You can choose to stick it out, but that might mean a miserable four or five years. Your other option is transferring and finishing out your athletic eligibility playing for another school. Warning: Transferring itself isn't a fun or easy process, but in the end you could have the college experience you were hoping for in the first place.

Here are the experiences of two former collegiate student-athletes who decided to transfer.

Emily

Emily, age twenty-three, was recruited to play volleyball at several colleges. Unfortunately, the one she chose ended up being a bad fit:

I played my freshman fall and then the coach left. I told the new coach that I was looking to transfer, I wasn't positive yet, and she was like, "OK,

"If you make the wrong choice the first time, try to make it right. I think sometimes when you spend four years at a place and it's not a good experience and you didn't appreciate it, I think you lose a lot. . . . If you feel like you made the wrong decision, don't hold back. Don't be like, 'Oh I have to stick this out because I made this decision.'"
—Jacque, 22, volleyball (NCAA Division I)

you're kicked off the team, you have to tell your teammates, I'm not going to tell them for you." I tried to use the weight room and the strength coach came up to me and told me that I was no longer an athlete there and I couldn't use their facilities.

Emily contacted her high school club volleyball coaches, and they put her in touch with the coaches at four universities who were interested in having Emily come play for them. Emily had four official visits left, but she only needed two to find the right school: "Transferring there [Wichita State] was one of best decisions I've ever made in my life. It was one of those things where I went on an official visit there and two hours into the trip I was like, 'This is where I want to be.' It's not something you have to sleep on. When you know it's right . . . I would give anything to have another year there."[39]

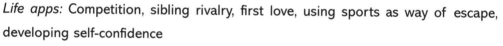

Good Read: Girls Got Game: Sports Stories and Poems

Sports: Softball, basketball, synchronized swimming, track and field, tennis, soccer, crew, football, baseball

Life apps: Competition, sibling rivalry, first love, using sports as way of escape, developing self-confidence

Summary: Girls Got Game is a collection of stories and poems written by and starring female athletes. The main characters model personality traits that high school female athletes have or want to have. The girls are competitive, hardworking, and good at what they play, though they recognize there's always room to improve and learn from coaches, grandparents, and teammates. Every one of the authors was or is involved in multiple sports, many before Title IX brought equality to high school and college sports participation. At the end of each story or poem is a short bio on the author, listing her accomplishments on the field, on the court, on the track, or in the pool. Girls, if you've been looking for sports fiction that is all about female athletes, this is it.

Henry Holt, 2001

152 pages

Lauren

Lauren, age twenty-two, was recruited to play basketball and then transferred after one year. When she transferred, Lauren changed her sport to track and field:

> My freshman year I was coached by a horrible coach that ruined the whole sport of basketball for me. I never could have predicted a bad coach could destroy the love I had for the game of basketball for the majority of my life. After that year I transferred schools, and transferring was difficult in itself. Coming into an athletic community where all of the people your age have had a year to start creating friendships before you got there is very difficult. You are trying to fit in as well as missing your friends at your old school.

Though the transferring process was hard, Lauren was ultimately glad she made the move, in large part because of the relationships she formed, both with the coaches and with her teammates. As she says, "When I graduated college, I knew I had created relationships that were lasting and extremely meaningful."[40]

Find Out More

Booklets/Information Packets

Miller Place Athletic Department. "The Student-Athlete's Game Plan," September 2008. This information packet was prepared for student-athletes at Miller Place High School in New York. It is available at www.millerplace.k12.ny.us/webpages/swhite/file_viewer.cfm?secFile=7816.

National Association of Intercollegiate Athletics. *NAIA Guide for the College-Bound Student-Athlete.* Kansas City, MO: Author, n.d. This guide only covers the requirements of the NAIA and is available at www.naia.org/fls/27900/1NAIA/membership/NAIA_GuidefortheCollegeBoundStudent.pdf?DB_OEM_ID=27900.

National Interscholastic Athletic Administrators Association. *A Guide for College-Bound Student-Athletes and Their Parents.* 13th ed. Indianapolis, IN: Author, 2008. This guide provides information on all three athletic associations: NCAA, NAIA, and NJCAA. You can purchase the forty-page booklet through the National Interscholastic Athletic Administrators Association at www.niaaa.org/publications.asp.

NCAA Eligibility Center. *2009–10 Guide for the College-Bound Student-Athlete.* Indianapolis, IN: Author, 2009. This guide only covers the requirements of the

NCAA and is available through the NCAA website at www.ncaapublications
.com/productdownloads/CB10.pdf.

Books

College Bound Sports. *The High School Athlete's Guide to College Sports:How to Market Yourself to the School of Your Dreams.* Lanham, MD: Taylor Trade, 2005.

Lauenstein, Ray, and David Galehouse. *The Making of a Student-Athlete.* 11th ed. Boston: Athlete's Advisor Press, 2012.

Wheeler, Dion. *The Sports Scholarships Insider's Guide: Getting Money for College at Any Division.* 2nd ed. Naperville, IL: Sourcebooks, 2009.

Websites/Organizations

College Athletic Associations

D3sports.com (www.d3sports.com).
NAIA Eligibility Center (www.playnaia.org).
National Association of Intercollegiate Athletics (www.naia.org).
National Collegiate Athletic Association (www.ncaa.org).
National Junior College Athletic Association (www.njcaa.org).
NCAA Eligibility Center (www.eligibilitycenter.org).

Financial Aid

College Scholarships (www.collegescholarships.org/athletic.htm).
FAFSA (www.fafsa.ed.gov).
Fastweb (www.fastweb.com).
FinAid (www.finaid.org).
Petersen's College Search (www.petersons.com/finaid).
Scholarships.com (www.scholarships.com).
Student Aid on the Web (www.studentaid.ed.gov).

Recruiting, Scholarships, and More

Athlete's Advisor (www.athletesadvior.com).
College Sports Scholarships (www.collegesportsscholarships.com).

National Athletic Combine (www.nationalathleticcombine.com).
National Letter of Intent (www.national-letter.org).
Under Armor Combines (combines.underarmour.com).
Varsityedge.com (www.varsityedge.com).

Scouting Agencies

From what I've heard and read, scouting agencies are not necessarily the best way to go. College coaches get overwhelmed with the number of letters, films, and so on from scouting agencies, and often put anything aside that looks like it came from an agency. Nonetheless I want you to know all your options; some of these websites also have links to other helpful information.

National Scouting Report (www.nsr-inc.com).
NCSA Athletic Recruiting (www.ncsasports.org).
Turn 2 Sports Consulting (www.turn2sportsconsulting.com).
Varsity Sports Group (www.govarsitysports.com).

Notes

1. Lenny Paoletti, "How to Get Recruited" (seminar, Holy Trinity Episcopal Academy, Melbourne, Florida, August 22, 2011).
2. College Sports Scholarships, "College Recruiting: How to Get a Scholarship," www.college sportsscholarships.com/ (accessed February 25, 2012).
3. Francois Fortin, ed., *Sports: The Complete Visual Reference* (Willowdale, ON: Firefly Books, 2000), 256; Human Kinetics, with Thomas Hanlon, *The Sports Rules Book: Essential Rules, Terms, and Procedures for 54 Sports*, 3rd ed. (Champaign, IL: Human Kinetics, 2009), 112; Nigel Smith, *Sports: Then and Now* (Brookfield, CT: Copper Beach Books, 1996), 5; NFL, "Chronology of Professional Football," static.nfl.com/static/content/public/image/history/pdfs/History/Chronology_2011.pdf (accessed March 31, 2012).
4. National Collegiate Athletic Association (NCAA), "History," www.ncaa.org/wps/wcm/connect/public/ncaa/about+the+ncaa/who+we+are/about+the+ncaa+history (accessed March 29, 2012).
5. NCAA Eligibility Center, "About the NCAA," web1.ncaa.org/ECWR2/NCAA_EMS/NCAA_EMS.html# (accessed February 20, 2012).
6. Jacque Davisson, interview with author, November 19, 2011.
7. J. Davisson, interview.
8. Statistics come from "Head-Count vs. Equivalency Sports," *STACK*, September 1, 2007, magazine.stack.com/TheIssue/Article/4714/HeadCount_vs_Equivalency_Sports.aspx (accessed February 21, 2012).
9. There are actually three divisions within Division I football: A, AA, and AAA. Only Division I-A is considered a head-count sport.
10. Statistics from "Head-Count vs. Equivalency Sports."

11. Noah Davisson, interview with author, February 3, 2012.

12. Alison Bell, "How to Get Recruited" (seminar, Holy Trinity Episcopal Academy, August 22, 2011).

13. National Interscholastic Athletic Administrators Association (NIAAA), *A Guide for College-Bound Student-Athletes and Their Parents*, 13th ed. (Indianapolis, IN: Author, 2008), 4–5.

14. Pat Coleman, "Why D-III?" D3sports.com, d3sports.com/columns/why-division-iii (accessed February 23, 2012).

15. U.S. Department of Education, "Confused about How to Pay for College?" www2.ed.gov/students/prep/college/thinkcollege/early/edlite-q-and-a.html (accessed February 21, 2012).

16. Coleman, "Why D-III?"

17. Anonymous, quoted by Pat Coleman, "FAQ: General," D3football.com, August 19, 2010, d3football.com/interactive/faq/general#2a (accessed February 23, 2012).

18. Polymer Science Learning Center, "Destination Mexico: Tlachtli," The Story of Rubber, www.pslc.ws/macrog/exp/rubber/aepisode/tlachtli.htm (accessed March 31, 2012); Smith, *Sports*, 8.

19. NAIA, "About the NAIA," www.naia.org/ViewArticle.dbml?DB_OEM_ID=27900&ATCLID=205323019 (accessed February 24, 2012).

20. NAIA Eligibility Center, *Quick Take: Student Registration* (video), www.playnaia.org/page/video_student.php (accessed February 23, 2012).

21. NJCAA, "History," www.njcaa.org/todaysNJCAA_History.cfm?category=History (accessed February 25, 2012).

22. NJCAA, "Stat," www.njcaa.org/athletesOfDistinction.cfm (accessed February 25, 2012).

23. College Scholarships, "Improve Your Chances for an Athletic Scholarship," www.collegescholarships.org/athletic.htm (accessed February 25, 2012).

24. NJCAA, "Stat," www.njcaa.org/careers.cfm (accessed February 26, 2012).

25. Josh Cohen, e-mail to author, March 10, 2012.

26. The suggestions in this section are largely based on two sources: the Miller Place Athletic Department's information packet "The Student-Athlete's Game Plan," available at www.millerplace.k12.ny.us/webpages/swhite/file_viewer.cfm?secFile=7816, and a seminar titled "How to Get Recruited," presented by Alison Bell and Lenny Paoletti at Holy Trinity Episcopal Academy (HTEA) in Melbourne, Florida, on August 22, 2011. Bell is the director of the college counseling program at HTEA, and Paoletti is the HTEA athletic director. By applying their own suggestions, Bell and Paoletti have helped 14 percent of HTEA graduates play at the college level. That's about one out of every seven student-athletes.

27. Emily Stockman, interview with author, November 19, 2011.

28. Dave Galehouse, "How to Create an Athletic Recruiting Resume," www.varsityedge.com/nei/varsity.nsf/main/recruiting+resume (accessed February 29, 2012).

29. Miller Place Athletic Department, "The Student-Athlete's Game Plan," September 2008, www.millerplace.k12.ny.us/webpages/swhite/file_viewer.cfm?secFile=7816 (accessed February 28, 2012). Figure 8.2 is adapted from page 9.

30. Bell, "How to Get Recruited."

31. Roger Bush, interview with author, December 22, 2011.

32. J. C. Kibbey, "Top 50 Recruiting Tips," *NCSA College Athletics Scholarships Blog*, March 9, 2012, www.ncsasports.org/blog/2012/03/09/top-50-recruiting-tips/ (accessed March 30, 2012).

33. College Sports Scholarships, "NCAA and NAIA Sports Recruiting," www.collegesportsscholarships.com/ncaa-recruiting-rules-contact-visits.htm (accessed March 29, 2012); check

out this link for details on the guidelines college coaches must follow throughout the recruiting process.

34. J. Davisson, interview.
35. Bell, "How to Get Recruited."
36. NIAAA, *Guide for College-Bound Student-Athletes*, 20–21.
37. NIAAA, *Guide for College-Bound Student-Athletes*, 20–21.
38. NIAAA, *Guide for College-Bound Student-Athletes*, 22.
39. Stockman, interview.
40. Lauren Young, e-mail to author, February 26, 2012.

9

SPORTS FOR LIFE

··

Even if you don't play your sport in college, high school doesn't have to be the end of the line. There are many opportunities to enjoy sports for life, both as a hobby and as a career.

Recreation Leagues

City and county recreational leagues are a great way to enjoy your sport long after you graduate from high school. Search your city's website for the parks and recreation department, community recreation division, or something similar. Then look for information on adult sports leagues. The most common adult leagues are for softball, basketball, soccer, and volleyball; ultimate Frisbee is also becoming popular. Some cities have coed leagues in certain sports (e.g., soccer and softball), and some cities have leagues for different levels of competition, divided either by age or skill level. If you don't see an adult league in the sport you want to play, talk to someone in the parks department and try to start one yourself.

If you want to keep playing at an intense, competitive level, that option is also available. In softball, for example, there are adult tournament teams—both coed and men's/women's—that travel every weekend to play against teams from other cities and states. You'd probably be surprised at the number of national sports organizations that have competitive leagues and tournaments for adults. Here are just a few examples:

- Amateur Softball Association of America (www.asasoftball.com/adult/index.asp).
- National Adult Baseball Association (www.dugout.org).
- United States Adult Soccer Association (www.usasa.com).
- United States Specialty Sports Association (http://www.usssa.com/sports). Adult tournaments include slow-pitch softball, flag football, and soccer.

Another option while you're in college is to look for intramural leagues on campus. They're basically campus recreational leagues. You can get more information from the college website, on dorm bulletin boards, in the campus newspaper, and so on.

History of Soccer

The game known as football, fútbol, and soccer has roots in many different cultures. Around 2,500 years ago, the Chinese played a game called *tsu chu* that involved kicking a feather-filled leather ball through a small goal. As with soccer today, players could not use their hands. The ancient Greeks and Romans also played a similar game; the Greeks called it *sphaira*, and the Romans called it *ollis*.

In other cultures, soccer may have started as a celebration of war victories. Winners chopped off the heads of the losers and then kicked them around the battlefield. This custom may have been started by the Danish who invaded England in the first century AD.

The game as we know it today developed in England in the mid-1800s. At first it was called association football; this was shortened to a-soc and then soccer. Soccer came to the United States with European settlers around 1850, but it didn't really grow in popularity until the 1970s. Today, soccer is considered the most popular sport in the world.[1]

It's even easier to stay involved in individual sports such as tennis, golf, Nordic skiing, alpine skiing, and snowboarding. Just grab your gear, a friend or two, and go.

Extreme Fitness

As mentioned in chapter 1, one of the benefits of sports is that they help you stay fit. You're burning calories and building muscle as part of every workout, practice, and game. Once you graduate and you're no longer going to the weight room or running with your team, it's easy to get out of shape. If this happens and you don't like the new you, one option is to start going to the gym, but that can get boring. Another option is to give yourself a fitness goal or challenge, and get a friend or two to join you.

Warning: The following can be categorized as extreme for a reason; each one involves intense physical exertion. Make sure you train safely, with plenty of water/sports drinks, and take breaks as needed.

History of Snowboarding

The first snowboard was actually made out of water skis. On Christmas Day in 1965, Sherman Poppen tied two water skis together so he and his daughter could "surf" the snow. Poppen called his creation the Snurfer. He licensed the design to a company that could mass-produce the board, and he sold over 750,000 Snurfers in the next fifteen years.

Here are a few more facts about the history of snowboarding:

- 1972: Dimitrije Milovich starts the first modern snowboard company: Winterstick.
- 1982: The first National Snow Surfing Championships take place in Vermont. There are 125 contestants. The next year it is renamed the U.S. Open Snowboarding Championships, as it is still known today.
- 1984: Ski resorts permit snowboarding on the slopes with skiers. During the 1984–1985 ski season, only 40 U.S. ski resorts allow snowboarders. By 1990, snowboarders are welcome at 476 resorts.
- 1998: Snowboarding becomes an Olympic event in Nagano, Japan.
- 2010–2011: Nearly 1,300 U.S. students (827 boys and 469 girls) compete on their high school's snowboarding team.[2]

Home Fitness Programs

Beachbody is one of several companies that sells home fitness programs. Basically you buy the program through the website, pop in the DVD, and perform each workout as part of a virtual class. The most popular Beachbody workouts are P90X, Insanity, and Asylum:

- *P90X* was created to help people lose weight and transform their bodies in just ninety days. There are twelve different workouts, including Chest & Back, Shoulders & Arms, Plyometrics (jumping, bounding, hopping, etc.), Cardio X, and Yoga X. According to the Beachbody website, to complete this program you just need a six-by-six-foot space, some dumbbells or resistance bands/tubes, a pull-up bar, and about an hour a day.[3]

- *Insanity* is a sixty-day total body conditioning workout. According to the Beachbody website, it might be "the hardest fitness program ever put on DVD." There are ten different workouts (e.g., Cardio Power & Resistance, Plyometric Cardio Circuit, Max Interval Circuit, and Max Cardio Conditioning) designed to increase your cardio fitness, balance, and overall strength through interval training.[4] You don't need any equipment. From personal experience, I can tell you this program is completely insane—but it works.
- *Insanity: The Asylum* is specifically designed to help athletes improve speed, agility, and strength. It's the first at-home fitness program that includes sport-specific training based on drills used by the pros. The workouts include Speed & Agility, Vertical Plyo, Strength, and Game Day.[5]

For more information on these and other Beachbody workouts, go to Beachbody.com.

Long-Distance Running

Many people take up running as a way to stay in shape. To make it more interesting, you could train for progressively longer distances and recruit a group of friends to join you. You could start with a 5K (3.1 miles) or 10K (6.2 miles) "fun" race and then progress to the more extreme races: the half marathon (13.1 miles), marathon (26.2 miles), and ultra-marathon (50 to 100 miles). There are websites and books with training tips and schedules to help you build up your daily and weekly mileage at a safe pace; see the Find Out More section for a few suggestions. Your local running or sporting goods store might have information on upcoming races as well as local training groups you can join.

Be a Volunteer

Another way to stay involved in sports for life is volunteering your time and knowledge. City youth leagues are often looking for coaches in baseball, softball, flag football, Pop Warner football and cheerleading, basketball, soccer, and more. If you've played a sport in high school and/or club, you can teach kids valuable skills and techniques they'll use throughout their years in sports.

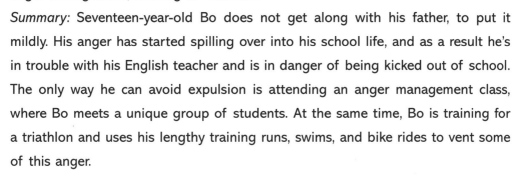

Good Read: Ironman *by Chris Crutcher*

Sport: Triathlon (swimming, cycling, running)

Life apps: Father-son relationship, friendship, anger management, training for triathlon

Summary: Seventeen-year-old Bo does not get along with his father, to put it mildly. His anger has started spilling over into his school life, and as a result he's in trouble with his English teacher and is in danger of being kicked out of school. The only way he can avoid expulsion is attending an anger management class, where Bo meets a unique group of students. At the same time, Bo is training for a triathlon and uses his lengthy training runs, swims, and bike rides to vent some of this anger.

Told from Bo's point of view, *Ironman* presents an honest and humorous account of his attempts to deal with his anger and start a new relationship with his dad.

Greenwillow Books, 1995

181 pages

Triathlons

Triathlons combine three events into one race requiring tremendous endurance. Participants swim first, then cycle, and finally run. There are several different distances, including the following:[6]

Name of Race	Swim	Bike	Run
Sprint	.5 miles	12.4 miles	3.1 miles
Olympic	.93 miles	24.86 miles	6.21 miles
Half (also called Half Ironman or 70.3)	1.2 miles	56 miles	13.1 miles
Full (also called Ironman)	2.4 miles	112 miles	26.2 miles

As with distance running, there are websites and books that can help you train safely and sufficiently. These resources can also teach you about the rules regarding transitions, allowable equipment, and so on.

Athlete Bio: Anthony Lowers, Basketball

In high school, Anthony played basketball and soccer, both because he enjoyed being part of a team and because he stayed fit without even trying. After he graduated, however, Anthony started getting out of shape; he wasn't part of a team with planned training and he wasn't really working out on his own. "I would start to work out but had no goal so I would just give up halfway in my workout and I didn't like that so I signed up for a triathlon," says Anthony, age twenty.

Anthony looked online for training information, since he had never done anything like a triathlon. He found a twelve-week program on the Triathlon Geek website (www.triathlongeek.com), adapted it to fit his schedule, and started training. His weekly routine involved two days of weight training, two days of swimming, three days of cycling, and four days of running; on most days he combined two of those activities. In October 2011, just eleven weeks after he started training, Anthony participated in his first triathlon, a sprint race that involved a .5 mile swim, a 12.4 mile bike ride, and a 3.1 mile run.

As of March 2012, Anthony was training for his second triathlon, a Half Ironman that is over twice as long as his first race. Anthony says, "[For the sprint] I did most of my training alone but every once in a while I got a friend to come with me. Now that I'm training for a 70.3 distance, everyone I ask says I'm crazy for doing that."[7]

Anthony says, "The most rewarding part I get from training [for a triathlon] is being able to do something that other people can't do." *Photo courtesy of Ryan Seeloff.*

Mud Runs and More

For a twist in the traditional running race, try a mud run. It's just what it sounds like: the courses involve running through the mud, as well as jumping over/climbing under other obstacles. These races are as much about teamwork and having fun as they are about actually running. Mudruns.net is a great place to start searching for mud runs in your area.

If you want to participate in "probably the toughest event on the planet," consider training for the Tough Mudder (toughmudder.com). According to the Tough Mudder website, these events are "hardcore 10–12 mile obstacle courses designed by British Special Forces to test your all around strength, stamina, mental grit, and camaraderie." As in the more traditional mud runs, the emphasis is on teamwork and making sure everyone finishes.[8]

Sports-Related Jobs and Careers

According to the NCAA (National Collegiate Athletic Association), your chances of becoming a professional athlete are pretty slim. Here's a breakdown by sport of the percentage of high school athletes who succeed in making a career out of playing their sport (stats as of 2011):[9]

Men's basketball	.03 percent
Women's basketball	.02 percent
Football	.08 percent
Baseball	.45 percent
Men's ice hockey	.32 percent
Men's soccer	.07 percent

That doesn't mean it's impossible; it just means you should probably think about other career options, and there are many that involve sports in some way. This section is intended to be an introduction to sports-related jobs and careers. I've listed a variety of the options (but definitely not all), along with a brief job description; you can do further research on education requirements, salaries, future job prospects, and more using the Internet or the books listed in the Find Out More section.

Athletic Director

Job description: This is the person at your high school who organizes, plans, and oversees the sports programs. The responsibilities include hiring and firing

Athletes Who Turned Pro as Teenagers

If playing professionally is a rare feat, turning pro as a teenager is even more so. Basketball player LeBron James is probably the most famous athlete who turned pro as a teenager; here are a few others:

- *Allyson Felix, track and field:* Felix was the first American track athlete to turn pro straight out of high school in 2003. At age seventeen, she signed a six-year contract with Adidas that included paying for her college education at the University of Southern California.[10]
- *Bryce Harper, baseball:* Harper took the GED (General Educational Development) test and started college when he was sixteen. He was drafted by the Washington Nationals in 2010 when he was seventeen, played in the minor leagues for a year, and finished his first season as a professional baseball player before he turned nineteen.[11]
- *Dwight Howard, basketball:* In 2004 Howard was named National High School Player of the Year and led his team to a Georgia state championship. Later that year, he was the first overall pick in the NBA draft. Dwight was only eighteen when he was drafted by the Orlando Magic.[12]
- *Michael Phelps, swimming:* Phelps was only fifteen years old when he competed in the 2000 Olympics. In 2001 at the age of sixteen, he signed a contract with Speedo, the swimsuit maker. By signing this endorsement contract, Phelps became a professional swimmer and gave up his college eligibility, but he still attended the University of Michigan.[13]
- *Jeff Skinner, ice hockey:* Skinner was born and raised in Ontario, Canada. As an eighteen-year-old, he was picked by the Carolina Hurricanes in the first round of the 2010 draft. Skinner won the NHL Calder Trophy, which is awarded to the rookie of the year.[14]
- *Michelle Wie, golf:* At the age of thirteen, Wie became the youngest golfer ever to qualify for an LPGA tour event, and she finished in the top ten. In 2005 at the age of fifteen she turned pro, though she still attended Stanford University and graduated in 2012.[15]

coaches, creating or dissolving athletic teams, helping student-athletes get college athletic scholarships, raising funds for the athletic department, and overseeing the team schedules. Colleges, universities, and even some middle and elementary schools employ athletic directors to handle the administration side of sports.

Other details: You might like this job if you are an organized people person with a good sense of humor and an ability to stay calm under pressure. Athletic directors tend to have strong leadership skills and an ability to be fair and impartial.[16]

Athletic Trainer

Job description: Athletic trainers are the injury prevention and rehabilitation experts that work with high school, college, and professional sports teams. They're the ones taping ankles, massaging cramped legs, and attending to injured athletes who are carried off the field. Athletic trainers also need to know the signs and symptoms of life-threatening injuries (concussion, broken neck, etc.) so they can keep a seriously injured athlete out of the game and potentially save a life. Athletic trainers are also called sports trainers.

Other details: You might like being an athletic trainer if you are interested in sports, value personal health and fitness, and enjoy helping people. If you're bothered by seeing people in pain, this might not be the job for you.

Sports Movies

There are literally hundreds of movies about sports—some fiction and some based on true, inspiring stories. Here's a short list of popular sports films since the 1970s. For a list of more than two hundred sports movies released between 1925 and 2010, see *Encyclopedia of Sports Films*, by K. Edgington and Thomas Erksine (Scarecrow Press, 2010).

- *Bend It Like Beckham* (2002): Fictional story of a girl who rebels against her orthodox Indian parents by secretly trying out for and making the English national soccer team
- *The Blind Side* (2009): Based on a true story—Michael Oher's journey from homeless teenager to professional football player

- *Breaking Away* (1979): Fictional story of four recent high school graduates who are trying to figure out what to do with their lives, and one of the guys dreams of being a professional cyclist
- *Brian's Song* (1971): Based on a true story—the friendship between Chicago Bears football players Gale Sayers and Brian Piccolo
- *Field of Dreams* (1989): "If you build it, he will come"—a key line from this fictional story involving Shoeless Joe Jackson, one of the eight White Sox players banned from baseball for throwing the 1919 World Series
- *Hoosiers* (1986): Based on a true story—an underdog Indiana basketball team that made it to the high school state championships in 1954
- *Invictus* (2009): Based on a true story—how the South African rugby team won the Rugby World Cup in 1995
- *Invincible* (2006): Based on a true story—how Vince Papale, a thirty-year-old bartender, succeeded in playing for the Philadelphia Eagles in 1976
- *A League of Their Own* (1992): "There's no crying in baseball"—famous line from this fictional story about the real-life 1940s–1950s women's professional baseball league
- *Miracle* (2004): Based on a true story—how the U.S. men's hockey team defeated the highly favored Russian team in the 1984 Olympics and went on to win a gold medal
- *The Natural* (1984): Fictional story of a man who returns to baseball as a middle-age player with incredible talent
- *Remember the Titans* (2000): Based on a true story—how a high school football team in Virginia overcomes racial tension to have a winning season
- *Rudy* (1993): Based on a true story—a young man named Rudy fulfills his dream of playing football for Notre Dame
- *We Are Marshall* (2006): Based on a true story—how a new coach helps rebuild the Marshall University football program after a plane crash kills most of the team

Coach

Job description: Coaching is probably the sports-related career you're most familiar with. There are paid opportunities at the high school, club, college, and professional levels, both for head coach and assistant coach positions. At the college and professional levels in particular, teams often hire multiple coaches, each of

Athlete Bio: Kirsten Frame, Softball

"When I was in high school me and [my high school coach] would always say one day we would coach together after I graduated college," says Kirsten, age twenty. And that's exactly what happened, though it was a little earlier than expected. After four successful years as a high school and travel ball pitcher, Kirsten was recruited to pitch at a Division II university. After two years, however, Kirsten quit and moved back home because the coach was taking all the joy out of playing.

Now she's sharing her knowledge of the game as the assistant coach of a girls' high school softball team. Kirsten's favorite part of this new role is helping the girls get better every day. She says, "I work with all the girls on every aspect of the game, whether I am throwing front toss and instructing, or if I am working with the pitchers on learning new pitches. . . . There is no better feeling than seeing your players improve and keep their love for the sport."

If there is a hard part to her job, Kirsten says it's having patience with her players: "Sometimes their focus goes off and they get distracted and their work ethic starts to fall. Otherwise the only other hard part is dealing with umpires and other coaches." *Photo courtesy of the author.*

Because she has so many years of playing experience, Kirsten can teach to just about every aspect of the game, both physical and mental:

Because I am a pitcher I have had many experiences so I can directly connect with all of the pitchers helping them with pitches. The biggest part of softball is the mental aspect, so I constantly am reminding the girls to relax. One thing we always are saying is, "don't think, just do" and that's the number one thing I've learned and want these girls to realize. The other important thing is for the girls to have fun and keep the sport fun, because the minute you start stressing about every aspect is the moment your game level decreases.

Even though she's not playing competitively anymore, Kirsten says coaching is a way to keep softball in her life, and she enjoys helping others keep their passion to play.[17]

whom focuses on a certain aspect of the team. For example, football teams hire defensive and offensive coordinators, a quarterbacks coach, a special teams coach, and more. A coach is responsible for arranging tryouts, calling plays, deciding which players start, deciding when to sub, teaching new skills, planning practices, scouting opponents, and much, much more.

Other details: You might enjoy coaching if you know and love the sport, are able to make quick decisions and stand by them, stay calm under pressure, and like to help and teach others.

Physical Education Teacher

Job description: You've probably had a few physical education (PE) teachers, so you know the job involves teaching the basics of various sports in a class setting. It also involves making lesson plans, evaluating the skill level of each class and revising instruction as necessary, encouraging students to stay healthy and fit, keeping track of equipment, communicating with parents, and more.

Other details: You might enjoy teaching PE if you value physical fitness for yourself and others, like to help and teach others, and have a lot of energy.[18]

Physical Therapist

Job description: A physical therapist is involved in a person's rehab following an injury, accident, or illness. After surgery to repair a torn ACL or rotator cuff, for example, an athlete usually goes to physical therapy where the therapist helps the person regain strength, range of motion, and flexibility through various exercises. The therapist teaches the person how to perform the same exercises at home.

Have You Ever Heard of Hurling?

- Hurling is the second most popular sport in Ireland, and it is growing in popularity in the United States. In 2009, Stanford and the University of California, Berkeley, played the first U.S. college–level hurling game.
- Hurling combines the skills of lacrosse, baseball, and hockey. The goal is to put the ball over the crossbar (one point) or into the goal (three points) using a curved stick called a hurley.
- Unlike hockey, players may use their hands to carry the ball (for up to four steps) or throw it to a teammate.
- Hurling has been called the fastest game on grass. A ball hit with a hurley can travel up to ninety miles per hour.[19]

Other details: You might like being a physical therapist if you're a people person and enjoy doing something different every day. However, you should know that part of the job involves stretching and moving the person's injured joint, which can cause the individual a lot of pain. Consider whether or not you can handle this.

Sports Agent

Job description: A sports agent represents a professional athlete and negotiates with the team manager and owner in order to get the best salary and playing arrangement for the player. The agent can also arrange speaking engagements, endorsements, and other business transactions on behalf of the athlete. An agent's salary is a percentage of the player's contract.

Other details: Agents are often lawyers or accountants, so you should pursue one of these majors in college if you think you might want to be an agent. Competition to be an agent is tough, but the pay is very good.[20]

Sports Announcer

Job description: A sports announcer is also known as a sportscaster, sports broadcaster, sports analyst, sports anchor, or color commentator.[21] Some sports announcers are hired to give play-by-play descriptions of a game; others are responsible for sharing stats, injury reports, biographical information, and funny stories to fill in the "dead" space between innings, during time-outs, and during other breaks in the action. Some sports announcers are responsible for interviewing players and coaches down on the field. Sports announcers can work on radio or television broadcasts.

Other details: You really have to know the sport you want to cover as a sports announcer. If you like doing research on stats, facts, interesting background stories, and so on, you might like the color commentary part of announcing. If you don't like talking in front of crowds, this job probably isn't for you.

Sports Official

Job description: Umpires and referees are the ones who make sure the game is played by the rules. They call fouls, initiate and stop the action, and regulate player substitutions. Officials are used at all levels of athletic competition: youth, high school, club, college, and adult. Officiating in youth and adult recreation leagues is a part-time job some people do in the evenings or on weekends.

Other details: You might like officiating if you appreciate clean, fair play in sports and can make quick decisions under pressure. You need to know the rules and be able to focus for long periods of time. To be an umpire or referee, you also

---

History of Tennis

Tennis originated in thirteenth-century France, where players would hit the ball over a low net using their hands. The French called this game *jeu de paume*, or game of palm. When the game was introduced in Wales (United Kingdom), people started using rackets instead of their hands. Around 1874, Major Walter Wingfield created the first set of tennis rules, which closely resemble those used today.

One big difference between the game played in the 1800s and the sport played today involves the players' "uniforms." Women used to wear long dresses and men used to wear long pants, both of which restricted the players' ability to move quickly around the court. Around 1919, professional French player Suzanne Lenglen starting wearing shorter, sleeveless dresses. Soon after, the men started wearing shorts, and today's uniforms evolved from there.[22]

need a "thick skin"; in other words, you have to be confident in your calls and ignore the yelling, booing, and negative comments from coaches, players, and the crowd.

Sports Photographer

Job description: Sports photographers capture the athletic action at all levels. Some photographers work for a certain newspaper or magazine; others work as free-lancers, which means they are self-employed and sell their photos to a variety of publications and/or websites.

Other details: Photography equipment is not cheap, and it takes years of experience to develop the skills needed to be one of those photographers you see

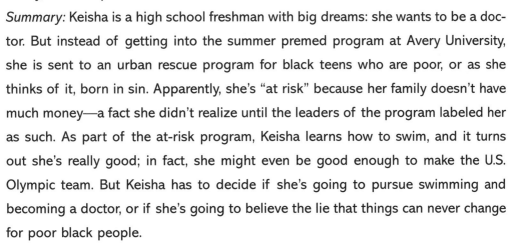

Good Read: Born in Sin by Evelyn Coleman

Sport: Swimming

Life apps: Pursuing a dream, poverty, race, family, friendship

Summary: Keisha is a high school freshman with big dreams: she wants to be a doctor. But instead of getting into the summer premed program at Avery University, she is sent to an urban rescue program for black teens who are poor, or as she thinks of it, born in sin. Apparently, she's "at risk" because her family doesn't have much money—a fact she didn't realize until the leaders of the program labeled her as such. As part of the at-risk program, Keisha learns how to swim, and it turns out she's really good; in fact, she might even be good enough to make the U.S. Olympic team. But Keisha has to decide if she's going to pursue swimming and becoming a doctor, or if she's going to believe the lie that things can never change for poor black people.

Keisha tells her story in an honest, sometimes angry, and often humorous voice. The plot is sometimes far-fetched—too many twists, coincidences, and so on—but overall it's a great story about not giving up on your dreams.

Simon Pulse, 2003

265 pages

courtside at a college basketball game or rimming the end zone of a NFL game. If you enjoy sports and photography, start your career now by taking photographs for your high school newspaper.[23]

Sports Physician or Surgeon

Job description: Also known as a sports medicine doctor or sports orthopedist, a sports physician is a doctor who specializes in caring for athletes with sports injuries such as sprains, strains, and tears. Some sports doctors work in sports medicine clinics; others work as trainers with a certain college or professional team. Sports surgeons spend most of their time in the operating room, repairing injuries such as a torn rotator cuff or torn ACL.

Other details: Becoming a sports doctor or surgeon requires many years of school in courses such as anatomy, physiology, biology, and chemistry. Doctors and surgeons spend their days talking to many different people with many different injuries. If you are patient, are able to make quick decisions in emergency situations, and like helping people, you might enjoy being a sports medicine doctor. If the sight of blood makes you sick, you probably don't want to become a sports surgeon.[24]

Sportswriter

Job description: Sportswriters (or sports journalists) work for newspapers, magazines, and websites and cover the news in sports. Writers sometimes report on a certain event, and sometimes they cover special interest topics such as the NFL draft, concussions in high school sports, a big steroids scandal, a tragic injury, and so on.

Other details: Sportswriters have to be pushy sometimes in order to get an athlete or coach to answer interview questions. If you really know sports, have strong writing skills, and don't mind working odd and long hours, sports journalism might be the job for you.[25]

As you can see, it's definitely possible to participate in sports for life. I hope you choose to do so!

Find Out More

Books

Field, Shelly. *Career Opportunities in the Sports Industry.* 2nd ed. New York: Checkmark Books, 1999.

Hietzmann, Ray. *Careers for Sports Nuts & Other Athletic Types.* 3rd ed. New York: McGraw-Hill, 2004.

——. *Opportunities in Sports and Fitness Careers.* Chicago: VGM Career Books, 2003.

Holland, Tom. *The 12-Week Triathlete.* 2nd ed. Beverly, MA: Fair Winds Press, 2011.

Pasternak, Ceel, and Linda Thornburg. *Cool Careers for Girls in Sports.* Manassas Park, VA: Impact, 1999.

What Can I Do Now? Sports. New York: Ferguson, 2007.

Whitsett, David A., Forrest Dolgener, and Tanjala Mabon Kole. *The Non-Runner's Marathon Trainer.* Indianapolis, IN: Masters Press, 1998.

Websites and Organizations

American Physical Therapy Association (www.apta.org).
Beachbody (www.beachbody.com).
Mud Runs (www.mudruns.net).
National Athletic Trainers Association (www.nata.org).
Totaltriathlon.com (www.totaltriathlon.com).
Tough Mudder (toughmudder.com).
Triathlon Geek (www.triathlongeek.com).

Notes

1. Francois Fortin, ed., *Sports: The Complete Visual Reference* (Willowdale, ON: Firefly Books, 2000), 242; Human Kinetics, with Thomas Hanlon, *The Sports Rules Book: Essential Rules, Terms, and Procedures for 54 Sports*, 3rd ed. (Champaign, IL: Human Kinetics, 2009), 208.
2. Paul MacArthur, "The Top Ten Important Moments in Snowboarding History," Smithsonian .com, February 5, 2010, 1–3, www.smithsonianmag.com/history-archaeology/The-Top-Ten -Most-Important-Moments-in-Snowboarding-History.html (accessed October 26, 2011); "2010–11 High School Athletics Participation Survey," 51.
3. Beachbody, "The P90X Home-Fitness System: What You Get," Beachbody.com, www .beachbody.com/product/p90x-what-you-get.do (accessed March 25, 2012).
4. Beachbody, "Insanity," Beachbody.com, www.beachbody.com/product/fitness_programs/ insanity.do (accessed March 25, 2012).
5. Beachbody, "About Shaun T," Beachbody.com, www.beachbody.com/product/fitness_ programs/insanity-next-level-asylum-workout.do (accessed March 25, 2012).
6. Totaltriathlon, "Triathlon Distances," totaltriathlon.com/triathlon-distances (accessed March 25, 2012).
7. Anthony Lowers, author's survey. December 14, 2011.
8. Tough Mudder, home page, toughmudder.com (accessed March 26, 2012).
9. NCAA statistics taken from University of Arizona, Office of Early Academic Outreach, "Estimated Probability of Competing in Athletics beyond High School," eao.arizona.edu/sites/

eao.arizona.edu/files/Early%20Academic%20Outreach%20Chances%20of%20Going%20
Pro%20Poster.pdf (accessed March 26, 2012).

10. Net Industries, "Allyson Felix Biography," biography.jrank.org/pages/2407/Felix-Allyson
.html (accessed October 9, 2011).

11. ESPN.com, "Bryce Harper Blows a Kiss at Pitcher," updated June 7, 2011, sports.espn
.go.com/mlb/news/story?id=6634378 (accessed October 9, 2011).

12. ESPN.com, "Dwight Howard Biography," espn.go.com/nba/player/bio/_/id/2384/dwight
-howard (accessed October 9, 2011).

13. Encyclopedia of World Biography, "Michael Phelps Biography," www.notablebiographies
.com/news/Ow-Sh/Phelps-Michael.html (accessed October 9, 2011).

14. ESPN.com, "Jeff Skinner," espn.go.com/nhl/player/_/id/5540/jeff-skinner (accessed October 9, 2011).

15. "Bio," on Michelle Wie's official website, michellewie.com/bio (accessed October 9, 2011).

16. Ray Heitzmann, *Opportunities in Sports and Fitness Careers* (Chicago: VGM Career Books,
2003), 39–40.

17. Kirsten Frame, e-mail to author, April 3, 2012.

18. *What Can I Do Now? Sports* (New York: Ferguson, 2007), 18.

19. *The Sports Book: The Games, the Rules, the Tactics, the Techniques* (London: Dorling Kindersley, 2007), 170.

20. Heitzmann, *Opportunities in Sports*, 154.

21. *What Can I Do Now?* 45.

22. Nigel Smith, *Sports: Then and Now* (Brookfield, CT: Copper Beach Books, 1996), 12; *The
Sports Book*, 176.

23. Heitzmann, *Opportunities in Sports*, 153.

24. *What Can I Do Now?* 69, 73.

25. *What Can I Do Now?* 91, 96.

Index

About the Author

Gail Fay grew up in Burbank, California, and started playing softball at age eight. In high school, she lettered in track, cross-country, and basketball, while playing softball and soccer in city leagues. Gail majored in English at UCLA, where she first combined her love of sports and writing by reporting on the fledgling women's soccer team. After graduation, Gail taught eighth grade English for ten years and then started a freelance editing business. She is the author of five nonfiction children's books—*Battles of the Civil War* (2011), *Economies around the World* (2012), *Using Money* (2012), *Malcolm X* (2013), and *Pocahontas* (2013). Gail still plays coed softball in Florida, where she lives with her husband, Bob, and their dog, Sedona.